NAG HAMMADI STUDIES

VOLUME VII

NAG HAMMADI STUDIES

EDITED BY

MARTIN KRAUSE - JAMES M. ROBINSON
FREDERIK WISSE

IN CONJUNCTION WITH

ALEXANDER BÖHLIG - JEAN DORESSE - SØREN GIVERSEN
HANS JONAS - RODOLPHE KASSER - PAHOR LABIB
GEORGE W. MACRAE - JACQUES-É. MÉNARD - TORGNY SÄVE-SÖDERBERGH
WILLEM CORNELIS VAN UNNIK - R. McL. WILSON
JAN ZANDEE

VII

VOLUME EDITOR

MARTIN KRAUSE

LEIDEN
E. J. BRILL
1975

LES TEXTES DE NAG HAMMADI

Colloque du Centre d'Histoire des Religions

(Strasbourg, 23-25 octobre 1974)

ÉDITÉ PAR

JACQUES-É. MÉNARD

LEIDEN
E. J. BRILL
1975

ISBN 90 04 04359 4

Copyright 1975 by E. J. Brill, Leiden, Netherlands

PRINTED IN BELGIUM

TABLE DES MATIÈRES

AVANT-PROPOS

Les communications recueillies ci-dessous furent présentées à l'Université de Strasbourg, entre le 23 et le 25 octobre 1974, lors d'un « Colloque sur la Bibliothèque copte de Nag Hammadi » organisé par le Centre d'Histoire des Religions de notre Université. Les Professeurs Böhlig et Krause, empêchés de se joindre à nous pour raisons de santé, participent néanmoins à nos échanges grâce aux textes qu'ils nous ont fait parvenir après le congrès. Nous leur adressons, ainsi qu'aux autres participants, nos plus vifs remerciements.

Comme le Président E. Trocmé nous le prédisait dans son allocution d'ouverture, l'assistance fut relativement peu nombreuse, mais l'atmosphère de nos séances n'en fut pas moins chaleureuse, ni le débat moins instructif. La place nous manque pour reproduire les discussions qui suivirent chaque exposé, et nous le regrettons. Cependant certains de nos collègues ont heureusement pallié cet inconvénient en répondant en note aux questions qui leur ont été posées.

S'il m'était permis de communiquer au public l'une des impressions que je tire de ce congrès, je dirais que, durant ces quelques jours, nous fûmes tous en mesure de ressentir la rapidité des progrès que l'institution par l'UNESCO d'un Comité international, chargé de la publication des planches photographiques, a fait faire à nos études pendant ces dix dernières années. Au risque d'offenser la modestie d'un homme qui a honoré l'Université de Strasbourg de son enseignement, comme professeur associé en 1970-1971, et nous-même, de sa bienveillance et de son amitié, nous n'hésitons pas à affirmer que ce succès est dû, pour une grande part, au dynamisme efficace du secrétaire de la commission, J. M. Robinson, « the man who gets things done », pour reprendre un des compliments qui lui furent adressés durant l'une de nos séances.

Grâce à la publication rapide des volumes de planches des textes de Nag Hammadi, la situation est entièrement différente aujourd'hui de ce qu'elle était, il n'y a pas dix ans. Nous n'avons plus à étudier des œuvres isolées et relativement peu nombreuses, c'est désormais la bibliothèque tout entière qui nous livre les richesses de ses quelque 50 traités. Du même coup, se posent des problèmes nouveaux, et tout d'abord celui de l'unité de cette bibliothèque. Il y a quelques années, nous eussions parlé de la « Bibliothèque *gnostique* de Nag Hammadi ».

Aujourd'hui, force nous est de constater que le terme *gnostique* ne fait plus l'unanimité. D'une part, certains traités ne peuvent être qualifiés de gnostiques, sans d'importantes réserves : c'est le cas, par exemple, des *Enseignements de Silvain*, étudiés ici par le Professeur J. Zandee. D'autres traités encore peuvent faire l'objet d'une double lecture : nous donnons, pour notre part, une *lectio gnostica* de *l'Exégèse de l'âme*, tandis que le Professeur G. Quispel a suggéré, au cours de la discussion, une lecture presque « origénienne » du même traité. Notre interprétation se rapproche ainsi de celle du Professeur M. Krause, mais elle diffère de celle du Dr. F. Wisse. D'autre part, il n'est même pas sûr, comme nous le rappelle le Professeur T. Säve-Söderbergh, que la Bibliothèque, dans son ensemble, ait été constituée par et pour des gnostiques. En attendant que le temps fasse son œuvre et nous aide à former d'autres hypothèses, il nous paraît préférable de dire que la Bibliothèque de Nag Hammadi n'est qu'une bibliothèque copte, et non une bibliothèque gnostique copte.

Les incertitudes qui se font jour quant à l'unité de notre Bibliothèque ne concernent pas seulement le fond des traités : l'examen attentif des faits matériels pose encore de nouveaux problèmes. D'abord au point de vue de la fabrication même des *codices*. Entre autres résultats très importants, acquis grâce aux travaux des papyrologues allemands et américains, J. M. Robinson attire notre attention sur la technique de reliure des papyri, qui nous oblige à les diviser en trois groupes, de provenance différente. Sans doute est-il trop tôt pour en conclure que nous n'avons pas affaire à une seule bibliothèque, comme nous l'avons cru tout d'abord, mais à trois bibliothèques, primitivement distinctes et secondairement réunies ; cependant, le problème se pose désormais avec acuité.

Le Professeur R. McL. Wilson, de son côté, nous faisant partager son expérience de traducteur, nous invite à réfléchir sur la langue de nos traités. Là encore c'est le règne de la diversité. Non point, pour l'essentiel, à cause des phénomènes de dispersion dialectale, mais surtout à cause de la qualité disparate de nos traductions coptes. Certains traités, par exemple, l'*Exégèse de l'âme*, sont traduits avec élégance et sensibilité ; d'autres traductions sont moins bonnes, par exemple l'*Asclepius*, dont M. J.-P. Mahé nous commente ci-dessous la première page, ou, cas extrême, mais très significatif, le fragment de la *République*, du codex VI, identifié et commenté récemment par le Professeur H.-M. Schenke.

Cependant la complexité des problèmes posés par l'ensemble de la

collection n'est qu'un prélude aux problèmes que pose l'étude proprement dite des différents traités. Il me semble que les contributions
de mes collègues nous en offrent déjà un assez bel échantillonnage.
Il y a d'abord les problèmes de reconstruction interne des mythes
et des systèmes gnostiques. Certains de nos traités se recoupent et se
complètent les uns les autres. Par exemple la *Trimorphos Protennoia*
qui apparaît fugitivement dans l'*Apokryphon de Jean*, fait l'objet
d'un traité complet dans le codex XIII. Mais les écrits gnostiques
ne doivent pas être seulement étudiés en eux-mêmes : ils doivent être
aussi confrontés à leur entourage culturel, et tout d'abord, au témoignage des Pères de l'Eglise. Cela n'est pas si simple, étant donné le caractère très mouvant de certains écrits, souligné par la conférence de
M. D. A. Bertrand sur la *Paraphrase de Sem* du codex VII et la *Paraphrase de Seth* connue d'Hippolyte. Il faut critiquer le témoignage
des hérésiologues, tenir compte de leurs habitudes rédactionnelles
et du caractère polémique de leur présentation : au cours des discussions le Dr. Wisse nous en a donné une preuve, en brossant un portrait
moral des sectes gnostiques qui tranche sur les accusations formulées
ordinairement par les Pères.

Au delà du contexte patristique, la culture grecque est omniprésente
dans nos textes. Non seulement leur langue originale peut avoir été
un grec plus ou moins teinté d'influences sémitiques, mais surtout,
l'un des modes privilégiés de cette présence consiste dans l'influence
de l'école grecque dont nous parle le Professeur A. Böhlig. L'usage
des anthologies, l'habitude d'un certain nombre de lieux communs,
de certains manuels (comme celui d'Albinus, cité par le Professeur
J. Zandee, à propos des *Enseignements de Silvain*), bref ce que W.
Bousset appelait déjà au début de ce siècle le *Schulbetrieb* d'Alexandrie,
confère à beaucoup de nos textes un certain air de famille qu'ils
partagent d'ailleurs avec telles ou telles œuvres de Philon ou de
Clément.

Reste enfin le problème le plus difficile : celui des influences orientales.
Non qu'on ne puisse trouver de l'Iran à l'Egypte des textes comparables
aux nôtres. Mais c'est une question de dosage ! Il s'agit d'apprécier
ce qui est ou n'est pas important, ce qui est décisif ou non. Parlons
par exemple des influences égyptiennes : tout le monde s'accorde pour
dire qu'elles sont minimes dans notre collection. J'ajouterai toutefois
deux réserves. En premier lieu les trois textes hermétiques conservés
dans le codex VI (voir les exposés du Professeur Säve-Söderbergh et
de J.-P. Mahé) sont précisément d'une couleur égyptienne plus appuyée

que beaucoup d'autres textes du *Corpus Hermeticum*. Deuxièmement, les Professeurs Quispel, Säve-Söderbergh et Zandee ont fait remarquer, avec raison me semble-t-il, au cours de nos débats, que l'influence égyptienne peut s'être conjuguée à d'autres influences sur des points très généraux intéressant tous les systèmes gnostiques : n'y a-t-il pas, par exemple, une certaine ressemblance entre la procession des Eons, deux par deux, et celles des divinités traditionnelles des Ogdoades et Ennéades égyptiennes ? Un problème beaucoup plus important et d'une solution encore plus difficile est celui des rapports entre le gnosticisme proprement dit et d'autres courants religieux, le manichéisme, le mandéisme, le judaïsme ou l'essénisme de Qumrân. On connaît les difficultés de cette entreprise dans un domaine où la documentation s'est entièrement renouvelée grâce aux découvertes de ces dernières années. On lira donc avec le plus grand intérêt la conférence du Professeur G. Quispel sur la *Brontè*.

En préparant ce volume pour l'impression, j'ai été saisi de la richesse des renseignements que j'ai recueillis, grâce à la généreuse participation de chacun. Il m'a semblé qu'en confectionnant des *indices*, qui viennent parfois préciser la pensée des auteurs, je rendrais ces richesses plus aisément accessibles au public, tout en m'acquittant, bien incomplètement d'ailleurs, de la dette que j'ai contractée à l'égard de tous les collègues qui ont bien voulu répondre à mon invitation.

Nous aimerions remercier enfin M. le Président Trocmé, ainsi que tous les membres du Centre de Recherches d'Histoire des Religions de l'Université des Sciences Humaines de Strasbourg, qui nous ont aidé à organiser ce Colloque, particulièrement, M. le Doyen Marcel Simon, Membre de l'Institut, et M. le Professeur Marc Philonenko. Que tous ceux qui nous ont fait l'honneur et l'amitié d'assister à nos séances et d'y participer pour notre intérêt à tous, trouvent ici l'expression de notre profonde gratitude. Que notre reconnaissance aille enfin à Annie et Jean-Pierre Mahé pour leur collaboration de tous les instants, soit lors du Colloque lui-même, soit, dans l'établissement des Indices qui viennent compléter ce volume. L'établissement de ces Indices a été rendu possible grâce au Conseil des Arts du Canada qui subventionne le projet d'édition française intégrale des textes de Nag Hammadi.

JACQUES-É. MÉNARD

PREMIÈRE PARTIE

L'ENSEMBLE DE LA COLLECTION : UNITÉ OU DIVERSITÉ ?

HOLY SCRIPTURES OR APOLOGETIC DOCUMENTATIONS?

The « Sitz im Leben » of the Nag Hammadi Library

BY

Torgny Säve-Söderbergh

Just before he died Professor John Barns submitted a contribution to the Labib Festschrift where he recorded the results of his analysis of the cartonnage of the bindings of the Nag Hammadi codices. His study revealed that the cartonnage contained Greek fragments of official accounts of Middle and Upper Egypt and that the covers, to judge from these texts, were probably manufactured by a Pachomian monastery. The details of Professor Barns's analysis and of his contribution to the Labib Festschrift are not known to me and my knowledge is restricted to what has been reported by Professor James Robinson in a circular letter to the International Committee for the Nag Hammadi Codices and in his manuscript of the Preface to Codex V.

This new evidence as well as the project to make an archaeological survey of the district in which the codices were in all probability found, 29 years ago, has led me to reconsider the « Sitz im Leben » of the Nag Hammadi library.

I hinted at the problems involved in my contribution to the Messina conference on the origins of gnosticism (Säve-Söderbergh 1967). Without going into details I underlined the heterogeneous character of the library. The dogmas of the different texts are impossible to bring under one single denominator and all the texts were hardly even acceptable as holy scriptures to one and the same congregation or single Gnostic believer. As I put it then « a detailed study of e.g. the attitude towards the OT or of central notions and ideas bears out the conclusion that the library cannot reflect the dogmas of one sect, however broadminded and syncretistic ».

The progress of the analysis of the different texts and theologoumena certainly bears out this point and I think that the heterogeneous character is now so generally accepted that I can content myself with quoting only one of the experts, Martin Krause, in his introduction to the anthology *Die Gnosis*, II

(Krause, 1971, pp. 10 f.) : « Wie bereits die Titel der Schriften, vor allem aber ihr Inhalt zeigen, gehören die 53 Texte zu verschiedenen religiösen Gruppen, den Gnostikern und zum kleineren Teil hermetischen Gemeinschaften. Gnostische und hermetische Schriften folgen sogar in einem Codex aufeinander (Codex VI). Zu diesem Beieinander von Schriften verschiedener, wenn auch miteinander verwandter Religionsgemeinschaften kommt hinzu, dass die gnostischen Schriften verschiedenen Schulen innerhalb der Gnosis zuzurechnen sind ». It is, as rightly stressed by Krause, difficult to assign the different texts to the sects known to us through the haeresiologists and a better way to categorize the texts is to divide them into groups according to their contents and general character. Thus we have two main categories : the non-Christian Gnostic texts and the Christian Gnostic texts. The first category can be subdivided into (a) texts with Gnostic ideas combined with OT and Judaic thoughts and (b) texts with philosophical-Gnostic ideas without references to the OT or to Judaism. The Christian-Gnostic texts again can be subdivided into those where the Christian notions are inherent parts already at the conception of the text, and, on the other hand, those which have been « Christianized » through Christian additions.

I have quoted Krause as he has here in a short form exposed the complex character of the library as a whole, and this is to my mind something of great importance to keep in mind when we try to understand for what purposes and under what conditions the Nag Hammadi library was assembled and why different codices are grouped together in the same binding.

The further analysis of the library bears out my remarks in Messina that we should not take it for granted, as has sometimes been done, that the texts were collected by a Gnostic congregation or by a Gnostic believer. « The library can have been brought together for haeresiological purposes, let us say by persons who like Epiphanius wanted to collect a Panarion against the Gnostics ».

An additional argument for the view that the library as a whole was not regarded as an anthology of holy scriptures is perhaps the colophon in Codex V introducing the text *Asklepius*. I mentioned it in Messina but without having access to the Coptic text and I therefore had to rely on the translation published by Doresse (1958, p. 166). Krause and Labib (1971, p. 187) have now edited the text and Krause (1967, p. 81) commented the text in his contribution to the Messina meeting giving the following translation : « Diese Abhandlung zwar (or ⲚⲦⲀϥ « of his » [Dr. F. Wisse orally]) habe ich geschrieben. Sehr zahlreich sind die, die in meine Hand gelangt sind. Ich habe sie nicht abgeschrieben, weil ich annehme, dass sie in eure Hände gelangt sind. Ich zweifle (TSS : ⲀⲓⲤⲦⲀⲌⲉ also = « ungewiss sein », « hesitate ») nämlich (γάρ) auch, während ich diese für euch abschreibe, ob sie vielleicht (schon) in eure Hände gelangt sind und die Sache euch ermüdet ; denn zahlreich sind die Abhandlungen des Hermes (? or : des Vaters, according to Krause and Labib 1971 or, according to Wisse [oral communication] « of this one », ⲘⲠⲎ), die in meine Hände gefallen sind ». Krause takes these words as a possible indication that *Asklepius* did not yet exist as one coherent text, but only in the form of several independent texts later combined into *Asklepius*. The main difference in Doresse's translation is the sentence starting with the verb *distaze*, which he rendered : « Car j'hésite à vous les copier en supposant qu'au cas où ils vous seraient déjà parvenus, ils vous ennuieraient ».

Whichever translation one prefers — and my preference is without doubt Krause's — the impression still remains that the scribe wants to avoid producing duplicates of the same texts in order not to bother (ⲢϨⲓⲤⲉ) those for whom he works. Such a reasoning would seem very strange if the texts copied were regarded as holy scriptures by the receivers. No Christian would react against receiving several copies of the Bible, and by analogy we can with great probability conclude that the Hermetic text « Asklepius » was not regarded as a holy scripture by those for whom it was copied [1].

Another passage which may indicate the same attitude of a nonbeliever to the Hermetic text is the introductory phrase of the Hermetic prayer which in the Coptic version precedes the *Asklepius* from which it is separated by the colophon just mentioned, whereas in the Latin text (*Corpus Hermeticum* II § 41) it marks the end of the whole composition. (The Coptic version of *Asklepius* ends already at § 29 of the Latin text.) The prayer is preceded in the Coptic text by the explanatory words : « This is the prayer which *they* said » (ⲠⲀⲓ ⲡⲉ ⲡϢⲗⲏⲗ ⲚⲦⲀⲨⲭⲟⲟϥ), where « they » does not allude to any persons already mentioned in the text. The Greek version starts with the prayer directly, but in the Latin text the prayer is preceded by a narrative section describing how Trismegistos and Asklepius start praying after

---

[1] As F. Wisse points out to me, the colophon can, however, have belonged to the Greek stage of the text and not to the Coptic writer.

having left the adytum of the temple (*De adyto uero egressi cum deum orare coepissent*, etc.). Of course the Coptic phrase ⲡⲁⲓ̈ ⲡⲉ ⲡϣⲗⲏⲗ ⲛ̄ⲧⲁⲩⲭⲟⲟϥ, « This is the prayer which they said » can be a fragment of such a narrative introduction, but as it stands it can also give the impression that a non-Hermetic scribe is explaining the Hermetic usage to another non-believer.

The remark at the end of the prayer is found both in the Coptic and in the Latin texts. In the Latin text the last phrase runs as follows : *haec optantes conuertimus nos ad puram et sine animalibus cenam*, thus with 1. pers. plur. (despite the form of the text preceding the prayer : *coepissent*, etc.). But the Coptic version again gives the impression of an observer, not of a partaker : « When they had (or have) said this praying they kissed (ⲁⲩⲣ̄ⲁⲥⲡⲁⲍⲉ) one another and went to eat their pure (holy : ⲉⲥⲟⲩⲁⲁⲃ) meal (ⲧⲣⲟⲫⲏ) in which there is no blood ». This is at least the impression of the text as it stands in the codex, the form in which the user of the codex had access to it, but this does not, of course, prevent the possibility or perhaps rather plausibility that the Coptic text was originally an excerpt from a larger context of the same nature as that of *Asklepius*.

To these arguments for a haeresiological interpretation of the library as an entity I should like to add some other aspects — the geographical environment and the Pachomian background.

Already in Messina Professor Wilson (Säve-Söderbergh, 1967, p. 560) stressed the fact that « the discovery was made in an area where there was a monastery of Pachomius ». « I remember » he continued « feeling at the time that it was rather strange that there should have been a gnostic community somewhere in the close vicinity of an orthodox Pachomian monastery. It may be that this would support your (Säve-Söderbergh's) point about the heresiological use ».

The Pachomian background was stressed long ago also by Doresse (1958, pp. 145 ff. esp. 155 f.) and this district of Upper Egypt and its Pachomian remains were described by L. Th. Lefort (1938) in his article « Les premiers monastères pachômiens » where he localized or tried to localize the monasteries of Pachom in the more or less immediate neighbourhood of the alleged finding place of the library.

Pachom's place of origin, Sheneset, where he converted and later founded one of these monasteries, Tabennese, where he founded his first monastery, and the later foundation Pbow were all in the neighbourhood of the cemetery of Qasr es-Sayyad, and his fourth foundation, Tmoushons, on the opposite bank of the Nile, was not far off either.

Thus this district was the real heart of monasticism in its first flouri-
shing period and if we are to believe the descriptions in the *Vitae
S. Pachomii* of the attitude of the monks to dissenters, disbelievers
or other opponents it must have been a rather uncomfortable neighbourhood for the assumed Gnostic congregation. We can e.g. recall
the brawl when the bishop tried to prevent the foundation of the
Pachomian monastery at Phnoum and when the large crowd assembled
by the bishop was victoriously driven away by Pachom and his monks.
When visiting the alleged finding-place near the Pharaonic tombs
of Qasr es-Sayyad Doresse (1958, p. 151) had the impression that a
cemetery at the foot of Gebel eṭ-Ṭârif was pagan and antedating the
Christian tombs which he thought are to be found in the neighbourhood
of Deir anba-Palamoun and Deir el-Malak near the river. Here, in
the flood-plain, there is a kind of geological « turtle back », a desert
hill separated from the desert mountain of Gebel eṭ-Ṭârif by cultiva-
tions, and this low desert would then correspond to the « mountain »
(ⲦⲰⲞⲨ) where the Pachomians buried their dead (*S. Pachomii Vita
Boh.*, p. 93[11]; Lefort 1943, p. 145).

This impression regarding the nature and date of the higher cemetery
was, however, founded only on surface finds of dubious value, and
a closer examination of the cemetery is of course needed to settle
this question.

Doresse (1958, p. 155) drew a parallel between the burial of the library
in pagan ground with what seemed to him an obvious fact from the
contents of the library, namely that those who possessed it and buried
it could never have been monks. His reconstruction, accepted by many
scholars, was that there was a Gnostic congregation in the neighbourhood and that they buried their library in pagan ground, when,
at the latest in the beginning of the 5th century, the Pachomian monasteries had come to dominate the region entirely.

Robinson (1974, p. 4), knowing from John Barns's discovery already
mentioned, that the library, or strictly speaking its bindings, were
indeed in all probability manufactured by a Pachomian monastery
and that the library had hence perhaps really belonged to Christian
monks [2], made the following attempt to reconcile the different facts:
« One usually assumes that the monks who copied such texts were

---

[2] This is a conclusion, however, to which Robinson does not subscribe. He, as well
as Wisse, at the colloquium pointed out that other interpretations are possible, e.g.
that the monks, for commercial reasons, bound books not belonging to them or sold
uninscribed books as stationery.

Gnostic Christians who had not yet been forced out of the monasteries. One can imagine that the Gnostic monks were expelled with their books as the monasteries came under orthodox censorship. The Gnostics might well have repudiated this wordly intervention from the distant capital of Greek culture, Alexandria. They might have felt they could best preserve the spiritualism of their otherwordly view by returning to the solitary caves in the cliff overlooking the desert, from which their predecessors had been enticed to enter the monasteries in the midst of the lush arable oasis. In any case they buried their holy books in a jar in the Greco-Roman cemetery at the foot of the cliff».

In favour of this reconstruction one could perhaps cite the fact that Pachom expelled some brothers whom he had, in a vision, seen as those who had lost contact with the light which led the others on the right path through the darkness of the world, this light being the Evangile, the divine truth. Whereas the righteous monks followed this light, others in the vision had gone astray in the darkness and led also others astray by crying out « the light is with us » and these represented the heretics, whereas as others again, believing that they approached the light, circled around columns in the darkness, the columns being the heretic leaders.

The Bohairic *Vita Pachomii* which contains the description of this vision (pp. 130 ff.; Lefort, 1943, pp. 173 ff.) tells us that he expelled the heretic brothers who did not repent, however, but persevered in their attitude and thus became strangers to the other brothers and to the eternal life of our Lord Jesus (cf. also the Greek version, ed. Halkin, 1932, § 102; and another section on dissenters (Lefort, 1943, pp. 171 f.).

A schismatic movement in the monasteries also led to the replacement of Horsiese by Theodoros as leader of the monasteries after the death of Pachom in 346 A.D. (Lefort, 1943, pp. 324 ff.; Halkin, 1932, pp. 80 f.).

I do not deny the theoretical possibility of Robinson's reconstruction of the background and history of the library, but to my mind it implies some difficulties. First of all, there is hardly any evidence that Gnostic Christians would ever have been tolerated in the Pachomian monasteries, at least not if we should believe the *Vitae* of S. Pachomios or the authenticity of the details of his writings. A percursory reading gives rather the impression that according to tradition Pachom was orthodox and intolerant when it came to upholding the rules and dogmas of the monasteries. Let us only remember the harshness with which he treated his successor Theodoros e.g. when some brothers had committed the sin to speak in the bakery (*S. Pachomii Vita Boh.*, pp. 82 f.; Lefort, 1943, pp. 138 f.).

This negative attitude towards all kinds of heretics is well attested in the textual tradition referring to the Pachomian monasteries (Lefort, 1956, pp. IV f.).

Doresse (1958, p. 155 f.) has collected some of the evidence on the fights of the Pachomian monks against Gnostics in their region.

In the year 367 A.D. Theodoros, the successor of Pachom, translated into Coptic and read the letter of S. Athanasios against the heretical books. Theodoros warned against reading such books written by the impure heretics and atheists, « these so-called apocryphal books (ⲛⲓϫⲱⲙ ⲛⲁⲡⲟⲅⲣⲁⲙⲟⲛ), to which they have attributed antiquity and given the name of the saints» (*S. Pachomii Vita Boh.*, p. 176; Lefort, 1943, p. 206).

Doresse (loc. cit.) also briefly mentioned the Pachomian fragment S³ (Lefort, 1943, pp. 370 ff.) where we read the refutation of « one of the books written by the heretics. They have given it under the name of the saints, as if these should have been the ones who wrote it». « It is said» the text continues « that he wrote in that book as follows : 'When Eve had been misled and she had eaten of the fruit of the tree, it was with the devil she conceived Cain' ».

The refutation consists of Bible quotations from *Genesis* and *Ecclesiasticus* proving that God had indeed declared that Adam was the father of Cain, that he gave Eve the name of Zoe, the mother of the living beings, and that Cain's evil character was not due to his birth but to his later evil acts.

Cerfaux (apud Lefort, 1943, p. 371, n. 79) assumed that we have here an allusion to the Gnostic Cainite sect, whereas Doresse (1950, p. 438) regarded the passage as a refutation of an authentic Sethian book.

Different variants of perversions of *Genesis* occur in several Nag Hammadi texts and the unnatural conception of Cain is narrated in *Apocryphon Johannis* (Krause and Labib, 1962, pp. 176 ff.), where the Protarchon defiles Eve who conceives two sons with him, Elohim and Jahve, one being the righteous ($\delta\iota\kappa\alpha\iota\sigma$), the other being the unrighteous ($\alpha\delta\iota\kappa\sigma$), and, as the text says, « he called them Cain and Abel». Cain was thus evil from his birth and this as well as other details shows a rather close connexion between the book refuted by the Pachomians and such texts as the *Apocryphon Johannis*.

Finally, Doresse (1958, pp. 155 f.) also mentioned the dispute between the « philosophers» and Theodoros, a dispute which of course ends with the complete defeat of the philosophers (Lefort, 1943, pp. 117 f.).

There are also other passages referring to the conflicts between the Pachomians and the heretics or the pagans. In this connexion it may be worth noticing that other fragments of S³ (Lefort, 1943, pp. 360 ff.) contain a long exposition on Adam and Eve and the origin of sin etc. according to *Genesis*, an exposition which gives the impression of being written *inter alia* to refute some Gnostic perverted version of *Genesis*.

Another Pachomian text is also of interest here as we just talked about *Asklepius* where the Coptic version as well as the Latin text (*Corpus Hermeticum* II, pp. 325 ff.) contains the famous passage regarding the statues of the gods.

As an antithesis to this we may recall the chapter κατὰ εἰδωλολατρείας in the Greek Pachomian *Paralipomena* (Halkin, 1932, pp. 161 ff.; cf. p. 42*) where the subject in both cases is man as creator of gods, in the Hermetic version in a possitive sense and in the Pachomian version naturally in a negative sense. There is no time here for a closer comparison of the two texts, but I should like to mention that the Pachomian version also alludes to *Genesis* as the true version regarding the creation and the first sin of man — which is also of interest because of the Gnostic anti-*Genesis* and other creation texts common in the Nag Hammadi library.

That the Pachomians abhorred the cult of statues or idols is natural enough and as textual evidence suffice it to recall the story in the Pachomian *Paralipomena* (Halkin, 1932, pp. 132 ff.), where a poor monk who was captured by the Blemmyes and forced by them to offer to their gods and idols was heavily punished by Pachom because he had yielded to their threats to kill him if he did not take part in their sacrificial rites.

Another instance of the antiheretical attitude is the episode (in the *Paralipomena*, Halkin, 1932, pp. 130 ff.; cf. *Vita Prima* quoted by Lefort, 1943, p. 353, n. 8), where Pachom from the bad smell of some visiting anachorets found out that they possessed the heretic writings of Origenes and told them to throw all these blasphemous books into the river and never again to read them.

To use this anathema as an indication that the Pachomians never possessed or studied heretic books would be an interpretation of the text which is contradicted both by the Pachomian passages mentioning the refutation of such books, and now also by the evidence of the bindings of the Nag Hammadi library.

But this text recalls another difficulty which must be taken into account when we try to analyze the Pachomian background of the library with the aid of the Pachomian texts in our possession.

To find out the historical events with the aid of an analysis of the contents of the Pachomian writings is difficult. There are indications that a source criticism, in the historical sense of the word, may yield results in favour of Robinson's assumption that the Christian monks were, to start with, not so orthodox and dogmatic as we meet them in the Pachomian writings and hence could perhaps originally have been more broadminded towards sects or dogmas which were later on regarded as heretic and unacceptable.

It is, I think, plausible to assume that large parts of the *Vitae* and other Pachomian texts were compiled some considerable time after the death of Pachom (see e.g. Halkin, 1932, p. 90*) and the texts could hence well be influenced by a more orthodox attitude than that of Pachom himself. That it is possible and perhaps plausible to assume such a change of attitude is shown by a comparison of the episode just mentioned, which was directed against Origenes, with the *Historia Lausiaca*, where Palladios gives a very positive description of the virtues of the monks of Tabennese, by whom he seems to have been well received. Now Palladios is known as an advanced adherent of Origenes and was expelled to Upper Egypt exactly for that reason. He would thus have been an abominable heretic in the eyes of the Pachomians, if these had, at the time of his sojourn in Upper Egypt, the same attitude towards Origenes as that described in the episode just mentioned. It is therefore reasonable (with Halkin, 1932, p. 105*) to ask, if, at the time Palladios wrote his chapters in the *Historia Lausiaca* on the monks of Tabennese, the *Vita Pachomii* already contained such passages where Origenes and his disciples were cursed in the crudest manner. Or, in other words, if at that time the Pachomians were so dogmatic and antiheretic as they are described in the texts preserved.

If this reasoning is accepted Robinson's theory is, of course, more plausible than if we take the Pachomian evidence at its face value. It is possible that a source-critical historical analysis may shed new light on this problem.

It is, however, time to come to some conclusions.

To me it seems doubtful if we are justified to assume that the Pachomians were originally *so* tolerant as to admit Gnostics and only gradually became orthodox, a change of attitude, which is still not possible to prove. If, instead, we regard the textual evidence as a true description of the attitude also of the early monks, contemporary with the copying and collecting of the texts into the Nag Hammadi library, and if a Pachomian monastery made the bindings and owned the library, then I have great difficulty to find any other explanation for the existence and character of the library as a whole than that it was brought together for heresiological purposes. It would then also be plausible to assume, that the heretical books were disposed of in a jar, buried in the desert, once they had served the purpose they had been collected for. (But again we have, of course, no certainty at what date this disposal of the books took place.)

To support this « heretical » view, which may be correct but which may also prove to be wrong in the light of new evidence, the following additional circumstances may be mentioned.

Some of the evidence in the Pachomian texts can perhaps be interpreted as indications that the Pachomians fought against heresies of just the type which we find in the Gnostic library, such as e.g. the Hermetic ideas about man-made god-statues or, again, the Gnostic anti-*Genesis*. In view of the fragmentary state and the late date of the Pachomian manuscripts and the fact that our Gnostic library should perhaps be regarded only as a random sample, the probability that the two groups of texts should coincide with regard to subjects treated is of course rather small, especially so if we assume that the Pachomians were up against anything like the 80 heresies, « comparable to wild animals and snakes », which Epifanius described in his *Panarion* of approximately the same date as the Gnostic library.

For the success of the Pachomian struggle against the heresies a thorough knowledge of their opponents was undoubtedly of importance — witness the whole heresiological literature of the Fathers of the Church — and even if they despised heretical books they could not avoid to study them in order to be able to refute them.

If some of the texts of their opponents were in Greek, they may have found it necessary to translate them into Coptic for a better understanding by those who should preach against the heresies in the native language. The Bohairic *Vita Pachomii* (Lefort, 1943, pp. 153 ff.) speaks about translations into Greek of Pachom's words, and it is reasonable to assume translations also from Greek into Coptic, the more so since the *Epistula Ammonis* (ibid., §§ 2 and 7) tells us that in the monastery of Theodoros there were some 600 monks, presumably more or less all of them Coptic-speaking, and twenty 'Ελληνισταί, who were acting as interpreters. There is little doubt that all or most of the texts of the Gnostic library were originally composed in Greek and it is not necessary to assume that the translations were always made by Gnostic believers — some of them may even have been translated by their opponents for a proper refutation.

The question may be raised if the Pachomians were literate and well educated enough to take such an interest in the heretic texts they wanted to refute. In this connexion we may refer to Lefort's very strong reaction against the assumption that the Pachomians were too illiterate to be interested e.g. in the writings of Origenes, and he quotes a passage in the Greek *Vita Prima* (Halkin, 1932, § 31) corresponding to the anti-Origenic episode in the *Paralipomena* just mentioned (Lefort, 1943, p. 353, n. 8).

With my contribution I have rather wanted to indicate the problems than to solve them and in my opinion much research is still necessary before the questions raised here can be answered with any certainty.

In addition to a closer study and a source-critical analysis of the Pachomian evidence to illustrate an aspect which has been shown to be of greater importance thanks to John Barns's discoveries, and continued efforts in the analysis of the different texts and theologoumena of the Gnostic library, which has already given rise to a great literature full of brilliant results (nobody mentioned or forgotten), the obvious thing which remains to be done is, of course, a thorough archaeological exploration and scrutiny of the district where the Gnostic library was found and where maybe the greatest contribution of the Coptic church to Christianity, the monasticism, came into being and from where it spread rapidly over the whole western world.

BIBLIOGRAPHICAL REFERENCES

Corpus Hermeticum. Tome II. *Asklepius.* Ed. A. D. NOCK and A.-J. FESTUGIÈRE, Coll. Budé, Paris 1945.

DORESSE, (J.), 1950. *Sur les traces des papyrus gnostiques : Recherches à Chénoboskion.* Acad. Royale de Belgique, Bull. Cl. Lettres 5, XXXVI (1950), 432-438.

——, 1958. *Les livres secrets des gnostiques d'Égypte.* Introduction aux écrits gnostiques coptes découverts à Khénoboskion, Paris 1958.

HALKIN, (F.), 1932, *Sancti Pachomii Vitae Graecae.* Ed. F. HALKIN (*Subsidia Hagiographica,* 19), Bruxelles 1932.

KRAUSE, (M.), 1967. *Der Stand der Veröffentlichung der Nag Hammadi Texte,* in : *Le Origini dello gnosticismo.* Ed. U. BIANCHI, pp. 61-89, Leiden 1967.

——, 1971. *Koptische Quellen aus Nag Hammadi. Die Gnosis.* Ed. W. FOERSTER II : 1, Zürich, Stuttgart 1971.

KRAUSE, (M.), LABIB, (P.), *Die drei Versionen des Apokryphon des Johannes,* (*ADIK,* 1), Kairo 1962.

——, 1971. *Gnostische und hermetische Schriften aus Codex II und Codex VI,* (*ADIK,* 2), Glückstadt 1971.

LEFORT, (L. TH.), 1943. *Les Vies coptes de Saint Pachôme et de ses premiers successeurs* (*Bibl. Muséon,* 16), Louvain 1943.

——, 1939. *Les premiers monastères pachômiens.* Exploration topographique; *Le Muséon* 52, pp. 379-407, Louvain 1939.

——, 1956. *Œuvres de S. Pachôme et de ses disciples.* Ed. L. TH. LEFORT. (*Corpus Script. Christ. Or.,* Script. Copt., 23), Louvain 1965.

S. Pachomii Vita Bohairice scripta. Ed. L. TH. LEFORT. (*Corpus Script. Christ. Or., Script. Copt.,* 7), Louvain 1953.

ROBINSON, (J. M.), 1974. *The Nag Hammadi Codices.* A General Introduction to the Nature and Significance of the Coptic Gnostic Godices from Nag Hammadi, Claremont 1974.

SÄVE-SÖDERBERGH, (T.), 1967. *Gnostic and Canonical Gospel Traditions,* in : *Le Origini dello gnosticismo.* Ed. U. BIANCHI, pp. 552-562, Leiden 1967.

ON THE CODICOLOGY OF THE NAG HAMMADI CODICES

BY

JAMES M. ROBINSON

Neither the science of codicology [1], nor that of papyrology [2], has devoted itself in any appreciable degree to the papyrus codex, much less to that of the Fourth Century. This is quite understandable, in view of the paucity of source material. But with the availability of the Nag Hammadi codices, this situation has changed considerably. Although the very fragmentary Codices X, XII and XIII cannot be adequately analyzed codicologically, the other ten codices were sufficiently intact or have been sufficiently reassembled to provide a wealth of source material for codicological analysis.

The current study of codicological features in the Nag Hammadi codices was carried out initially in the interest of establishing criteria for determining pagination and the placement of fragments [3]. But as this activity reaches its termination, codicological matters increasingly become significant in their own right. And as one seeks by various

---

[1] Cf. e.g. the program of the Colloque de paléographie grecque et byzantine at Paris 21-25 October 1974. It is amusing to note that at the dawn of the modern period the theory was offered that the codex rather than the roll was the original form when papyrus was employed. JAMES BRUCE, *Select Specimens of Natural History Collected in Travels to Discover the Source of the Nile in Egypt, Arabia, Abyssinia, and Nubia* (Dublin: Zachariah Jackson, etc. 1790), VI, p. 9 : « ... the shape of the book where papyrus is employed was always of the same form with those of the moderns ... It is written on both sides, so never could be rolled up as parchment was, nor would the brittleness of the materials when dry, support any such frequent unrolling ».

[2] Such a standard work as L. MITTEIS and U. WILCKEN, *Grundzüge und Chrestomathie der Papyruskunde*, I. *Historischer Teil*, 1. *Grundzüge* (Leipzig and Berlin: B.G. Teubner, 1912) limits its treatment to five lines (p. XXXI). E. G. TURNER has begun a serious investigation of the papyrus codex, in such matters as the sizes of the leaves.

[3] FREDERICK WISSE took the first important steps in this regard with the Nag Hammadi codices. See his codicological analyses of Codex III, « Nag Hammadi Codex III : Codicological Introduction », *Essays on the Nag Hammadi Texts in Honour of Pahor Labib* (*Nag Hammadi Studies*, 6; Leiden: E. J. Brill, 1975), and of Codex VII in *Nag Hammadi Codex VII* (forthcoming in The Coptic Gnostic Library, *Nag Hammadi Studies*).

criteria to ascertain the extent to which sub-classifications can be
established, codicological considerations should be included.

I. Previous Groupings within the Nag Hammadi Library

A first way of grouping the Nag Hammadi codices is in terms of
the history of their transmission. The local tradition near the site
of the find reflects a unity of the library in terms of a single finder :
El Samman (deceased) had fled to the caves in the hills on avenging
the murder of his father, and came upon the codices in a jar buried
in a tomb. But the local tradition already reports separate lots.
Local bedouin report the find consisted of eight books, and eight codices
were once in the hands of Abouna Makarios and his son Tanios of Dechneh (both deceased). Three were seen by Abouna Daoud at Chenoboskion
near Nag Hammadi who in his futile attempt to translate them jotted
notes on one. (In the extant material such a note occurs only at IV,
49, where the first line of the Greek title of the *Apocryphon of John*,
« according to John », is glossed in Arabic « Gospel of John ».) They
were acquired by a local carpenter who sold them in Cairo at such a
profit that he was able to set himself up in business there and did
not have to return home. Helmi Sahoun, teacher of mathematics
and inspector at the Elementary School of Nag Hammadi, reported
that a single volume was offered for sale to his father (deceased),
who, however, did not acquire it. Although early reports that two
were burned to cook tea may be dismissed as a trait of such legends,
other reports that in the '60s a couple were still in the area are at
least tantalizing.

The Cairo tradition indicates that the material was still further
subdivided in the process of transmission. In March 1946 two codices
were put on consignment at the antiquities shop of Mansoor near the
old Shepheards Hotel by two Arabs. Here Jacques Schwartz and
Charles Kuentz of the Institut français d'archéologie orientale saw
and bid for them unsuccessfully. Snakes were drawn on the cover of
one (= Codex II) and one contained an Apocalypse of Peter and several
references to Seth (= Codex VII). They with five others of the same
lot, under group ownership or control, were bought by the antiquities
dealer Phocion J. Tano. He then negotiated unsuccessfully through
an agent with a grain merchant at Nag Hammadi for Codex I. But
his collection included in addition to the seven codices presumably
from Dechnah 18 leaves of Codex I as well as a still smaller part of

Codex XII, the bulk of which remains lost, the eight leaves of Codex
XIII put in antiquity inside the front cover of Codex VI, and two
other more or less complete codices. Codex III was shown to George
Sobhy and thereupon sold on 26 October 1956 to the Coptic Museum by
Ragheb (son of) 'Afandi' Andrawus (son of) Priest Abd El-Said, the
headmaster of the Coptic School of Dechneh and a native of El Kasr
El Sayyad. The antiquities dealer Albert Eid of Cairo in conjunction
with a colleague Ed. E. Anawati of Alexandria had in consignment
41 leaves and the cover of Codex I as early as December 1946; on
gaining access to a second lot of 11 leaves from the same codex, he
acquired both in 1948. The leaves were sold by his estate to the Jung
Institute in 1952, and are being given by the heirs of C.G. Jung to the
Coptic Museum tractate by tractate as they are published. Thus the
history of the transmission of the material indicates that there were
a number of lots into which the library was divided. The various
groups seem to be fortuitous, but the existence of these groups calls
for an examination of other groupings, to verify if the library is to be
conceived of as a single collection and is not to be separated along
such lines into a series of distinct collections. For just as it is in theory
possible that other manuscripts were part of the same find (e.g. Bodmer
papyri), it is at least theoretically possible e.g. that one or more of the
thirteen codices is not part of this find.

A further classification into groups is in terms of dialect. The library
is written in two distinct dialects, the majority in Sahidic of various
colorations (which have not yet been studied synoptically to an extent
permitting sub-classification) and a minority in Sub-Achmimic. The
Sub-Achmimic material is Codices I and X and the first two tractates
of Codex XI, whereby I, *4* is distinctive in dialectal variants from the
other Sub-Achmimic tractates, according to an analysis carried out
by Rodolphe Kasser.

Another classification is in terms of scribal hands. They have been
analyzed tentatively by Martin Krause [4]: Codices II, III, XII and
XIII are each by a different scribe. The scribe who wrote most of
Codex I (tractates *1, 2, 4* and *5*) wrote Codex X and the scribe who wrote
I, *3* wrote the first two tractates of Codex XI. The scribe who wrote
the last two tractates of Codex XI also wrote Codex VII. A single
scribe wrote Codices IV, V, VI, VIII and IX. Subsequent study has
indicated that the scribe who wrote I, *1, 2, 4* and *5* is not the scribe

---

[4] MARTIN KRAUSE, «Zum koptischen Handschriftenfund bei Nag Hammadi», *MDAIK*
19 (1963) 110-111.

of Codex X. A rapid survey of the majority hand by M. Manfredi indicates only VI and VIII are very similar hands, with IV somewhat less similar to VI and VIII, whereas V and IX are clearly by different scribes.

A grouping of the codices in terms of the construction of their leather covers seems possible. One group consists of Codices IV and VIII, and to a lesser extent Codex V; another consists of Codices VI, IX and X, and to a lesser extent Codex II; a third, more heterogeneous group consists of Codices I, III, VII and XI [5].

Attempts have been made to group the material in terms of contents, e.g. as typified by a particular school of Gnosticism, such as Codex I as Valentinian and Codex III as Sethian. But the Valentinianism e.g. of I, *1* has been challenged, as has the Sethianism of some of Codex III, and other materials are Valentinian (e.g. XI, *1* and *2*) and Sethian (e.g. V, *5* and VIII, *1*). Whether Codex II is to be regarded as reflecting the gnostic tradition of Thomas, Philip and Matthew (cf. II, *2*, *3* and *7*) as recorders of the Savior's sayings [6] depends in part upon whether Matthew or Matthias is to be read, but also upon how one reconciles such a theory of the composition of Codex II with the presence of the other four tractates of the codex. Grouping in terms of contents seems to be limited to smaller units, e.g. the obvious literary affinities between II, *4* and *5* and between III, *3* and *4*. The size of a tractate may have been more decisive in determining whether it should be included at a certain place than was content (within of course certain limits).

Perhaps a more relevant observation in terms of contents, though negative, is that no codex contains the same tractate twice, a fact which would seem to reflect an understandable desire to avoid duplication. Nor is there any duplication within a single scribal hand. This then raises the question as to whether the duplication that occurs in the library is due to originally separate collections having been secondarily combined. The following duplication occurs: I, *2*=XII, *2*; II, *1*=III, *1*=IV, *1*; II, *5*=XIII, *2*; III, *2*=IV, *2*; III, *3*=V, *1*. This data correlates to a degree with the three groups into which the leather

---

[5] See my article on « The Construction of the Nag Hammadi Codices », *Essays on the Nag Hammadi Texts in Honour of Pahor Labib* (*Nag Hammadi Studies*, 6; Leiden: E. J. Brill, 1975), 170-190.

[6] See *Pistis Sophia* 42.

covers may be classified, since there is no duplication within any one of the three groups.

II. CODICOLOGICAL OBSERVATIONS

The Nag Hammadi Codices are single-quire codices, with the exception of Codex I. A quire is made from two or more rolls (except for the one-roll quires that follow upon the first quire in Codex I). A roll is constructed of papyrus sheets called *kollemata* (sg. *kollema*) stuck together at joins called *kolleseis* (sg. *kollesis*). (It is of course indeterminate whether the rolls from which the sheets were cut were in fact ever rolled; since some [especially Codices IV and V] use crude papyrus, they may never have been intended to be rolled, but only to be cut for a codex. Hence the following usage of the concept of rolls is not intended to preclude the possibility that they may have existed only as strips but not as scrolls prior to cutting.) A quire is constructed by cutting rolls into sheets which are stacked and then folded so that each becomes two leaves or folios; each leaf is written on both sides and thus provides two pages; a sheet thus provides four pages. The rolls are here numbered from below in terms of the position of the sheets into which they are cut in the unfolded stack of sheets comprising a quire.

A *kollema* is constructed by laying with a slight overlap strips of the stringy pith of the papyrus stalk side by side and then laying a second layer on top at right angles to the first. When the papyrus is pressed, rolled, or pounded the natural sap pastes the material together. The size of a *kollema* is limited by the working surface and the press. Whereas some of the *kollemata* in the Nag Hammadi library are small, hardly broader than a leaf, others extend to a breadth of more than a meter. This large size is quite unusual, indeed seems hardly known to papyrology [7]. It is thereby a distinguishing trait of most of the Nag Hammadi codices.

A series of *kollemata* is stuck one to the other with an overlap of a few centimeters to make a roll. Traditionally the left *kollema* overlaps the right *kollema*. When in the Nag Hammadi codices the reverse is sometimes the case, it is here assumed that the roll has been rotated

---

[7] Such experienced and varied papyrologists as E. G. TURNER, ANTON FACKELMANN and HASSAN RAGAB have indicated they had not previously encountered *kollemata* of this length.

horizontally 180° before or after cutting, i.e. that the roll itself was made in the traditional way.

a) *Fibre directions*

In the traditional roll the surface with horizontal fibres is facing up and the surface with vertical fibres facing down. This practise is reflected in the Nag Hammadi codices, in that before being folded the sheets present the horizontal fibres facing up with but few exceptions. One exception is Codex XII, where sheets alternate between horizontal and vertical fibres facing up. This is a practise more common in parchment codices, where the hair side and the flesh side differ considerably in appearance; a marked aesthetic improvement is achieved by having facing pages always use the same side of the skin. In the case of papyrus the effect is that facing pages always have the same fibre direction. Another exception is the fourth roll of Codex II, where the whole stack of cut sheets seems to have been turned over (or the roll was turned over and cut with vertical fibres facing up). This was apparently done since the top sheet of roll three was a protocol (see below) with vertical fibres facing up, and it seemed undesirable to reverse again the fibre direction.

A further instance of vertical fibres facing up is Codex XIII, though this is only an apparent exception. Normally when a roll is cut into sheets to make a quire, the height of the roll becomes the height of the sheet, and the length of the piece cut out of the roll becomes the breadth of the sheet in the codex. Thus the stack of sheets in the quire before it is folded has the same fibre directions as did the roll. But in the case of Codex XIII the sheets were rotated horizontally 90° after being cut. Thus the height of the roll became the breadth of the sheet (before it was trimmed), and the length of the piece cut out of the roll became the height of the sheet. The result is that the upper surface in the stack of sheets, though it is the same surface that had horizontal fibres in the roll, has become the surface with vertical fibres in the codex.

b) *Protocols*

In the case of a script written from left to right such as Greek or Coptic, it is natural for the columns of a roll to follow each other from left to right. As a result when one wrote or read, the left edge of the roll would be the beginning of the roll and the right edge would be its end. It would be rolled up from right to left and unrolled as one read from left to right. The first *kollema* on the left would be on the outside exposed to view and to wear. This first *kollema* (hence called the *proto-kollon* or protocol) was often attached with reversed fibre directions to avoid having on the outside vertical fibres that fray. As if it were a dust jacket, it was originally left uninscribed; in the Byzantine period the name of the manufacturing firm could be listed on the inside.

Most of the rolls from which the Nag Hammadi codices were made either lacked a protocol, or the protocol was discarded when making a quire. The uninscribed pastedown originally covering the inside of the front and back covers of Codex V lacks continuity of horizontal fibres with the front flyleaf and hence may or may not be part of the first roll (only in Codex VII is it clear that a pastedown is part of the first roll). Since the left edge (pasted to the leading edge of the front cover) has reversed fibre directions, it is presumably a protocol. This would indicate a sensitivity at least on the part of the person(s) responsible for Codex V that a sheet with a protocol is defective and should be used for surfaces not intended for writing. However there may be as many as four extant protocols to be found within the quires of the codices.

The first leaf of the second roll of Codex V has the unusual situation of a *kollesis* connecting the first *kollema*, which has reversed fibre directions, to a second *kollema*, which has normal fibre directions. Whereas a *kollesis* is usually such a smooth join that it is hardly noticeable to the eye or pen, the first *kollema* is so thick that its edge, near the center of the writing surface, rises noticeably above the surface of the second *kollema*. Usually a stationer obscures such a noticeable defect when it occurs in a *kollesis* by pasting a strip of papyrus over the seam. Perhaps he did not do so here on the assumption that the writing in the roll would not have begun until after the *kollesis* joining the protocol and the second *kollema*. The stationer who used this in a quire may have had a similar sensitivity that the protocol was not to be inscribed, since the sheet on which it occurs is about 2.5 cm. narrower than it otherwise should have been. The sheet could have been cut narrow so as to waste only a minimum of the second *kollema* on the leaf not intended for writing. In view of the coarseness of the protocol, it would not have been considered useable at the fold. Hence a minimum of the next *kollema* would be needed at the inner margin. The stationer may hence have cut the sheet only wide enough for the *kollesis* to begin well within the inner margin of p. 67 (and end

near the center of the verso, p. G). The scribe wrote on the first side
of the leaf in question, in spite of its narrowness. The surface is smooth
enough to invite this decision, even though the protocol, on which
most of the writing occurred, was in part unusually dark. But on turning the narrow page the scribe decided not to write on the verso, no
doubt because of its unevenness and darkness, and perhaps in recog-
nition that it had not been constructed for writing.

Codex VIII has a leaf (pp. 89/90) with reversed fibre directions,
whereas its conjugate leaf (pp. 51/52) has the normal fibre directions.
A *kollesis* must have joined them, but is now lost in the lacunae at
their inner margins.

In both these cases the protocol seems to lie at the right end of the
roll, since each lies in the second half of the quire. The rolls seem to
have been cut from right to left, since the left edge of one sheet joins
the right edge of the next sheet above it. But since in each case the
kollema on the right overlaps that on the left, which is the reverse
of what one would expect, one may assume that each roll has been
rotated 180°. Hence in each case the *kollema* with reversed fibre directions originally lay at the left end of the roll, where one would expect
a protocol.

In Codex II there is a whole sheet (pp. 49/50 and 91/92) having the
reversed fibre directions (the vertical fibres facing up in both cases).
But at the outer edge of p. 92 there is the beginning of a *kollesis* joining
a *kollema* with normal fibre directions (the *kollesis* apparently ended
in the material trimmed off at the outer edge of this sheet or in the
outer edge of the next sheet below to which it joined, though this
happens to be a missing uninscribed leaf C/D, which seems to have been
2.2 cm. too narrow, which could explain why it was not inscribed).
Since that sheet pp. 49/50 and 91/92 clearly is not continuous with
the next sheet above (though both sheets have vertical fibres facing
up—see below), nor is it when turned over continuous with the next
sheet below it (pp. C/D and 93/94), it is antecedently more probable
that it is a protocol than that it is a single sheet with part of a *kollesis*
or a vertical strip at one end. Since on the *kollema* that begins in the
outer margin of p. 92 the vertical fibres are exposed and the horizontal
fibres hidden, it has been impossible to trace horizontal fibre continuity
from this *kollesis* to the next sheet below. But Anton Fackelmann
has succeeded in separating from the outer edge of p. 92 the beginning
of a *kollema* so that its horizontal fibres can be seen. The frayed
condition of these fibres prevents a definitive conclusion, especially

since the next leaf in the roll C/D was uninscribed and so has become lost after having been photographed in 1958 by Søren Giversen, so that fibre continuity would have to be traced over this gap to the conjugate leaf 93/94. But on the basis of the available evidence Fackelmann judged the edge of a *kollema* on p. 92 to be part of the same *kollema* as pp. 93/94. The edge of the *kollema* has in the final conservation not been put back onto p. 92 but rather just beside it, so that others can study the problem. In Codex I there may be a similar beginning of a *kollesis* that joins a *kollema* with reversed fibre directions, on the first leaf of the roll comprising the second quire, the inner edge of p. 85. But only full access to the part of Codex I still in Zürich will make an explanation possible.

c) *Stubs*

It is not necessarily the case that the length of a roll was an exact multiple of the breadth of the sheets into which it was cut. Hence there arose the problem that when the roll had been cut the last sheet that remained was not always broad enough. If the remnant were no broader than a leaf, it would have to be discarded, since it could not be bound in. But if it were merely a few centimetres broader than a leaf, there would be enough papyrus for the binding thongs passing through the center of the quire at the fold to pierce the half-sheet and bind it into the quire. Thus the one leaf would be conjugate with a narrow stub lying roughly in the position of an inner margin. Three such stubs are extant, one at the end of the first roll of Codex VII conjugate with pp. 13/14 lying between pp. 114 and 115, one at the end of the second roll of Codex VII conjugate with pp. 99/100 lying between pp. 28 and 29, and one in Codex VIII conjugate with pp. 13/14 lying between pp. 128 and 129. The third is unusual in that the left edge of the first roll of Codex VIII (which was cut from right to left) is the left or outer edge of pp. 13/14 rather than an edge of the conjugate stub; the half-sheet must have been shifted from a position flush with the right edge of the stack of sheets of the roll where one might expect it to its present position flush with the left edge. This might have been done so as to retain equal sizes for the two halves of the quire, in view of the fact that there is a (missing) stub at the end of the second roll conjugate with pp. 111/112 lying between pp. 30 and 31 in the first half of the quire.

A missing stub may also be conjectured at the end of the first roll of Codex V conjugate with pp. 19/20 lying between pp. 67/G and 69. One may conjecture a further missing stub at the end of the second roll of Codex III conjugate with pp. 131/132 lying between pp. 18 and 19. One may conjecture still another missing stub in Codex XI conjugate with pp. 15/16 lying between pp. 56 and 57 at the end of the first roll. This is another instance of the half-sheet having been moved from a position flush with the right edge of the stack of sheets of the roll where one might expect it (since the roll was cut from right to left) to a position flush with the left edge; the end of the roll is actually not the stub but rather the left edge of the conjugate leaf. Perhaps one preferred for a stub to fall in the back half of a book.

One may also conjecture a missing stub conjugate with pp. 29/30 lying between pp. 98 and 99 at the bottom of the stack of sheets cut from the third roll of Codex VII. The problem is that one would expect a half-sheet only as the remnant at the end of the roll when the last cut was made, rather than at the beginning of the cutting process, which normally lies at the bottom of the stack of sheets of a roll. Since the stub is missing, one could also conjecture that it was a full leaf, as one would expect at the beginning of the cutting process. But since in that case it was unnumbered and uninscribed, but would hardly be a protocol (since it is the right end of the roll), this alternative is hardly preferable to the assumption of a stub. One could explain this unusual position for a stub as due to the stationer turning the roll over before he began to cut or turning each sheet over as he cut, and then turning the completed stack back over, thus moving the half-sheet that was cut last from the top to the bottom of the stack.

It is also possible that there was a missing stub in Codex II conjugate with pp. 145/E lying between the front cover and the front flyleaf A/B. Since this position is at the bottom of the stack and would normally be that of the first sheet cut, one may again wonder whether what is missing was a complete leaf. But then one would need to explain why there were two uninscribed front flyleaves. It is possible that this first sheet was the pastedown, since pp. 145/E seems to have been stuck to the back cover [8], at least at the inner margin. The pastedown of Codex VII was also the bottom sheet of the first roll (in most codices too little of the pastedown is extant to form a judgment; in Codex III

---

[8] JEAN DORESSE, « Les reliures des manuscrits gnostiques coptes découverts à Khénoboskion », Revue d'Égyptologie 13 (1961) 45.

it is probable the pastedown was not part of the first roll). The blotting or migration of ink from p. 1 onto p. B, the verso of the front flyleaf, is much fainter near the inner margin than on the rest of p. B. This suggests that the inner part of the page was more protected from the dampness in the cover or the air penetrating the cover than the rest of the page, which would be the case if a stub, but not a full leaf, lay between the cover and the front flyleaf. If there were a stub, one would then have to assume, as in the preceding case, that the roll prior to cutting, or each sheet as cut, was turned over, and then the whole stack turned back over after cutting. Furthermore the half-sheet would have been moved from a position flush with the left edge of the stack of sheets of the roll where one might expect it (since the roll, though cut from right to left, was rotated 180º and thus came into a position as if cut from left to right) to a position flush with the right edge; the end of the roll is actually not the stub but rather the right edge of the conjugate leaf.

d) *Cutting the roll*

Usually the right edge of the roll lies at the bottom of the stack of sheets for the quire and would hence seem to have been cut first. To be sure, one can conceive of procedures that would produce the stack as we find it, even if the cutting were from left to right. If the roll were cut from left to right, each sheet turned over as it was stacked, and the completed stack of sheets turned back over, then the right end of the roll would be on the bottom, as we in fact find it. Or if the roll were turned over to the right before cutting and unrolled from beneath to the left, so that the vertical fibres faced up, then what is the outer edge of the roll when rolled up would be on the right and the roll would be cut from right to left (when seen from above—but from left to right when seen from below facing the horizontal fibres). If, after cutting, the stack of sheets were turned back over so that the horizontal fibres face up, the right end of the roll (in terms of its normal position with horizontal fibres facing up) would be at the bottom of the stack of sheets, as we in fact find it. Or the roll could have been rerolled from left to right before cutting, so that the outer edge of the roll would be the right edge, with the result that it would then be cut from right to left and stacked without turning over. Or the roll could have existed as a strip that was not rolled at all. Although it is not known which of these (or other) alternatives was actually followed, the present analysis uses language consistent with the third or fourth alternatives as fraught with the least complexities and gratuitous assumptions.

A minority of rolls seems to have been cut from left to right rather than from right to left. For when the roll is cut from right to left, the left edge of one sheet joins (if one may ignore the amount trimmed away at the outer margins) the right edge of the next sheet above it. But when the reverse is true, i.e. when the right edge of one sheet joins the left edge of the next sheet above it, one would assume the roll had been cut from left to right. This is the situation with regard to the first roll of Codex V and the first roll of Codex VII. But in the case of the first roll of Codex VII the *kollemata* on the right side overlap those on the left, so that one may assume that, before or after cutting, the roll or stack of sheets had been rotated in a horizontal plane 180°. If this rotation was done after cutting, then the roll was cut and stacked in the normal direction from right to left.

The converse phenomenon also occurs, where the left edge of one sheet joins the right edge of the next sheet above it, so that one would be led to assume that the roll was cut from right to left, except that the *kollemata* on the right side overlap those on the left, so that the roll must have been rotated 180° before or after cutting. Roll three (=quire two) of Codex I, roll one of Codex II, roll two of Codex V, roll four of Codex VIII, both rolls of Codex IX and of Codex XI seem on first glance to belong with the majority that were cut from right to left. But since in each case the *kollemata* on the right side overlap those on the left, one may assume (though other alternatives may not be excluded) that, before or after cutting, the roll or stack of sheets had been rotated 180°. If one may assume it was standard to cut from right to left, then one should assume the roll was first rotated 180° and then cut from right to left.

In order to reconstruct the rolls of Codex XII, in which fibre directions alternate, one must assume that the alternate sheets with vertical fibres facing up had been simply turned over (rotated 180° from one side to the other in a vertical plane). By returning these alternate sheets to their original positions with horizontal fibres facing up the original sequence of the rolls can be reconstructed as in other codices. The second extant roll of Codex XII displays the *kollemata* on the right side overlapping those on the left. One may assume the roll was rotated 180° in a horizontal plane before or after cutting, although the roll is so fragmentary that it cannot be determined which edge of one sheet joined which edge of the next sheet above it, and hence the direction in which the roll was cut. There is a similar indeterminateness with regard to the overlap of *kollemata* in the cases of Codices X and XIII. The only instance where it seems evident that a roll was cut from left to right is the first roll of Codex V, where the *kollemata* on the left side overlap those on the right and the right edge of one sheet joins the left edge of the next sheet above it. It may be that the second roll of Codex V was cut in the same direction in which case it would have been rotated after it was cut.

e) *Building a Quire*

It is in principle difficult to distinguish a lack of horizontal fibre continuity from one sheet to the next that is due to the presence of the end of one roll and the beginning of another roll, from a lack of fibre continuity due to a *kollesis* that was trimmed off just beyond the outer margins between two adjoining sheets. But in some instances one may conjecture that the discontinuity is due to a shift from one roll to another. When there is a shift from one quire to another in Codex I, it seems reasonable to attribute the discontinuity of fibres to a shift from one roll to another. When there is a case of reversed fibre directions, it is probable that it is a protocol and hence the beginning of a roll. When there is a stub, it is probable that the end of a roll is involved, especially when the stub, exempt from the general trimming of the quire, is where one otherwise would have to expect a *kollesis*. (Of course a stub not be due to the ending of a roll, but to unusable papyrus having been cut off any sheet, but none of the stubs in the Nag Hammadi library seems best explainable on this basis.) If the crude writing at the top of IV, 72 that was already present when the text was inscribed is a stationer's figures, it would mark the beginning (outside) of a roll. Sometimes a shift from one roll to another is confirmed by the fact that a relatively standard length of the *kollemata* shift (suggesting a third roll in Codex IV); or the pattern of the *kolleseis* shifts from left over right to right over left (between quire one and quire two of Codex I, between the two rolls of Codices V and XII, and between the third and fourth rolls of Codex VIII) or the converse (between the second and third quires of Codex I, and between the first two rolls of Codices II and VII). Such relatively clear instances of the beginning and end of rolls then provide some precedent for estimating approximately where a roll might be expected to end thus for choosing which alternative is more probable to explain a lack of fibre continuity from one sheet to the next. Of course such a procedure of necessity overlooks irregularities of very long or short rolls (or even single sheets), the possibility of whose existence cannot in reality be excluded.

On the basis of these considerations it seems probable that the first quire of Codex I and Codices V, VI, IX and XI each made use of two rolls, Codex IV of three (?) rolls, Codices II, VII and VIII of four rolls, and Codex III of six rolls. Codices X and XII made use of at least two rolls, but are too fragmentary for one to ascertain whether more rolls were involved. Codex XIII made use of at least one roll, but since only eight leaves were preserved, one cannot readily assess the original size of the codex as a whole. Although Codex I has not been made fully available for such analyses, it may have consisted of three quires, the second and third of which would have consisted of a single roll each. Rodolphe Kasser conjectures a fourth quire consisting perhaps of a single sheet. However any serious analysis of Codex I by others must await full access to the material.

f) *Cutting the sheets*

The number of sheets that could be cut from a roll depended not only on the length of the roll but also upon the breadth of the sheets. Hence it may be no coincidence that cases of the fewest sheets cut from a roll occur in the codices with the broadest sheets : 7 1/2 sheets in roll two of Codex VII and 4, 6 1/2, 7, 7, 7 and 7 sheets in the six rolls of Codex III (though quire three of Codex I is a roll of 6 sheets). This in part accounts for the fact that Codex III has more than four rolls, though not a significantly larger codex in number or pages than the codices with four rolls and that Codex VII has fewer pages than the other codices with four rolls. Similarly one finds the most sheets cut from a roll in one of the codices with the narrowest sheets : 13 sheets in roll two of Codex V. (This might indicate that the 15 sheets above the crude lettering that may be a stationer's marking on IV, 72 need not be conjectured to be derived from two rolls, but rather from a single roll cut into the narrow sheets of Codex IV.) Actually the broadest sheets must have occurred in Codex XII and the narrowest in Codex X, but both are too incomplete to calculate the number of sheets per roll. However the fact that Codex X has the narrowest sheets and hence could have the most sheets from a roll makes it possible to conceive of it as having consisted of at most two rolls, even though vestiges of at least 19 sheets survive.

There would seem to be also some correlation between the number
of sheets cut from a roll and the position of those sheets in a codex.
One may well assume that the sheets were trimmed at their outer
margins after being bound into the cover. Since the sheets on the top
of the stack would be separated from the spine by the intervening
sheets in the stack, they would, if of the same breadth as the sheets
lower in the stack, be trimmed more heavily, with a resultant increase
in waste. It may have been possible to avoid some of this waste by
cutting a roll with somewhat narrower sheets for use higher in the
stack nearer the center of the quire. Such a possibility gains some
support from a trend for rolls used higher in the stack nearer the center
of the quire to be cut into more sheets. For this would suggest that
these sheets were narrower (unless shorter rolls were employed). Codices
that tend to support such a conjecture are the first quire of Codex I,
whose rolls produce 10 and 11 sheets, Codex II with 8, 9, 11 and 10
sheets, Codex V with 10 1/2 (or 11 1/2, if the pastedown were part of
the roll) and 13 sheets, Codex VI with 9 and 11 sheets, Codex VIII
with 7 1/2, 8 1/2, 10 and 10 sheets, Codex IX with 9 and 10 sheets,
and Codex XI with 8 1/2 and 10 sheets. In such a fragmentary codex
as X such considerations may in turn permit a conjectural division
into rolls of 9 and 10 sheets. The second and third quires of Codex I
use only one roll each and hence cannot be included in such a study,
nor can Codices XII and XIII, which are too fragmentary.

The two broadest codices, VII and III, may be exceptions to the
pattern here indicated. The inclusion of the pastedown in the first
roll of Codex VII means that the rolls of this codex produce 8 1/2,
7 1/2, 8 1/2 and 9 sheets. The facts that the first roll includes five
kollemata and the second only three, while the third and fourth include
each four, tend to indicate rolls of varying length, although the pattern
of *kollemata* in the codices is too irregular to be accorded much weight.
In Codex III the rolls produce 4, 6 1/2, 7, 7, 7, and 7 sheets. Rolls
three through six measure 216.8, 212.0, 205.7 and 201.7 cm., which
suggests rolls of approximately the same length were cut into sheets
of a standard size which were then subjected to wider and wider
trimming as one moved toward the top of the stack of sheets. However
there is no standardized length of the *kollemata* to add support to
the conjecture of rolls of the same length. Both the theory that each
successive roll was cut into narrower sheets, producing more sheets
per roll as one moved higher in the stack of sheets (as in most codices)
and the theory that all rolls of a codex were cut into sheets of a stan-

dardized breadth, only to be subjected to ever widening trimming as one moved higher in the stack of sheets (as in rolls three through six of Codex III), remain hypotheses with no more weight than their inherent plausibility and their usefulness in explaining observed phenomena.

III. CONCLUSIONS

Such a first overall survey of codicological features in the Nag Hammadi library is of necessity incomplete, both in the observation and collection of data and in the critical sifting into relevant categories of analysis. Only more mature study of this library and a broader spectrum of papyrus codicology will permit definitive conclusions. However some first impressions from the above data may be indicated.

There was a minimum of 36 rolls used in the Nag Hammadi codices; if Codices XII and XIII were complete, no doubt the total would be greater. One improvement of the codex format over that of the roll is that the papyrus could be inscribed on both sides. When put into codex format, 36 rolls would have the writing surface of 72 rolls. To be sure this gain would be in part balanced by the loss of more space in margins, the spine and the trim in the codex format than in that of the roll. Yet with a minimum of 52 tractates, it is easier to correlate the number of tractates with the number of rolls than with the number of codices. Put otherwise, the tractates more nearly average the length of a roll than of a codex (VIII, *1* and X being the major exceptions). Since each codex not only utilized both sides of the roll but also contained more than one roll, the codex format, at a time when many texts had been written with the roll in view, invited the collection of essays.

Much of the data forms patterns that seem purely fortuitous, e.g. the random distribution of the seven stubs and five protocols, the exceptions to the rules that at a *kollesis* the left *kollema* overlaps the right and that rolls are cut from right to left. The exceptions to the rule of horizontal fibres facing up that have been noted in Codices II, XII and XIII neither share a pattern that would bring them together nor do they lend themselves to a theory that would disassociate them completely from the rest of the library, to which they are related by duplicates (II, *5*=XIII, *2*; XII, *2*=I, *2*), although one could argue that duplication indicates membership in distinct sub-groups or even existence outside the Nag Hammadi library (cf. BG 8502). The fact that Codex I has multiple quires does not provide an adequate basis for separating this codex out, since it shares a scribal hand with Codex XI and through it with Codex VII. Thus much codicological information does not readily aid in sub-classifying the material.

Of the 36 or more rolls comprising the 13 codices, at least 28 include long *kollemata* extending more than the breadth of two sheets (though such rolls often contain also short *kollemata* especially at the ends of the roll). Only six or seven rolls seem to lack one or more long *kollemata* : The two or three rolls of Codex IV, the two rolls of Codex V, roll four of Codex VIII, and roll one of Codex XI. (Codex XII is too fragmentary to permit a judgment.) This may provide a significant correlation with the first group of covers characterized by the absence of a flap on the leading edge of the front cover (Codices IV and VIII) as well as other traits associating these two covers with each other and with that of Codex V, e.g. that they are approximately the same height, noticeably shorter than the other codices. These three codices also share another trait in their quires : the top or center sheet is in each case uninscribed.

THE TRIALS OF A TRANSLATOR

Some Translation Problems in the Nag Hammadi Texts

BY

ROBERT McL. WILSON

A German-speaking colleague once remarked that in his opinion
it was easier to make a literal translation from Coptic into French
than into either German or English. Strangely enough, a French
speaker about the same time gave *his* view, that it was easier into
German than into French or English. Neither of them, unfortunately,
offered any examples in support of his opinion. Now it is not my
purpose here to adjudicate between them, or to draw up a comparative
table of difficulty — although for one who has to work in English
there is a certain rueful satisfaction in the fact that English in both
cases appears on the more difficult side of the equation ! The aim of
this paper is rather to indicate some of the problems which arise, for
one reason or another, and to raise some questions for consideration
and discussion.

At the very outset there is the fundamental question : What kind of
translation are we aiming at ? Is it to be literal, or literary ? Is our
concern to be fidelity to the original text, or the bringing out of its
meaning ? Ideally, of course, the translator ought to let his author
speak as clearly and fluently and correctly in the translation as in
the original language, but with ancient languages it is no longer possible
to check with the author as to what he meant to say, and an attempt
to bring out the meaning may involve the introduction of an element
of interpretation, or even the reading into the text of something that
is not there. On the other hand, a literal translation may be so faithful
to the original, in terms of sentence structure, word order, and so on,
that it is practically unreadable — or only to be read with a great
expenditure of patience.

Our decisions here will inevitably be influenced by the purpose
for which the translation is being made. A polished literary rendering
may be appropriate in the context of an anthology of texts, where
the main interest is in the ideas and not in the detail of the document;

but it will not help the student who is trying laboriously to translate the original, and it may even be positively misleading for those who have to work with the translation alone — because the translator has introduced something from an alien context to bring out the meaning, and that element of interpretation sets the reader off on the wrong track altogether. For example, in the NEB translation of 1 *John* 2:2 ἱλασμὸς περὶ τῶν ἁμαρτιῶν ἡμῶν is rendered « the remedy for the defilement of our sins ». Anyone who, on the basis of this translation, forges a link with the φάρμακον ἀθανασίας of Ignatius, and through that with ideas in the pagan world, will be led very far astray ! For a « working » text, the translation should be as literal and accurate as possible, within the limits of reasonable style in the translation language, and where paraphrase or interpretation is necessary the literal version should be noted. We have to sail between the Scylla of unreadability with a literal version and the Charybdis of misunderstanding with a literary one. It has been said that the best commentary is a good literal translation, but all too often the most faithful literal translation still requires a commentary if it is to be understood.

A second problem is presented by the state of the text. If the manuscript is complete and undamaged, there is of course no problem — apart from those of decipherment, punctuation and so on. With a damaged manuscript it is another matter. Some lacunae can of course be filled without much difficulty : if we have ΠΑΡΑ before and ΙϹΟϹ after, and the context fits, it is no problem to restore ΠΑΡΑ[ΔΕ]ΙϹΟϹ. Where the lacunae are longer, however, or more frequent, as at the bottom of nearly every page in the *Gospel of Philip*, it is quite another matter. A continuous text together with the surviving letters may provide clues to the proper restoration, but cases remain in which any restoration must be regarded as highly conjectural. For example, five sacraments are mentioned in the *Gospel of Philip*, but in paragraph 60 in Schenke's original translation [1] the number of the « mysteries » is given as seven. Till [2] notes that this restoration is very uncertain, but adds « what other word ending in ϥ fits both the lacuna and the syntax ? ». More recent versions such as those of Ménard

---

[1] *Koptisch-gnostische Schriften aus den Papyrus-Codices von Nag-Hamadi*, Hamburg-Bergstedt 1960, 48.

[2] *Das Evangelium nach Philippos*, Berlin 1963, p. 77.

and Krause [3] present a completely different reconstruction of the passage.

On this question of the lacunae there are at least two quite different approaches. According to the one, it is the editor's duty and responsibility to make good the deficiencies of the text, to fill the gaps, by conjecture if necessary. According to the other view, only what is clear and certain should appear in the text, any reconstruction or restoration — apart of course from those which require only the replacement of a letter or two — being relegated to the notes where the problems and the possibilities can be discussed at length. The trouble here is that some people persist in ignoring brackets and other critical marks, and thus quote as firm text what is in fact conjectural. It is salutary to recall the case of the famous Oxyrhynchus Logia papyri, one of which was split down the middle so that only half the column was preserved. Scholars attempted to make good the text over a period of some twenty years, producing in the process some very plausible reconstructions, and then later, in 1959, the *Gospel of Thomas* was published. The Coptic matches very closely with what remains of the Greek, but if Thomas at this point is a Coptic version of the Oxyrhynchus Logia then none of the attempts at reconstruction was anywhere near the mark.

Reference to the *Gospel of Thomas* prompts a warning — against allowing oneself to be unduly influenced by association with existing material. Schenke for example divided the *Gospel of Philip* into 127 *Sprüche*, apparently under the impression that it was a kind of counterpart to Thomas. Later, of course, he adopted the more non-committal term « paragraph », and the general trend of discussion since has been towards the view that this document is not just a string of disconnected sayings, however abrupt the transitions may sometimes appear to be. Another example may perhaps be the opening lines of the *Acts of Peter and the Twelve*, reconstructed by Dr. Krause [4] in the form « [These are the wor]ds which [C]ephas [and the apostle]s spoke : It [came to pass] ... ». Now this is entirely possible — but the extant remains are in line 1 ϫⲉ ⲉⲧ, in line 2 ⲉϥⲁⲥ, and in line 3 what appears to be a *semma* (*sigma*) followed by a colon and ϫⲉ ⲁⲥⲱ. In line 3 I should

---

[3] MÉNARD, *L'Évangile selon Philippe*, Strasbourg 1967; KRAUSE in *Gnosis* (ed. W. FOERSTER) vol. II, Zürich and Stuttgart 1971 (ET Oxford 1974).

[4] *Gnostische und Hermetische Schriften aus Codex II und Codex VI*, Glückstadt 1971, p. 107.

regard the restoration ⲁⲥⲱ[ⲱⲡⲉ] as very probable, while in line 2 the name [ⲕ]ⲉⲫⲁⲥ is certainly possible. The Greek form of the name seems to be normally κηφᾶς, but the form with *eie* (epsilon) does occur in Coptic manuscripts, and may be merely an orthographical variant. The rest however is conjectural, and the opening words appear to have been suggested by the beginning of the *Gospel of Thomas*. It may well be that the original text was something entirely different.

Thirdly, there is a whole cluster of problems arising from the nature of the Coptic language. My German-speaking colleague, for example, might have adduced the fact that Coptic, like French, has only two genders, whereas English and German have three. In a French translation the gender of adjectives and pronouns is determined by that of the noun to which they refer, and there is no problem, as there is in English and German, of determining whether a third person singular pronoun should be « he », « she », or « it ». It may be, of course, that other complications arise for our French colleagues, because for example a Coptic word is masculine and its French equivalent feminine, but that is by the way. Again, there is the fact that Coptic has no passive, and has to use an impersonal third plural of the active. Occasions therefore arise on which the translator has to determine whether a third person plural is a straight third person referring to some subject already mentioned, or impersonal, or a substitute for the passive. In some such cases the choice may not make much difference to the sense of the passage; it does make a difference to the form of the translation.

Another cluster of problems relates to vocabulary. Here I need mention only in passing the problem of identifying the particular Coptic form with which we are concerned amid the sometimes bewildering variety of dialect variants and other modifications in the pages of Crum's *Dictionary*. Sometimes one is reduced to the expedient of conjecturing what the English ought to be, or the underlying Greek might have been, and then looking up the relevant index — only to find the word where one least expected it ! Not all of us have undergone the rigorous training required of a specialist in the Coptic language.

A further problem is presented by the range of meaning which can be covered by the same Coptic word, or perhaps I should say the same group of Coptic letters, arranged in the same order. A few minutes with the Dictionary will show several examples. ⲉϩⲣⲁⲓ, disconcertingly, can mean either « upward » or « downward », although in this case the correct meaning is quite often dictated by the context. But

on successive pages there is a verb ⲤⲰⲚⲦ, meaning « to found, create »,
a noun ⲤⲰⲚⲦ meaning « creature, creation », another noun ⲤⲰⲚⲦ
meaning « custom » and a verb ⲤⲰⲚⲦ meaning « to look ». Or there
is the verb ϨⲈ « to fall », with the cognate noun « fall, destruction »,
and another sense of the verb « to light upon, find », and a different
noun meaning « manner ». Such cases may be multiplied. Verbs may
be used transitively or intransitively, sometimes with a difference
of meaning, as with ⲤⲰⲔ « flow as water, move on swiftly, glide,
also draw, be drawn » and transitively « to draw, beguile, gather,
impel ». As this last example shows, the translator is sometimes faced
with an embarrassing range of choice of English equivalents ! And the
same Coptic term may serve as the equivalent of half a dozen Greek
words. I can recall an occasion on which I was confronted by a Coptic
word for which the dictionary offered the equivalents « redeemer, deli-
verer, saviour » — and the context was such that choice between them
would materially affect the translation, and the reader's understanding
of the passage. Did it carry the religious associations connected with
the title « saviour », or was it merely deliverance or liberation in a
more or less neutral or secular sense ? [5] For light on that question I
checked Dr. Schenke's German translation to see what he had made of
it, but a further check with a German dictionary under *Erlöser*, the
term he used, yielded the same three English equivalents !

This prompts a further warning, or rather two : first, that it is not
always enough simply to put down an English, French or German
equivalent for the Coptic word. It may be necessary to consider what
the translation will suggest to the mind of a modern reader, and whether
that is what the original author really intended. And second, that it
is dangerous to assume that words in different languages have the
same significance, simply because they can be rendered by the same
English word. A case in point is the Coptic ⲘⲚⲦⲢⲘⲚϨⲎⲦ, for which
in some contexts « wisdom » is a fairly adequate equivalent. It is,
for that matter, the only equivalent offered by Professor Metzger in
his word list [6]. Now the reader who sees the word « wisdom », and either
knows or has reason to suspect that the Coptic was translated from a

---

[5] Dr. NKRUMAH's adoption of the title « saviour » offers an analogy. It has been pointed
out that the African word does not necessarily carry the religious associations of the
English « saviour » (see J. S. MBITI, in *Christ and Spirit in the NT*, ed. *Lindars* and *Smalley*,
Cambridge 1973, p. 400).

[6] *Lists of Words occurring frequently in the Coptic NT*, Grand Rapids 1961, p. 21.

Greek original, will almost inevitably and automatically think of one Greek word, σοφία — which could have quite considerable implications in a gnostic context. But the blunt fact is that σοφία is not among the equivalents for ΜΝΤΡΜΝ2ΗΤ listed in Crum's *Dictionary*, nor according to Wilmet's *Concordance* is it rendered by ΜΝΤΡΜΝ2ΗΤ in the Sahidic New Testament. Indeed there are two cases (*Col.* 1.9; *Eph.* 1.8) where σοφία as a loan-word appears alongside the Coptic term, in the phrase 2Ν ϹΟΦΙΑ ΝΙΜ 2Ι ΜΝΤΡΜΝ2ΗΤ. The argument might seem to be weakened by the fact that the Codex II version of the *Apocryphon Johannis* twice has ΜΝΤΡΜΝ2ΗΤ (Krause 15.22, 20.3-4) where the corresponding Berlin text has σοφία (BG 44.3, 50.4), with in one case the support of Codex III (in the other there is a lacuna). But in three other cases BG has σύνεσις as the equivalent twice (56.3,15) and ΜΝΤϹΑΒΕ once (68.3). ΜΝΤΡΜΝ2ΗΤ does not occur at all either in the Berlin text or in Codex III. The cases where the Berlin text and Codex III have σοφία as an equivalent therefore do not necessarily invalidate the main point. Any judgment on the use in the *Apocryphon of John* would require a comparative study of the relationship between the four versions and the possible reasons for their divergence in the use of these words, but at the very least we should be cautious in drawing conclusions based on our understanding of ΜΝΤΡΜΝ2ΗΤ as « wisdom ».

A problem of a different kind is posed by paragraph 3 of the *Gospel of Philip*, with its reference to inheriting the living and the dead. The Greek word κληρονομεῖν may mean either « inherit » with a direct object, or « be heir to », which immediately presents in theory two different renderings for each of the seven occurrences of the word in this passage. Again, Coptic has two genders only, and it is not always possible to determine whether the reference is to a person or a thing : the dead could be dead persons, or dead things, and the living could be either « what is living » or « the living (one) ». Ringing the changes on the various possibilities, one could produce a whole crop of variant translations of this one passage — but what did the original author mean ?

A similar case occurs in the *Gospel of Truth* (33.11-14), in the admonition « Take heed to yourselves alone. Take no heed for others, those whom you have cast away from yourselves ». Some editors, like the *editio princeps*, take « others » as neuter, and understand it to refer to the ἀλλότρια, all that is alien to the gnostic, and this admittedly fits very well with the following lines about not returning to that which one has vomited forth. But were these lines *intended* to be read so closely together, or are these following words not meant to be taken as a quite separate admonition ? The translator can only make his choice and set down the rendering he thinks best, arguing the case in his notes if he is allowed any.

A fourth and final group of problems arises from the fact that in most if not all of the Nag Hammadi texts we have to do not with original Coptic compositions but with translations from the Greek. In one case a hitherto unidentified treatise has now been recognized as a somewhat defective translation of part of Plato's *Republic* [7]. This immediately prompts the question : How good is the Coptic version ?

In general the translators appear to have been fairly reliable and faithful to the original, even to the point where occasional lapses allow us to suspect what the original underlying Greek must have been. But this in turn raises a further problem for the translator : Is he to translate the Coptic as it stands, obscurities and all, or the Greek which he can more or less confidently suspect to lie behind it ? The answer must surely be « Translate the Coptic » — and put the hypothetical Greek text — or better still the patristic parallel — in the notes for comparison. There are for example in the *Gospel of Philip* some passages, particularly paragraph 67, which are only comprehensible in the light of Valentinian theory. And there are passages in the Fourth Treatise from the Codex Jung which in the light of parallel passages from Irenaeus and others not only become clear and meaningful, but show us how the Coptic translator went about his work.

A few ambiguities in the latter document are listed in a note to the preface [8], and more could be added. At 73.6 the text could mean « giving himself to them » or « giving it (the Spirit) to them ». The French and English versions choose the first, the German the second. At 75.23 a different division of words produces a very different translation : « he is one (unique), not being from the Father » or « he is not one, nor is he from the Father ». As it happens, the printed text here requires the first translation, but the French version opposite, with the English, gives the second. The German translation renders the printed text, but in the critical notes (p. 297) the translators suggest the restoration

---

[7] *Gnosis und Neues Testament*, ed. K.-W. Tröger, Berlin 1973, p. 53 : H. M. Schenke discovered that tractate VI. 5 is « eine fehlerhafte Übersetzung von Platons Politeia 588 bis 589b ».

[8] *Tractatus Tripartitus Pars I*, ed. Kasser, Malinine et al., Berne 1973, p. 8, n. 1.

of a negative. When the same result can be achieved by following the second division of the words, without conjectural restoration, and this seems to fit the context, it would seem better to adopt the second version. At 84.9 all three versions translate ⲁϫⲛ- as « without », but the notes (p. 302) indicate two other possible meanings, either of which would make a difference to the sense of the passage as a whole.

It will be noted that in two of these cases the French and English versions agree against the German, which may have something to do with the following comment that in general the French and English translators have preferred to sacrifice literalism to clarity, whereas in the German version the opposite course was adopted [9]. How far they have succeeded is a matter for others to judge, but it should perhaps be stated that it was the deliberate policy of the translators to make the English version as literal and accurate as possible, within the limits of reasonable English style. Where a paraphrase was introduced, or an element of interpretation, the literal sense is provided in the notes.

A united effort like the work on the Jung Codex documents presents a number of special problems. A single translator makes up his own mind and presents his own version. Two or more must find some means of reaching agreement, and the problem is complicated further when it is a case not of one translation but of three separate versions into different languages. One possible solution is to make one the master version and conform the others to it, but it then becomes a question how far the others are really translations of the original, and not just versions at second or third hand. It has been suggested that in the *editio princeps* of the *Gospel of Truth* the English translation was made from the French, but of that I am by no means sure. There are passages which I think could only have come direct from the Coptic, and not through the French translation. But « howlers » such as « the verb » for « Word » or « Logos » in the opening lines show that the English was coordinated to the French by someone not completely familiar with the English language and the English Bible.

A second possibility is to make independent translations and circulate them for consideration. The danger here is that, having accepted

---

[9] Loc. cit., lines 24-28 of the note. The note however immediately adds : « L'opposition entre ces deux procédés de traduction, cependant, et leurs résultats, n'a jamais été poussée à l'absolu ». Even the German sometimes includes an element of interpretation, while passages in the French and English versions remain obscure.

the version proposed by his French or German colleagues and amended his translation accordingly, the English translator may in the end discover that his colleagues have chosen to accept his version! Ideally, any proposed changes should also be circulated and, if possible, agreed upon, and there should be no amendment at proof stage — apart of course from the correction of printing errors. To have one co-ordinator responsible for the oversight of the whole is obviously an advantage, but this demands a high level of linguistic competence (in the case of the Jung Codex in at least six languages!), to say nothing of the time and effort required. As it happens, the Jung Codex project is almost completed, and it is unlikely, on grounds of cost alone, that anything on this scale will be undertaken in the future.

This paper has not in fact taken the course that was originally envisaged, but it may serve a useful purpose in indicating why it can be said that there is no such thing as a perfect translation, and showing some of the reasons why translations can differ so widely one from another.

DIE GRIECHISCHE SCHULE
UND DIE BIBLIOTHEK VON NAG HAMMADI [1]

VON

ALEXANDER BÖHLIG

Im Rahmen des Göttinger Sonderforschungsbereiches 13, der Fragen des Synkretismus im Vorderen Orient behandelt, hat die Außenstelle Tübingen unter anderem zur Zeit die Aufgabe, den hellenistischen Einfluß auf die Texte von Nag Hammadi zu bearbeiten. Dabei werden die Ergebnisse in drei umfassenden Monographien vorgelegt werden : Der Einfluß 1. auf die Metaphysik von A. Böhlig, 2. auf die Anthropologie von R. T. Updegraff, 3. auf die Ethik von F. Wisse.

Für den Historiker ist es dabei eine unabdingbare Voraussetzung, nach dem Weg zu fragen, auf dem griechisches Gedankengut zu den Verfassern der Schriften gelangt ist, die in Nag Hammadi gefunden worden sind. Hier bietet sich die griechische Schule als Stätte der Vermittlung an. Gerade bei ihrer Wanderung in den Vorderen Orient haben die Griechen viele Schulen gegründet, zumal dem Hellenismus auch an einer Verbreitung der Bildung besonders gelegen war. Autochthone Kreise in den eroberten Ländern haben sich dieser Bewegung geöffnet. So kann man in Ägypten von Gräkoägyptern sprechen, die aus der einheimischen Bevölkerung stammend sich ein mehr oder weniger großes Schulwissen aneigneten. Viele Stellen in den Nag-Hammadi-Texten lassen sich nur von jemandem verstehen, der die griechische Schule besucht hat, und die Griechen, vermehrt um die Gräkoägypter, bieten ein an Zahl genügendes Publikum, aus dem sich bereits für die griechisch geschriebenen Vorlagen unserer Texte hinreichend Interessenten finden konnten.

In der koptisch-gnostischen Bibliothek begegnen Elemente aus allen Stufen der Schule, der Elementarschule, der höheren Schule, den Spezialschulen genauso wie aus der Rhetoren- und Philosophenschule.

---

[1] Der vorliegende Beitrag ist das Resümee einer gleichzeitig in den *Göttinger Orientforschungen*, Reihe Hellenistica, unter Band 2 (*GOF* VI, 2), erscheinenden Studie (S. 9-53).

Ein schönes Beispiel ist die Schrift des Codex X über die Konsonanten und Vokale (NH X, *2*). Mit der Terminologie des Dionysios Thrax und teilweise des Aristoteles wird hier eine wissenschaftliche Lautlehre gegeben, die einen tieferen Sinn, die Erklärung des Kosmos, hat, eine übrigens echt griechische Tendenz. Bei dieser Darstellung finden sich auch Beispiele für die Art, wie man Kindern das Alphabet und die Verbindung von Konsonanten und Vokalen beibrachte entsprechend den auf Papyrus gefundenen Schreibübungen.

Die klassischen Schulschriftsteller bilden einen Stoff, den jeder Gebildete zu kennen hat. Deshalb kann in der *Exegesis der Seele* (NH II, *6*) der ποιητής ebenso wie die Bibel zitiert und zur Verdeutlichung gnostischer Wahrheiten herangezogen werden. Ebenso setzt die titellose Schrift des Codex II (NH II, *5*) die Vertrautheit mit der *Theogonie* Hesiods voraus, auch wenn man ihn gleichzeitig stellenweise angreift. Abgelehnt wird die Ursprünglichkeit des Chaos. Bekannt ist auch der Titanenkampf und der Tartaros. Breit ausgeführt wird die an Eros und Himeros sich anschließende Thematik. Eros und Psyche sind in ihrer Zusammengehörigkeit bekannt.

Die Disziplinen der ἐγκύκλιος παιδεία werden im Hellenismus immer mehr zu Fachwissenschaften, so daß man in der Kaiserzeit zum Verständnis Platons erst Mathematik nachlernen mußte. Deshalb schrieb Theon von Smyrna ein Buch über die zu diesem Zweck nötigen Anfangsgründe der Arithmetik, Musik und Astronomie. Immerhin hat sich in den gnostischen Schriften ein Gefühl für die Bedeutung erhalten, die der Zahl zur Erfassung des Kosmos zukam. Schon Pythagoras hatte die Arithmetik über eine nützliche Kenntnis für Kaufleute hinaus zu einer wirklichen Wissenschaft gemacht. Auch aus der großen Tradition griechischer Medizinerschulen, die es zu ihrer Zeit noch gab, schöpften die Gnostiker. In einer ausführlichen Schilderung, welche die Erschaffung des Menschen zum Gegenstand hat, begegnen soviele griechische anatomische Termini, daß hier die Abhängigkeit von griechischer Medizin ganz eindeutig ist.

Für das eigentliche Hochschulstudium gab es zwei Alternativen, die Rhetorenschule und die Philosophenschule. Die letztere hatte dabei aber genügend Elemente auch der ersteren aufgenommen. Die Gnostiker machten dies ebenfalls. Im *Rheginusbrief* (NH I, *3*) haben wir einen seinem Aufbau nach wohlgesetzten Kunstbrief vor uns. Aber auch die Schilderung von «wunderbaren Ereignissen» scheint aus dieser Schule von den Gnostikern übernommen zu sein. Die Metamorphose wird auf Personen des mythischen Geschehens angewandt.

Topoi wie die wunderbare Selbsterneuerung des Phönix (NH II, *5*) oder die von Helena auf Eva übertragene Verwandlung und Schaffung eines Scheinbildes (NH II, *5*) können nur aus der griechischen Rhetoren- schule stammen.

Die Philosophenschule dürfte aber den größten Beitrag zum griechi- schen und hellenistischen Einfluß auf die Gnostiker geleistet haben. Daß die Gnostiker von der Schule her philosophisches Wissen aus Anthologien bezogen, scheint die an Thales anklingende Stelle (NH VI, *4*) und das verdorbene Stück aus Platons *Politeia* (NH VI, *5*) zu erweisen.

Die Probleme der Erkenntnis werden von den Gnostikern eingehend behandelt. Die Terminologie des stoischen Erkenntnisvorganges, κατάληψις, φαντασία, συγκατάθεσις, ὁρμή, läßt sich nachweisen (NH II, *1*). Das platonische Denkmodell Urbild—Abbild kehrt immer wieder. Auch die in Platons *Kratylos* gestellte Frage nach der Richtig-- keit der Namen findet sich (NH II, *3*). Neben solcher sprachphilo- sophischer Frage wird die Etymologie als Prinzip der Hermeneutik verwendet.

Weil der Gnostiker für sein Heil eines Wissens darüber bedarf, woher er stammt, gibt es nicht nur Darlegungen über die ἀρχή des Menschen, sondern auch die ἀρχή überhaupt. Der Gedanke, daß vor dem Kosmos eine Lichtwelt da war, die noch jetzt existiert und in die der Gnostiker zurückzukehren strebt, läßt mythische Vorstellungen entstehen, die von Gedanken griechischer Philosophenschulen genährt sind. Der fremde Gott, der in unbeschreibbarer Einsamkeit übertrans- zendent vorhanden ist, ist das …, das vor dem Zählen steht. Die maß- gebliche Rolle, die ihm Plotin eingeräumt hat, läßt sich grundsätzlich bis auf Platon zurückverfolgen. Die negative Darstellung kann wie bei Plotin auch im Gnostizismus in positive Füllebeschreibung um- schlagen. Dieses ἕν hat in sich die Potentialität, in ihm ist eine innere ἐνέργεια. Die platonische Vorstellung ist verbunden mit einer pytha- goreischen. Nach letzterer können Zahlengrößen auseinander hervor- gehen, die δυάς aus dem ἕν, die τριάς aus der δυάς. Im Platonismus bildet die Dyas ein Materialprinzip, wofür es in den gnostischen Texten ebenfalls Beispiele gibt. Die Bezeichnung πνεῦμα ἀόρατον stammt aus stoischer Terminologie. Ein gleiches Nebeneinander von Platonismus und Stoa liegt in der Konkurrenz von λόγος- und νοῦς- Theologie vor, die sich in gnostischen Schriften findet. Die Verschärfung des Dualismus läßt die Hyle aus einem Materialprinzip im Gnostizis- mus noch stärker zu einem gottfeindlichen Prinzip werden. Die φύσις als unbegrenzte Urmaterie entspricht ihr (NH VII, *1*).

Doch die Welt ist nicht gänzlich negativ zu werten. Zwar ist der
Mensch von den Archonten geschaffen, um ein Faustpfand in ihrer
Hand zu bilden, doch auch diese Vorstellung ist nur eine dualistische
Umformung der Schaffung durch die Demiurgen im *Timaios*. Die
Würdigung die Fixsternhimmels entstammt aristotelischem Denken.

Die Ambivalenz der Seele, die im *Timaios* dargestellt wird, entspricht
der Fähigkeit der Seelen, sich zu entscheiden und dafür gerichtet zu
werden. Es geht darum, daß die himmlische Seele den Heimweg findet
und wieder zum *νοῦς* kommt. Eingehend werden die Affekte behandelt.
Auch in der Seelenlehre kann der Gnostizismus soweit gehen, daß
zwischen sterblichen und unsterblichen Seelen geschieden wird (z.B.
NH VII, 3). Doch liegen auch hierfür die Grundlagen bereits im
Timaios.

Wer die griechische Schule nicht besucht hatte, konnte die gnostischen Texte kaum verstehen. Solche Texte verfassen, konnte er auf
keinen Fall.

DEUXIÈME PARTIE

A TRAVERS DIFFÉRENTS TRAITÉS

CODEX II, VI ET VII

DIE SAKRAMENTE IN DER «EXEGESE ÜBER DIE SEELE»

VON

Martin Krause

Obwohl der Gnostiker keine Sakramente nötig hat, sind in späten gnostischen Schriften Sakramente bezeugt. Hier liegen offensichtlich Einflüsse anderer Religionen vor, der Mysterienreligionen oder des christlichen Kultus. Hans-Georg Gaffron hat diesem Fragenkomplex zuletzt ausführlich in seiner Dissertation *Studien zum koptischen Philippusevangelium unter Berücksichtigung der Sakramente* erörtert [1]. Er konnte dabei leider nur die bisher veröffentlichten Texte aus Nag Hammadi bzw. Angaben über veröffentlichte Schriften aus diesem Handschriftenfund berücksichtigen [2] und daher eine weitere Schrift, die damals unveröffentlichte [3] *Exegese über die Seele* in Codex II von Nag Hammadi, in der ebenfalls Sakramente bezeugt sind, nicht in seine Untersuchung einbeziehen.

Die *Exegese über die Seele* zählt m.E. zur Gruppe der christlich-gnostischen Schriften [4]. Sie enthält neben gnostischem sehr viel christliches Gedankengut, wie wir noch sehen werden. Wie bei allen Texten dieser Gruppe muß daher untersucht werden, ob eine ursprünglich nichtchristlich-gnostische Schrift durch Hinzufügung christlichen Materials verchristlicht wurde, was bei einer Reihe christlich-gnostischer Schriften, z.B. dem *Evangelium der Maria*, der *Sophia Jesu Christi*

---

[1] H.-G. Gaffron, *Studien zum koptischen Philippusevangelium unter besonderer Berücksichtigung der Sakramente*, Theol. Diss. Bonn 1969.

[2] Gaffron, aO. 71-76 (Gnosis und Kultus. Überblick über den Befund in den Nag Hammadi Schriften).

[3] Inzwischen veröffentlicht in: M. Krause u. P. Labib, *Gnostische und hermetische Schriften aus Codex II und VI*, Glückstadt 1971 (= *Abh. d. Deut. Archäol. Inst. Kairo*, Kopt. Reihe Bd., 2), 68-87; deutsche Übersetzung auch in: *Die Gnosis*. Zweiter Band. *Koptische und mandäische Quellen eingeleitet, übersetzt und erläutert* v. M. Krause u. K. Rudolph, mit Registern zu Bd. I und II versehen und herausgegeben von W. Foerster, Zürich und Stuttgart 1971, 127-135.

[4] M. Krause, «Der Stand der Veröffentlichung der Nag Hammadi-Texte», in: *Le origini dello gnosticismo*. Colloquio di Messina 13-18 Aprile 1966, Leiden 1967, 72.

und dem *Apokryphon des Johannes* nachweisbar ist [5]. J. Doresse [6] scheint dieser Meinung zu sein, denn er rechnet den Text zu den Offenbarungsschriften der Propheten der Gnosis von Seth bis Zoroaster, also reinen gnostischen Schriften. Die christlichen Elemente sind nach seiner Ansicht wohl Zusätze eines Redaktors. Auch William C. Robinson will in einem in *Novum Testamentum* erschienenen Aufsatz [7], dessen Manuskript er mir freundlicherweise zur Einsicht sandte, eine heidnische Erzählung herausschälen, deren genauen Umfang er zu bestimmen versuchte [9]. Diese sei durch Stichwortzitate aus dem biblischen Schrifttum und Paränesen angereichert worden [10]. Diese Erzählung ist aber — wie er selbst zugestehen muß — nicht fortlaufend, sondern die verschieden langen Teile enthalten Wiederholungen [11]. Außerdem unterschätzten sowohl Doresse [12] als auch Robinson [13] die feste Verzahnung von Erzählung und Zitaten [14] und die Tatsache, daß auch die Zitate den Fortgang der Handlung und Erzählung beeinflussen. Dieselbe Art der Exegese, die in diesem Text durchgeführt wird, hat Alv Kragerud [15] kürzlich bei der Untersuchung der *Pistis Sophia* festgestellt.

---

[5] KRAUSE, aO. 74 f.

[6] J. DORESSE, *The Secret Books of the Egyptian Gnostics*, London 1960, 190 f.

[7] W. C. ROBINSON, Jr., « The Exegesis on the Soul », *NT* 12 (1970) 102-117.

[8] ROBINSON, aO. 104-110 (Composition), 117 : « The narrative seems to be pagan ».

[9] ROBINSON, aO. 106 : « narrative (127,22-129,5; 131,13-134,32; 137,4-11) » und 107-110 : auch der erste Teil der Paränese gehöre noch zur Erzählung. Aus der Erzählung müßten noch alle Zitate ausgeschlossen werden.

[10] ROBINSON, aO. 105 : « The exegetical composition seems therefore to be a redactional insertion into the narrative *Vorlage* ». Zu den Paränesen (hortatory I und II) vgl. aO. 107 : in die erste Paränese, die « integral with the narrative » sei (aO. 107), seien noch Zitate eingearbeitet worden, die zweite sei von dem Redaktor, der die Zitate in die erste Paränese einarbeitete, angefügt worden. Ebenso seien alle Zitate sekundär. Diese Zufügungen müßten aber nicht auf einen einzigen Redaktor zurückgeführt werden : « the tractate's literary history may have been more complex ».

[11] ROBINSON, aO. 107.

[12] DORESSE (aO. 190 f.) vertritt die Ansicht, der « compiler of the manuscript » habe « various eclectic glosses and references » in den Traktat eingearbeitet.

[13] ROBINSON, aO. 105 ff., vgl. A. 10.

[14] Vgl. M. KRAUSE, « Aussagen über das Alte Testament in z.T. bisher unveröffentlichten gnostischen Texten aus Nag Hammadi » in : *Ex orbe religionum*. Studia G. Widengren oblata I, Leiden 1972 (= *Studies in the History of Religions*, XXI), 449-456, 453 ff.

[15] A. KRAGERUD, *Die Hymnen der Pistis Sophia*, Oslo 1967, 212 f.; vgl. dazu G. WIDENGREN, « Die Hymnen der Pistis Sophia und die gnostische Schriftauslegung », in : *Liber Amicorum*. Studies in Honour of Prof. Dr. C. J. BLEEKER, Leiden 1969, 269-281; H. L. JANSEN, « Gnostic Interpretation in the Pistis Sophia », in : Proceedings of the

Ich bin daher der Überzeugung, daß keine literarische Überarbeitung einer ursprünglich gnostischen Schrift vorliegt, sondern daß der Verfasser, ein christlicher Gnostiker, bei der Ausarbeitung seiner Abhandlung versucht hat, die verschiedensten Gedanken, vor allem gnostische und christliche, miteinander zu verbinden [16], wie wir das z.B. bei Philo [17] und im frühchristlichen Schrifttum finden [18]. Dazu bediente sich der Verfasser des Traktates der exegetischen Methode, was auch bereits der Titel, die *Exegese über die Seele* [19], aussagt. Inwieweit ihm das von ihm benutzte gnostische Material schriftlich vorlag, werden wir nicht mit Sicherheit erschließen können.

Der Verfasser zeigt seine gute Allgemeinbildung durch Zitate bzw. Anklänge an das Schrifttum Homers [20]. Er weiß, daß die « Weisen » der Seele einen weiblichen Namen gegeben haben [21] und die Seele sogar eine $\mu\acute{\eta}\tau\rho\alpha$ besitzt [22], was auch Philo [23] bezeugt, usw.

Zu den gnostischen Lehren rechne ich vor allem die Aussage von der (erschlossenen) Spaltung [24] der mannweiblichen Seele in zwei Teile, deren weiblicher Teil in den Körper fällt [25], den Herabstieg des männlichen Teiles [26], seine Wiederverbindung mit dem weiblichen Teil im Sakrament des Brautgemaches [27] zur Erlösung des gefallenen Teiles und damit die Wiederherstellung des Anfangszustandes [28].

IXth International Congress for the History of Religions, Tokyo and Kyoto 1958, 1960, 106-111; K. RUDOLPH, « Gnosis und Gnostizismus, Ein Forschungsbericht », in: *ThR* 34 (1969) 225-231; H. L. JANSEN, Rez. von KRAGERUD in: *Temenos* 3 (1968) 180-183 (dazu RUDOLPH, aO. 231).

[16] KRAUSE, « Aussagen », aO. 455.

[17] J. CHRISTIANSEN, *Die Technik der allegorischen Auslegungswissenschaft bei Philon von Alexandrien*, Tübingen 1969 (= *Beitr. z. Gesch. d. bibl. Hermeneutik*, 7).

[18] Belege bei WIDENGREN, aO. 275 ff.

[19] II 127,18 und 137,27.

[20] II 136, 28 ff.; vgl. KRAUSE u. LABIB, aO. 86.

[21] II 127, 19 f.; vgl. auch H. JONAS, *Gnosis und spätantiker Geist* I, Göttingen ²1954, 192 f.

[22] II 127, 22.

[23] *Leg all.* III 180; vgl. JONAS, aO. II, 1, 39 A. 1.

[24] Der Terminus ΠⲰⲢ{ⲭ} « spalten » wird nicht verwendet. Der Text spricht davon, daß der weibliche Teil den männlichen *verlor* (II 133,5) bzw. daß die Seele ihren Gatten *verläßt* (II 137,6).

[25] II 127, 24 ff.

[26] II 132, 8 ff.

[27] II 132, 13 ff.

[28] II 133, 6 ff.; 134, 6 ff.; vgl. C. COLPE, « Die 'Himmelsreise der Seele' außerhalb und innerhalb der Gnosis », in: Colloquio di Messina, aO. 429-447, 439.

Das christliche Gedankengut ist nicht nur bei weitem umfang-
reicher als das gnostische, sondern auf ihm ruht auch der Nachdruck
der Aussagen. Dazu gehören neben den Zitaten aus dem biblischen
Schrifttum [29], die etwa ein Drittel des Textes ausmachen, innerhalb
der Erzählung folgende Aussagen : entsprechend dem Handlungsablauf
muß an erster Stelle die *Buße* genannt werden. Nicht nur die Seele
tut Buße [30], sondern auch die Menschen müssen Buße tun, um von
Gott gerettet zu werden [31] : « Der Anfang des Heils ist die Buße.
Daher kam Johannes vor der Parusie Christi, indem er die Taufe der
Buße verkündete » [32]. Die Rettung erfolgt dann, weil *Gott sich erbarmt* [33]. Gott wird beschrieben als « der des großen Erbarmens » [34],
als « guter Menschenfreund, der die Seele, die zu ihm ruft, erhört und
ihr das Licht zur Rettung schickt » [35]. Der männliche Teil der Seele
kommt nicht von selbst zur Rettung der Seele, sondern wird *von Gott*
gesandt [36]. Auch die Reinigung der Seele wird *von Gott* vorgenommen [37].
Christlich ist ebenfalls die Terminologie der Reinigung : die Taufe [38].
Auch die Vereinigung der beiden Teile versucht der Verfasser aus dem
biblischen Schrifttum zu belegen. Der Same, den die Seele im Brautgemach empfängt, wird in neutestamentlicher Ausdrucksweise als
« Geist, der lebendig macht » beschrieben [39]. Dazu gehören auch die
Bezeichnung der Erneuerung der Seele als « Wiedergeburt » [40] und
ihre Rückkehr als « Auferstehung » [41]. Die Wiedergeburt wird außerdem
eine Gnade und ein Geschenk Gottes genannt [42].

---

[29] KRAUSE in : Colloquio di Messina, aO. 72 u. A. 10 ff. und KRAUSE u. LABIB, aO.
71 ff.

[30] $\mu\epsilon\tau\alpha\nu\omicron\epsilon\hat{\iota}\nu$, II 128, 7.30; 131, 18-19; 137, 10.

[31] II 135, 8; 137, 23.

[32] II 135, 21 f.

[33] ⲚⲀ : II 129, 4; 131, 19.

[34] II 135, 18; vgl. auch II 135,14 : « damit er (Gott) sich unser erbarme » und die
Zitate, in denen vom Erbarmen die Rede ist : II 129,32; 134,23; 135,18; 136,10.

[35] II 135, 26 ff.

[36] II 132, 7.

[37] II 131, 19 f.

[38] II 132, 2.

[39] *Joh.* 6,63; 2. *Kor.* 3,6 : II 134,1 f.

[40] II 134, 29.

[41] II 134, 12.

[42] II 134, 32 f.

Die Abhandlung gipfelt — wie im *Philippusevangelium* [43] — in Aufrufen an die Leser oder Hörer, eingeleitet durch ϣϣⲉ « es ziemt sich ». Es finden sich drei solcher Aufforderungen. Sie gelten der Wiedergeburt der Seele [44] und zweimal dem Gebet [45].

Nicht als Kriterien für literarische Überarbeitungen des Textes dürfen verschiedene Aussagen angesehen werden, z.B. die Tatsache, daß am Anfang der Schrift die Rede vom Fall der Seele ist [46], später vom Fall aus dem Hause ihres Vaters [47], von der Flucht der Seele aus dem Jungfrauengemach [48], vom Verlust des männlichen Teiles durch den weiblichen [49], davon, daß Aphrodite die Seele aus ihrer Stadt [50] gebracht habe. Diese verschiedenen Ausdrucksweisen sind das Ergebnis der Exegese des Verfassers, sind abhängig von gnostischen Lehrsätzen, an die sich Zitate als Belege und Erklärungen anschließen [51], die angeführt werden, um den Fall der Seele zu illustrieren.

Die gnostische Lehre vom Fall der Seele und ihre Selbsterlösung durch ihren männlichen Teil ist also in unserem Text wesentlich verändert : jetzt rettet *Gott* die Seele mit Hilfe von Sakramenten.

Das zuerst genannte Sakrament ist die *Taufe*. Sie ist notwendig, um den in den Körper gefallenen weiblichen Teil der Seele von den erlittenen Verunreinigungen zu säubern. Sehr drastisch wird die Nahrungsaufnahme als Hurerei bezeichnet [52]. Als die Seele Buße tut und nachdem sich Gott ihrer erbarmt hat, wendet er ihre Gebärmutter, die sich — wohl infolge ihres Falles — außerhalb des Körpers befindet wie die männlichen Geschlechtsorgane, wieder nach innen [53]. Dadurch erhält die Seele ihre Individualität ($\mu\epsilon\rho\iota\kappa\acute{o}\nu$), wird getauft und reinigt sich von der Befleckung der Außenseite, die man auf sie gepreßt hatte. Dieser Vorgang wird veranschaulicht durch das Bild schmut-

---

[43] II 52 (= Taf. 100), 28; 66 (= 114), 17; 67 (= 115), 13.16.17.19; 69 (= 117), 12; 70 (= 118), 3; 71 (= 119), 3.14; 72 (= 120), 3; 75 (= 123), 22; 76 (= 124), 18; 80 (= 128), 8; 82 (= 130), 29.

[44] II 134, 6 ff.

[45] II 135, 4 ff. u. 136, 16 ff.

[46] II 127, 25 ff.

[47] II 132, 20 f.

[48] II 129, 1 ff.

[49] II 133,5 f.

[50] II 137, 2 ff.

[51] Vgl. KRAUSE, « Aussagen », aO. 453 (mit Lit.) und die in A. 15 genannte Literatur.

[52] II 130, 23 ff.

[53] II 131, 16 ff.

ziger Gewänder, die durch Waschen wieder sauber werden [54]. Dieses
Reinigen der Seele wird beschrieben als « Empfangen ihrer Neuheit
ihrer früheren physischen Beschaffenheit » [55]. Die Seele wendet sich
dann wieder. « Das ist die Taufe » [56]. Die Taufe wird also als eine
Waschung, als Reinigung der Seele von erlittener Befleckung, als
Rückwendung der $\mu\acute{\eta}\tau\rho\alpha$ von außen nach innen verstanden. Wie im
Philippusevangelium wird das Äußere negativ, das Innere positiv
bewertet [57].

   Damit ist die Seele aber noch nicht gerettet. Die Rettung findet
erst im Brautgemach statt — wie wir noch sehen werden —, wenn
durch die Vereinigung der beiden Teile miteinander der Zustand vor
dem Fall der Seele wieder erreicht wird. Die Taufe hat also nur eine
vorbereitende Wirkung und damit denselben geringen Wert wie im
Philippusevangelium [58]. Dort wird bekanntlich die Salbung als
wertvoller als die Taufe beschrieben [59] und vor ihrer Überbewertung
gewarnt [60]. Aus dem Kontext kann nicht erschlossen werden, ob die
Taufe für die christlichen Gnostiker, die die *Exegese über die Seele*
lasen, ein *Sakrament* darstellte oder nur eine Waschung als Vorbe-
reitung auf das Sakrament des Brautgemaches war. Unklar ist auch,
ob und wie sie vollzogen wurde. Bezeugt ist aber der Ort der Handlung.
Aus der Aussage : « sie (nämlich die Seele) reinigte sich im Brautgemach » [61] möchte ich schließen, daß sie im Brautgemach stattfand.

   Ob die Formulierung : « sie (die Seele) füllte es (das Brautgemach)
mit Wohlgeruch » [62] als Hinweis auf eine anschließende Salbung — wie
sie im *Philippusevangelium* [63] bezeugt ist — gedeutet werden kann,
ist mir dagegen zweifelhaft.

   Die Rettung der Seele findet dann im *Brautgemach* statt. Den männ-

---

[54] II 131, 31 ff.

[55] II 135, 35 f.

[56] II 132,2.

[57] Vgl. II 68 (= Taf. 116), 4 ff.; 79 (= 127), 8 ff.; 84 (= 132), 26; 85 (= 133), 4;
ebenso z.B. im Thomasevangelium log. 22 u. 89; vgl. dazu W. SCHRAGE, *Das Verhältnis
des Thomasevangeliums zur synoptischen Tradition und zu den koptischen Bibelübersetzun-
gen*, Berlin 1964 (= *BZNW*, 29), 171.

[58] GAFFRON, aO. 117-140, 221.

[59] II 74 (= Taf. 122), 12 ff.

[60] II 73 (= Taf. 121), 5 ff.

[61] II 123,13.

[62] II 123,13 f.

[63] GAFFRON, aO. 140-171, 221.

lichen Teil der Seele, der auch als « Erstgeborener » [64] und « ihr Bruder » [65] bezeichnet wird, sendet Gott vom Himmel zu ihr ins Brautgemach. Seit ihrem Fall kennt sie zwar nicht mehr sein Aussehen, doch sie träumt von ihm nach dem Willen des Vaters. Durch die Vereinigung der beiden Teile werden sie «ein einziges Leben» [66], was nach Ansicht des Verfassers bereits der « Prophet » [67] über den ersten Mann (= Adam) und die erste Frau (= Eva) in *Genesis* 2,24 b gesagt hat : « sie werden ein einziges Fleisch werden » [68]. Damit wird die anfängliche Vereinigung der beiden Seelenteile bei Gott vor dem Fall des weiblichen Teiles wiederhergestellt [69]. Der männliche Teil wird als « physischer Herr » [70] des weiblichen bezeichnet, was der Verfasser bereits in *Genesis* 3,16 b und *Psalm* 44,11-12 vorhergesagt findet, wo vom « Herrn » die Rede ist.

Wie dieses Sakrament, die Vereinigung im Brautgemach, vollzogen wird, bleibt unklar. Es wird nur betont, jene Hochzeit sei « nicht so wie die fleischliche Hochzeit, bei der die, die miteinander geschlechtlichen Umgang haben, sich an diesem Umgang zu erfreuen pflegen » [71]. Ähnliche Aussagen finden wir im *Philippusevangelium* [72]. Es wird ferner betont, das sei die « große, vollkommene Wiedergeburt, daß diese Hochzeit sich nach dem Willen des Vaters vollziehe » [73].

Es heißt zwar, die « Seele habe bei der Vereinigung den Samen empfangen » [74], dieser wird aber als « Geist, der lebendig macht » [75] gedeutet. Daraus möchte ich schließen, daß die Feier des Sakramentes des Brautgemaches der gnostischen Gruppe, die die *Exegese über die Seele* benutzte, die Verleihung des lebendigmachenden Geistes bedeutete. In welcher Form dies vollzogen wurde, bleibt ungesagt.

Auch im *Philippusevangelium*, in dem das Sakrament des Brautgemaches bekanntlich bezeugt ist [76], bleibt unklar, wie wir uns die Feier

---

[64] II 132,9.
[65] II 132,8.
[66] II 132,35.
[67] II 133,1.
[68] II 133,3.
[69] II 133,3 ff.
[70] II 133,9.
[71] II 132,27 ff.
[72] II 129 (= Taf. 81), 34 ff.
[73] II 134,4 ff.
[74] II 133,35 f.
[75] *Joh.* 6,63; 2. *Kor.* 3,6 : II 134,1 f.
[76] GAFFRON, aO. 191-219, 222.

dieses Sakramentes vorstellen müssen. Daß es sich um einen Kuß
handelte, den der Myste vom Mystagogen erhielt — wie H.-M. Schenke [77] meinte — wird von Gaffron [78] m.E. zu Recht bestritten. Aber
auch für die Deutung des Sakramentes des Brautgemaches als Sterbesa-
krament, als Salbung des Sterbenden durch Gaffron [79] bietet der
Text keine Stütze. Die Aufforderung an den Gnostiker, daß sich seine
« Seele wiedergebären soll » [80], was eine Folge des Vollzuges des Sakramentes des Brautgemaches ist, verbietet eine solche Deutung dieses
Sakramentes, sie legt vielmehr die Auffassung nahe, daß das Sakrament
sofort nach der Bekehrung, der Buße des Gnostikers und zusammen
mit der « Taufe » vollzogen wurde, da ja die Taufe im Brautgemach
stattfand.

Die Seele soll sich selbst wiedergebären, so daß sie wieder wie vor
ihrem Fall wird, wieder zu dem Ort zurückkehrt, an dem sie früher
war. Das wird als « Auferstehung von den Toten, die Erlösung aus
der Gefangenschaft, das Hinaufsteigen zum Himmel, der Weg hinauf
zum Vater » [81] beschrieben.

Diese Aussage erhellt eine Reihe von Aussagen des *Philippusevangeliums* : Hier wird bekanntlich die Meinung der Großkirche
bekämpft, daß der Herr zuerst gestorben und dann auferstanden sei.
Er ist « zuerst auferstanden und starb (dann) » [82]. Daher — so wird
gefolgert — wird jemand, der nicht zuerst die Auferstehung erwirbt,
sterben [83]. Dieser Ausspruch kehrt ähnlich wieder : « Wenn man nicht
die Auferstehung bei Lebzeiten erhält, wird man nichts erhalten,
wenn man stirbt » [84]. Daraus wird gefolgert : « Solange wir in der Welt
sind, ziemt es sich für uns, uns die Auferstehung zu erwerben, damit,
wenn wir das Fleisch ablegen, wir in der Ruhe gefunden werden ... » [85].
Auch aus II 74 (= 122), 12 ff. ergibt sich, daß die Auferstehung eine
Folge des Sakramentes des Brautgemaches ist.

---

[77] H.-M. SCHENKE in : LEIPOLDT-SCHENKE, *Koptisch-gnostische Schriften aus den
Papyrus-Codices von Nag Hamadi*, Hamburg-Bergstedt 1960 (= *Theologische Forschungen*, 20), 38.

[78] GAFFRON, aO. 212 ff.

[79] GAFFRON, aO. 218.

[80] II 134,6 ff.

[81] II 134,11 ff.

[82] II 56 (= Taf. 104), 16 f.

[83] Eine andere Übersetzung vertreten W. C. TILL, *Das Evangelium nach Philippos*,
Berlin 1963 (= *PTS*, 2), 17 und J.-É. MÉNARD, *L'Évangile selon Philippe*, Paris 1967, 57.

[84] II 73 (= Taf. 121), 3 ff.

[85] II 66 (= Taf. 114), 16 ff.

Wir müssen noch einmal zurückkehren zu der Aussage, die Rückkehr
der Seele zu Gott sei « die Auferstehung von den Toten » [86] und « die
Erlösung aus der Gefangenschaft » [87]. Mit « Erlösung » ist koptisches
cⲱⲧⲉ übersetzt worden, das griechischem ἀπολύτρωσις entspricht.
Die Apolytrôsis ist bekanntlich bei manchen Gnostikern als Sakrament gefeiert worden und begegnet auch im *Philippusevangelium*
als 4. Sakrament [88]. Es wird dort in Beziehung zum Sakrament des
Brautgemaches gebracht [89]. In der *Exegese über die Seele* ist die Apolytrôsis kein Sakrament, sondern die Folge des Sakramentes des Brautgemaches. Dieselbe Bedeutung hat sie m.E. auch im *Philippusevangelium* und ist nicht « als Einleitung zum Sakrament des Brautgemaches » zu verstehen, wie Gaffron [90] meint.

Diese Erlösung findet der Verfasser wieder im Alten Testament
vorausgesagt. Er zitiert daher *Psalm* 102,1-5, wo nach Vers 4 Gott
das Leben aus dem Tode « errettet » hat.

Diese Rettung der Seele wird auch noch als « Wiedergeburt » bezeichnet [91]. Sie begegnet auch im *Philippusevangelium* [92]. Die Wiedergeburt
wird als Gnade und Geschenk Gottes bezeichnet [93].

Zusammenfassend läßt sich sagen, daß von den fünf Sakramenten
des *Philippusevangeliums* zwar drei namentlich oder indirekt genannt
werden, aber nur bei einem, dem Sakrament des Brautgemaches,
ein Vollzug feststellbar ist, während bei der Taufe Unklarheit besteht,
ob sie als Sakrament galt. Das *Wie* des Vollzuges des Sakramentes
des Brautgemaches bleibt im Dunkeln. Dafür wird deutlich, welche
wichtige Rolle die Sakramente bei der Rettung der Seele spielen.

---

[86] II 134,11 ff.

[87] II 134,13.

[88] GAFFRON, aO. 185-191, 222.

[89] II 69 (= Taf. 117), 23.26 f. (KRAUSE in : *ZKG* 75 [1964] 177); diese Lesung ist
inzwischen auch von H.-M. SCHENKE in : *ThLZ* 90 (1965) 329 f. und J.-É. MÉNARD,
aO. 82 übernommen worden.

[90] GAFFRON, aO. 191.

[91] II 134,29.

[92] II 67 (= Taf. 115), 12 f.

[93] II 134,32 f.

L'«ÉVANGILE SELON PHILIPPE»
ET L'«EXÉGÈSE DE L'ÂME»

PAR

JACQUES-É. MÉNARD

La réunion de l'âme à son parèdre céleste, l'esprit, exprime dans les gnoses en général la perfection que l'âme atteint en se reconnaissant elle-même. Cette union est symbolisée dans l'*Évangile selon Philippe* et dans l'*Exégèse de l'âme* du Codex II par celle des époux dans la chambre nuptiale. Il y a lieu de rapprocher cette représentation de celle des Valentiniens et des Naassènes. Ce sont ces rapprochements que j'aimerais exposer devant vous aujourd'hui.

I. LA SYMBOLIQUE DU MARIAGE DANS LE VALENTINISME

On ne comprend vraiment la notion de mariage spirituel dans le valentinisme qu'en la remettant dans le large contexte de ce système gnostique, c'est-à-dire dans la structure syzygique du pneumatique et dans le développement du processus cosmique à ses trois niveaux : celui du pneumatique ou du Plérôme, celui du psychique ou du milieu, l'endroit où résident le Démiurge, créateur du monde, et ses anges, et celui du hylique et du monde terrestre et provisoire [1]. Ce qui est et ce qui se passe en dehors du Plérôme est considéré comme une contre-façon du monde supérieur, de ses personnages et de ses événements mythiques. La Sophia-Achamoth est la copie de sa Mère au Plérôme, sa chute et sa rédemption sont des événements archétypaux, qui se renouvellent dans la souffrance et la libération définitive des pneu-matiques. Le Démiurge est une copie du Dieu Très-Haut, ses anges, des copies des Éons du Plérôme, et sa puissance encercle la sphère psychique et hylique. L'Église des gnostiques a son archétype dans l'Éon-Ekklesia, le baptême salvifique des gnostiques a le sien dans celui des anges, et le sacrement de la chambre nuptiale, dans la syzygie du Plérôme. Si cette structure de pensée comporte l'idée de l'image pure

---

[1] Cf. K. MÜLLER, *Beiträge zum Verständnis der valentinianischen Gnosis* (*NGG*, phil.-hist. Kl.), 1920, pp. 208-221.

et simple renfermée dans les créatures inférieures et dans leurs comportements, qui sont des manifestations de Déficience, elle n'en manque pas moins de souligner la possibilité pour les images de renouer leur lien avec le monde supérieur. Puisque le gnostique reconnaît sa propre destinée dans celle de Sophia, il peut être assuré de son salut. Ainsi, les mystes du valentinien Marcos, anticipant grâce à l'image de leur union à Charis leur mariage eschatologique [2], n'ont pas à craindre les attaques du Juge. Et l'*Évangile selon Philippe* peut aller jusqu'à considérer la chair méprisable comme une chair semblable à celle du Christ; elle peut être sanctifiée par l'Eucharistie et être rendue digne de résurrection (sent. 23, 108). Semblablement, Philippe reconnaît dans les sacrements des symboles sans doute méprisables et faibles, mais qui sont, au titre d'images d'une réalité supérieure, le lien entre ce monde-ci et celui de l'Au-delà. Aussi sont-ils porteurs de salut.

Rien de surprenant alors que Philippe ait vu dans l'union mystique de la chambre nuptiale l'image la plus parfaite de la « Vérité ». En elle doit se réaliser l'Unité que le gnostique a perdue et qu'il tente avec nostalgie de retrouver. Pour employer un langage moderne, il parvient ainsi à son identité avec soi-même. Il peut être d'autant plus assuré de la réalité de cet événement que celui-ci n'est que la réalisation des syzygies supraterrestres et du mariage du Soter et de la Sophia, et il est introduit dans son état de sauvé par le sacrement [3].

La revalorisation salvifique des sacrements constitue une étape ultérieure dans l'évolution de la pensée valentinienne. Ce qui n'était, pour des maîtres comme Valentin, Ptolémée et Héracléon, que des événements eschatologiques pouvant être anticipés dans un acte de connaissance, devient à la deuxième génération un déploiement cultuel. L'acte intellectuel paraissait à cette deuxième génération d'une atteinte trop peu facile et même insuffisamment certaine. Ce qui est concret, le geste, le signe, les paroles et les formules, tout cela procure une assurance plus grande. Nous savons des Marcosiens que l'expérience de cérémonies mystériques jouait chez eux un rôle décisif. Les religions à mystères connaissaient des pratiques de ἱερὸς γάμος permettant au myste de prendre part à l'événement du salut, et lui promettant

---

[2] Cf. IRÉNÉE, *Adv. Haer.* I, 13, 1; 13, 4.6.

[3] Cf. H.-G. GAFFRON, *Studien zum koptischen Philippusevangelium unter besonderer Berücksichtigung der Sakramente.* Inaugural-Dissertation zur Erlangung der Doktorwürde der Evangelisch-Theologischen Fakultät der Rheinischen Friedrich-Wilhelms-Universität zu Bonn, Bonn 1969, p. 198.

une libération de ses peines, ἐκ πόνων σωτηρία [4]. Pourquoi les gnostiques n'auraient-ils pas emprunté à d'autres des rites, quand il leur suffisait d'y verser un contenu nouveau ? Quelques gnostiques ont suivi cette voie, — comme on peut le constater pour les trois sacrements de baptême, d'onction et d'eucharistie, mentionnés à la sentence 68 de l'*Évangile selon Philippe* —, et ils ont eu les sacrements en honneur, à l'exemple des chrétiens de la Grande Église. Mais ils ne se sont pas limités à emprunter ces sacrements, ils ont essayé, dans un esprit de créativité, de les dépasser en leur adjoignant d'autres rites, comme celui du mariage spirituel. Ce dernier acquérait toute sa valeur d'acte salvifique, dans la mesure où il permettait au gnostique d'exprimer par lui sa nostalgie du monde parfait de l'Unité céleste.

II. LE MARIAGE SPIRITUEL DANS L'«ÉVANGILE SELON PHILIPPE»

L'homme de l'*Évangile selon Philippe* est tombé de son Unité primordiale, de cette Unité qui était présente en Adam. En effet, l'homme et la femme étaient liés, aux débuts, dans une syzygie androgynique. C'est seulement quand la femme s'est séparée de l'homme que s'est produite la rupture qui détermine maintenant toute l'existence du monde et de l'homme. La puissance qui subjugue tous les êtres, c'est la mort (sent. 71, 78). Le chemin qui conduisait à cette Unité, à la Vie, est dorénavant fermé par le voile cosmique ; il faut attendre qu'il se déchire pour que la réunion des deux sphères soit rendue possible. Alors, ceux d'en-haut, c'est-à-dire le Sauveur et sa cour angélique, pourront descendre vers ceux d'en-bas, les gnostiques, et les reconduire vers l'Unité primordiale (sent. 125 = p. 85, 5-13) [5].

Cette ἀποκατάστασις s'est réalisée lors de la venue du Christ (sent. 67 = p. 67, 18 ; p. 52, 19.35 ; 53, 10 ; 55, 6.12 ; 63, 24.29 ; 67, 31 ; 68, 20 ; 73, 23 s). Le Christ apporte à l'homme le pain du ciel, parce que l'homme manquait de nourriture spirituelle (sent. 15, 93). Il est venu racheter, sauver et délivrer, « ceux qui étaient étrangers, il les a rachetés, il les a faits siens » (sent. 9 = p. 53,3 s). Il est venu, sous les traits d'un

---

[4] Cf. FIRMICUS MATERNUS, *De errore profanarum religionum* 22, 1.

[5] Contrairement à la pagination que nous avions suggérée dans notre édition de l'*Évangile selon Philippe* (cf. J.-É. MÉNARD, *L'Évangile selon Philippe*. Introduction, texte, traduction et commentaire, Paris 1967), nous adoptons celle qui est maintenant communément admise. Notre méprise était due aux deux pages blanches, 3 et 4, du ms. La pagination arabe est faussée à compter de la p. 5, laquelle est en fait la p. 3.

teinturier miraculeux, transformer les couleurs du monde en la seule couleur qui soit, la couleur blanche céleste, et rassembler les couleurs, mêlées à la multiplicité des coloris (sent. 54 = p. 63, 25-30). Il est « venu corriger à nouveau la séparation qui existait depuis le début, les réunir à nouveau (l'homme et la femme) et vivifier ceux qui étaient morts dans la séparation et les unir » (sent. 78 = p. 70, 13-17). C'est lui qui a réparé la chute des débuts (sent. 83 = p. 71, 18-21). Il reconstitue en lui-même l'Adam original. De même que celui-ci est né de la παρθενός, la Sophia considérée comme l'esprit vierge, et de la terre vierge [6], le Christ est né d'une Vierge qui n'a pas été entachée du commerce sexuel instauré par les créateurs du monde (sent. 83 = p. 71, 16-19). Parce qu'il vient de la grande chambre nuptiale, il révèle, il ouvre aux siens, les disciples, qui sont prisonniers de l'ignorance et de l'erreur (sent. 123 = p. 84, 6 s), l'entrée de la chambre nuptiale dont ils sont sortis (sent. 82 = p. 71, 7-15). La voie est maintenant libre, mais la réunion définitive est encore à venir : « ceux qui sont séparés *seront* ac[couplés] et *seront* remplis » (sent. 126 = p. 85, 31). Cette réunion est éternelle (sent. 126 = p. 86, 3 s) : elle n'a rien à voir avec le « mariage de la souillure », qui est l'expression de l'ἐπιθυμία et des ténèbres. Elle est pure, elle est l'accomplissement suprême de l'homme dans la lumière parfaite et sainte (sent. 122 = p. 82, 4-10 ; sent. 127 = p. 86, 17 s) qui se répandra à la fin sur tous : alors, le « Saint des Saints » se révélera, toute méchanceté, et l'esclavage avec elle seront abolis (sent. 125 = p. 85, 19-29).

On jugera d'après cette esquisse que la pensée de Philippe place, contrairement au témoignage des hérésiologues, tout l'événement du salut et de la damnation sous le signe de la séparation et de la réunion. Pour Philippe la chambre nuptiale n'est pas seulement une dimension eschatologique, mais elle est aussi une dimension préexistante, parce qu'il se représente tout le monde céleste comme une grande « chambre nuptiale ». Et c'est dans cette perspective nouvelle, pour nous qui étions habitués à celle des hérésiologues, que nous devons envisager la révélation apportée par le Christ. Celui-ci occupe chez Philippe une place beaucoup plus importante que chez les gnostiques d'Irénée ou de Clément d'Alexandrie. Sur la christologie et la doctrine de la rédemption, notre Évangile se rapproche en plusieurs points de la notion irénéenne de récapitulation, sans

---

[6] Cf. J.-É. MÉNARD, *op. cit.*, p. 203.

abandonner pour autant l'idée spécifiquement gnostique de révélation et de rédemption.

Le but du sacrement du mariage est de protéger le gnostique, lors de sa remontée vers l'Unité que toutes les Puissances cherchent à détruire. La foi populaire appelle ces Puissances des démons, mais, pour le gnostique, elles doivent être identifiées aux Archontes. Ceux-ci veulent pousser l'homme aux vices mentionnés dans la troisième partie de la sentence 61 : le désir (sexuel), la crainte, l'envie. Si le gnostique est uni à son archétype céleste par la συνουσία, ils sont sans force, car il leur est alors supérieur (ϥϫⲟⲥⲉ, p. 65, 29) [7]. Ce sont eux également qui essaient de se saisir du gnostique, lorsqu'il quitte le monde (sent. 63, 127), pour l'empêcher de remonter vers sa patrie céleste ; ⲉⲙⲁϩⲧⲉ ou ⲁⲙⲁϩⲧⲉ sont les expressions employées par l'*Évangile selon Philippe* pour décrire cette attitude des Archontes désirant entraver l'ascension des âmes défuntes (p. 65, 8.28.32 ; 70, 7 ; 76, 23.25 ; 85, 1 ; 86, 6). Ce vocabulaire est d'ailleurs communément gnostique [8].

Une deuxième allusion évidente au sacrement de mariage est celle de la sentence 77 (p. 70, 5-9) : « Ceux qui ont revêtu la lumière parfaite ne sont pas aperçus par les Puissances, et ils ne peuvent être retenus par elles. Or, on revêtira cette lumière dans le mystère, dans la syzygie ». On pourrait rapprocher ce passage, ainsi que le fait Gaffron [9], de la sentence 127 (p. 86, 4-9). Pour se soustraire à l'emprise des Archontes (δύναμεις), le gnostique doit revêtir le vêtement céleste de lumière dans le « mystère » dont le but est la réunion. Ce « mystère » ne peut être autre que le sacrement de mariage. Si quelqu'un l'a reçu, les Archontes ne peuvent rien contre lui, « même s'il est dans le monde » (sent. 127 = p. 86, 10 s). Celui qui reçoit la lumière devient ainsi « enfant du mariage » (p. 86, 4 s), c'est-à-dire qu'il est d'ores et déjà lié à la « chambre nuptiale », au Plérôme. L'expression « fils de la chambre nuptiale » semble avoir été un *terminus technicus* pour désigner tout gnostique qui s'est soumis au sacrement du mariage ; on retrouve par exemple, la même notion à la sentence 66, où il semble, malgré la lacune, que les deux époux soient l'âme et l'esprit. De plus, à la sentence 102 (p. 76, 4 s), nous lisons, à propos de l'Esprit-Saint et du Fils de l'homme : « Ceux-ci sont le lieu où se trouvent les enfants de la cham-

---

[7] Cf. *Apocryphon de Jean*, fol. 65, 8-16 Till ; *Évangile selon Marie*, fol. 16, 5-21 Till ; Ptolémée, *Lettre à Flora* 6, 1 Quispel ; *Évangile de Vérité*, p. 32,31 - 33,32 Ménard.

[8] Cf. *Extraits de Théodote* 1, 2 ; 22, 4.7 ; 37 ; 39 Sagnard ; *Pistis Sophia*, p. 23, 5-10 ; 146, 7-10 Schmidt-Till ; II *Livre de Ieoû*, p. 314, 27 Schmidt-Till.

[9] Cf. *op. cit.*, p. 104 s.

bre nuptiale». Le « lieu » est évidemment le monde céleste. Et le sacrement de mariage a ici encore une signification eschatologique. Dans
le cas présent Gaffron a sans doute raison : le « mariage » est davantage
chez Philippe un sacrement de l'Au-delà.

Il semble, à ce propos, qu'il faille citer presque dans son intégralité
la sentence 67 (p. 67, 9-18) :

> La Vérité n'est pas venue
> dans le monde nue, mais elle est venue dans
> les types et les images. Il ne la recevra pas autrement.
> Il y a une régénération et une
> image de régénération. Il faut vraiment
> que l'on renaisse par l'image. Quelle
> est la résurrection ? Et l'image par l'image,
> il convient qu'elle ressuscite ; le fiancé et l'image
> par l'image, il faut qu'ils pénètrent dans
> la Vérité, qui est la restauration.

La notion-clé de ce passage est celle d'εἰκών ; sa double signification
a donné l'occasion à Philippe de se livrer, comme de coutume, à des
jeux de mots spirituels, mais difficiles à saisir pour des non-initiés.
Εἰκών désigne d'une part l'image de l'ange, c'est-à-dire le gnostique
(p. 58, 14 ; 65, 24) ; d'autre part, comme synonyme de τύπος, elle
signifie le mode de révélation de ce qui est caché [10]. Les deux sens sont
souvent juxtaposés chez Philippe. La Vérité n'est pas accessible à la
connaissance naturelle, elle est cachée (p. 85, 12 s), elle est un mystère
(p. 84, 20 s). Elle est quelque chose de puissant et de vénérable, alors
que les choses visibles sont méprisables et faibles (p. 85, 14-15). Elle
a un nom propre qui est inconnu du monde (sent. 12), mais elle veut
être connue. C'est pourquoi elle sort de son mystère, et, quand elle
se révèle, elle est reconnue (p. 84, 4 s). Les moyens dont elle se sert
pour se révéler sont les noms ; ils sont en même temps le moyen pour
le gnostique de reconnaître la Vérité (p. 54, 13-18). Il ne faut pas
toutefois prendre les noms pour la Vérité elle-même ; car ils ont une
fin dans l'Éon (p. 54, 4 s). Ils ne sont en quelque sorte que le miroir
de la réalité la plus élevée et ils n'ont plus aucune raison d'être, lorsque
celle-là se révèle elle-même et qu'elle se dévoile. C'est ainsi que les
noms de Dieu, du Père, du Fils, de l'Esprit-Saint, de la Vie, de la lumière, de la résurrection ne sont que l'expression imparfaite de ce qu'ils

---

[10] Cf. p. 84, 21 ; εἰκών : p. 69, 37 ; 86, 13 ; 65, 12 ; τύπος : p. 85, 15 ; 75, 16 ; l'expression
« symboles et images » se retrouve dans l'*Epistula ad Rheginum* (*De Resurrectione*),
p. 49, 6 s Malinine ; PTOLÉMÉE, *Lettre à Flora* 5, 9 ; 6, 5 ; IRÉNÉE, *Adv. Haer.* I, 12, 1.

désignent ; ils peuvent être mal interprétés, et ils ne concèdent en aucune manière une totale connaissance de la Vérité (sent. 11-13, 103 ; 19, 33, 47).

Il en va de même des symboles et des images dont se sert la Vérité dans sa Révélation. Comparés à la « beauté parfaite », ils ne sont que des êtres fantomatiques négligeables, et ils ne reproduisent la véritable nature de l'archétype que dans un terne éclat (p. 85, 13-16). Ils renferment pourtant en eux-mêmes quelque chose de la puissance et de la beauté de l'archétype, qui permet à celui qui le reconnaît de participer de la réalité archétypale (p. 85, 17 s). La Vérité ne se révèle pas nue, mais sous un voile. Elle ne se livre pas au monde, mais elle conserve en elle-même et pour elle-même sa nature cachée. Le monde ne serait d'ailleurs pas en mesure de la saisir telle qu'elle est en réalité ; aussi s'exprime-t-elle dans des images et des symboles identiques aux « noms ». Lorsqu'il est dit dans notre Évangile : « [Il (le Seigneur) s'est manifesté en ce] lieu-ci dans des [symboles et des images] » (sent. 69), on pourrait entendre par là que les paroles kérygmatiques du Maître doivent être rangées parmi ces noms. Mais nous avons affaire ici à un langage technique : les symboles et les images sont les sacrements. Jésus révèle la beauté de la Vérité d'une manière mystérieuse, dans des images (sent. 68 s). Celui qui porte tout en lui-même (sent. 20), le Christ, connaît le chemin de la Vérité, puisqu'il la rend accessible aux hommes par le baptême, l'onction, l'eucharistie, l'ἀπολύτρωσις et le mariage (sent. 68). Celui qui reçoit les sacrements a déjà reçu la Vérité dans les images (p. 86, 12 s). Le monde n'est plus pour lui une puissance qui l'opprime et qui l'asservit : désormais il est mort, sa méchanceté est supprimée et il est sans force [11]. Le monde de la Vérité, dans lequel le gnostique est introduit grâce aux images, est un monde de plénitude et de perfection. Ce monde est devenu Éon (p. 86, 13). Il est l'Éon, le temps infini. « Ce Jour-là ou sa Lumière ne se couchent pas » (p. 86, 3-4). Celui qui a reçu la Vérité est déjà entré dans la Vérité (p. 67, 17 s ; 85, 14 s). Il ne vit plus dans le temps, mais il est entré dans l'ère eschatologique.

Tel est le contexte de révélation, de salut et de plénitude dans lequel il faut remettre la pensée de la sentence 67, citée plus haut. Si l'analyse des sentences 69, 124, 125, 127 peut nous laisser douter de la

---

[11] La sent. 123 expose l'idée qu'une chose est reconnue bonne ou mauvaise dès son apparition.

signification qu'elles donnent aux τύποι et aux εἰκόνες, le sens de la sentence 67, lui, est clair.

Lorsque Philippe y oppose la régénération à la régénération en image, il ne peut s'agir, dans le cas de la première régénération, que d'un événement spirituel qui se réalise dans l'image sacramentelle. Cette régénération n'est pas celle du baptême, comme dans le N.T. (*Jn* 3, 5 ; *Tit.* 3, 5). L'ἀποκατάστασις est la reconstitution de l'Unité primordiale obtenue avant tout par le sacrement de mariage. En lui, enfin, l'image rencontre son ange. Et cette rencontre est décrite comme une régénération en image, ou, ce qui revient au même dans la pensée de Philippe, comme une résurrection. La triple répétition du verbe ϢϢⲈ, « il convient », « il est nécessaire », insiste sur la nécessité pour le gnostique d'une appropriation du salut « par l'image ». Cette dernière tournure elle aussi revient trois fois dans cette sentence 67. Dans la célébration du sacrement de mariage, la Vérité se révèle au gnostique en image, du fait qu'il la reconnaît lors de sa réunion à son ange, et qu'il s'unit à elle. C'est ainsi que nous lisons, à la sentence 123 (p. 84, 11-14) : « Si nous reconnaissons la Vérité, nous trouverons les fruits de la Vérité en nous-mêmes. Si nous nous unissons à elle, elle recevra notre Plérôme ». En la personne du fiancé, la Vérité elle-même vient vers le gnostique et s'unit à lui (ϨⲰⲦⲢ est l'expression même pour désigner la syzygie) [12] ; il entre alors avec elle dans la chambre nuptiale (p. 67, 17). Cette συνουσία du gnostique avec la Vérité, réalisée par son union avec son ange, restitue l'Unité primordiale. C'est l'ἀποκατάστασις. L'entrée finale dans le Plérôme est anticipée dans l'acte sacramentel. C'est pourquoi les Puissances d'erreur et d'ignorance n'ont plus aucune emprise sur le gnostique unifié, ni pendant sa vie terrestre, ni au moment de son entrée définitive dans le monde céleste. Nous lisons à la sentence 63 (p. 66, 16-20) : « Pendant que nous sommes en ce monde, il nous convient d'acquérir la résurrection, afin que, si nous nous dépouillons de la chair, nous soyons trouvés dans le repos (et) que nous n'errions pas dans le milieu ». Ou encore : « Si quelqu'un ne la (la lumière) reçoit pas », grâce à laquelle il devient enfant de la chambre nuptiale, « tandis qu'il est en ces lieux, il ne pourra la recevoir dans l'autre Lieu » (sent. 127 = p. 86, 6 s). Mais on reçoit cette lumière dans « le mystère, la réunion » (sent. 77), c'est-à-dire dans la chambre nuptiale en image (sent. 61).

Ainsi que le démontrent tous ces arguments, le mariage spirituel a,

---

[12] Cf. sent. 26, 61, 74, 77, 78, 79, 80, 82, 103, 113, 126.

avant tout, dans l'*Évangile selon Philippe* une dimension eschatologique. Mais il est inexact de le réduire à cette dimension, comme le propose Gaffron [13]. Si l'union du gnostique avec son ange ne se réalise
en plénitude qu'au moment de sa remontée au ciel, — c'est l'aspect
eschatologique de la Gnose qu'on oublie trop souvent —, il faut ajouter
que le gnostique est aussi d'ores et déjà sauvé, — et c'est l'aspect
actualisé de son salut. A vouloir l'ignorer, on ignore la valeur réelle
du sacrement en tant qu'image, quel que soit d'ailleurs l'acte grâce
auquel il est administré : baiser (sent. 31, 55) ou le mariage lui-même,
dont la sentence 122 nous décrit bien toute la sacralité. Les Valentiniens
reconnaissaient d'ailleurs à ce mariage une valeur sacramentelle [14].
Son opposition à la chambre nuptiale céleste ne doit pas faire difficulté :
elle est ancienne et classique, pour ne pas dire usée. Il ne faudrait pas
non plus oublier que, dans l'Antiquité, l'image est toujours liée à
un archétype, ainsi que l'ont démontré en d'autres domaines Jervell
et Schwanz [15]. L'image ne se définit que par rapport à un archétype.

III. La remontée du gnostique et l'« Exégèse de l'âme »

Mais comment s'effectue cette réunion dans l'Au-delà ? Plus explicite-
ment encore que l'*Évangile selon Philippe*, l'*Exégèse de l'âme* enseigne
que c'est entre l'âme et le *pneuma* que se réalise ce mariage. L'âme
est féminine, lisons-nous à la p. 127, 19-20 [16] :

> Les sages (σοφός) avant nous donnèrent (ὀνομασία)
> à l'âme un nom féminin.

Et cette âme s'est livrée à la prostitution dans la chair avec les
Égyptiens, symbole du monde matériel [17] (p. 130, 19-20) :

> Tu t'es livrée à la prostitution (πορνεύειν) avec les fils d'Égyptiens
> qui sont tes voisins, qui ont une grande chair.

---

[13] Cf. *op. cit.*, pp. 209 s.

[14] Cf. J.-É. Ménard, *op. cit.*, p. 28.

[15] Cf. J. Jervell, « *Imago Dei* ». *Gen 1, 26 f. im Spätjudentum, in der Gnosis und in
den paulinischen Briefen* (*FRLANT*, NF 58), Göttingen 1960; P. Schwanz, *Imago Dei
als christologisch-arthropologisches Problem in der Geschichte der Alten Kirche von Paulus
bis Clemens von Alexandrien* (*Arbeiten zur Kirchengeschichte und Religionswissenschaft*,
2), Halle 1970.

[16] Cf. M. Krause, Pahor Labib, *Gnostische und hermetische Schriften aus Codex II
und Codex VI* (*Abhandlungen des Deutschen Archäologischen Instituts Kairo*, Koptische
Reihe 2), Glückstadt 1971.

[17] Cf. J.-É. Ménard, « Le Chant de la Perle », *RevScRel* 42 (1968) 289-325.

Mais lorsqu'elle se retourne sur elle-même, elle redevient pure (p. 131, 27-30) :

> Lorsque la matrice (μήτρα) de l'âme (ψυχή)
> d'après la volonté du Père
> se retourne sur elle-même, elle se plonge (βαπτίζειν) et devient
> immédiatement pure de l'extérieur.

Elle est alors comparée, comme dans l'*Évangile selon Philippe*, à la femme qui était originellement unie à son époux. Elle et le mari redeviennent Un (p. 133, 3-10) :

> Ils deviendront une seule chair (σάρξ). Ils
> étaient en effet (γάρ) d'abord unis dans le Père,
> avant que la femme ne quitte l'homme qui
> est son frère. Ce mariage (γάμος)
> les a à nouveau (πάλιν) réunis, et l'âme (ψυχή)
> s'est unie à son véritable bien-aimé, son
> Seigneur naturel (φυσικός), comme (κατά) il est écrit :
> Le maître de la femme en effet (γάρ) est son mari.

Ce mari, c'est le πνεῦμα. Se retournant sur elle-même et retrouvant son bien-aimé, l'âme est semblable en cela à la Sophia, retrouvant son maître et remontant au ciel. C'est en cela que consiste la résurrection (p. 133,33-134,14). Et les enfants issus de ce mariage sont les gnostiques :

> ... l'âme (ψυχή) rencontra à nouveau son bien-aimé.
> Et [lui aussi] l'aima. Et
> lorsqu'elle entra en communion (κοινωνεῖν) avec lui, elle reçut
> de lui la semence (σπέρμα) — c'est-à-dire l'esprit (πνεῦμα),
> qui rend vivant — de sorte qu'elle engendre de lui des enfants
> qui sont bons, et elle les garde en vie.
> Car (γάρ) c'est là la grande (et) parfaite
> naissance merveilleuse (θαῦμα), puisque (ὥστε) ce mariage (γάμος)
> s'accomplit selon la volonté du Père. Mais (δέ) il convient que l'âme (ψυχή)
> s'engendre elle-même (à nouveau) et qu'elle devienne à nouveau
> ce qu'elle était originellement. L'âme se meut maintenant
> seule. Elle a reçu le divin du Père,
> de sorte qu'elle devient veuve, pour qu'à nouveau elle remonte
> dans le lieu où elle était depuis le commencement. Telle est
> la résurrection (ἀνάστασις) des morts.
> Tel est le salut de l'emprisonnement (αἰχμαλωσία).
> Telle est la montée (ἀνάβασις) dans le ciel.

Et c'est grâce au *pneuma* intérieur que s'opère la μετάνοια, qui est avant tout une conversion de la πλάνη (p. 135, 1-10) :

« Personne ne peut venir à moi, si (εἰ μήτι)
mon Père ne l'attire et ne me l'apporte,
et moi-même je le réveillerai au dernier
jour ». Il convient par conséquent de prier le Père et de
le supplier de toute notre âme (ψυχή). Non avec les
lèvres, (de) l'extérieur, mais (ἀλλά) dans l'esprit (πνεῦμα)
qui est à l'intérieur, qui est venu
de la profondeur (βάθος), pour que nous gémissions et fassions pénitence (-μετανοεῖν)
à cause
de la vie que nous avons menée, pour que nous confessions (ἐξομολογεῖν)
les péchés, pour que nous reconnaissions l'erreur (πλάνη) vide …

Contrairement à bien des textes gnostiques, l'*Exégèse de l'âme* ne
conçoit pas la μετάνοια simplement comme un retour, une conversion
sur soi-même, mais aussi comme une pénitence. Cette double signification du terme provient des influences différentes, aussi bien bibliques que grecques [18], qui se sont exercées sur l'*Exégèse*. La séparation
de l'âme de son πνεῦμα est comparée à un adultère (p. 129, 8-14)
comme en *Jér.* 3, 1-4. L'âme dans notre traité est également comparée
à l'épouse bien-aimée d'*Osée* 2, 4-9 qui s'est livrée à la prostitution
(p. 129, 23 s), ou encore à celle d'*Ézéchiel* 16, 23-26 a (p. 130, 11-20).
Cette prostitution, Paul l'interdisait aussi en 1 *Cor.* 5, 9-10 (p. 131, 4-8),
ou encore en *Ephés.* 6, 12 (p. 131, 9-13) ; elle est la prostitution avec
les Archontes cosmiques, comme l'interprètent tous les textes gnostiques.

Cette conversion de l'âme doit être, d'une part, une conversion des
péchés (p. 135, 31-136, 27), ainsi que le recommandent *Is.* 30, 15.19-20 ;
Ps. 7, 19 ; *Jér.* 11, 20 ; 17, 10 ; *Apoc.* 2,23, mais elle est, d'autre part,
un retour à la patrie qu'a quittée Ulysse (p. 136, 29 s), séduit par les
beaux discours et les tromperies de Calypso (*Odyssée* 1, 48 s ; 4, 555 s ;
5, 82 s ; 151 s). Elle est aussi le retour d'Hélène, dans l'*Odyssée*
(4, 261 s), vers Ménélas, qu'elle avait quitté (p. 136,36 - 137,5) sous
les instances d'Aphrodite, maîtresse de ce monde de générations.

Le mythe qui se cache derrière toutes ces relectures de la Bible ou
d'Homère est un mythe androgynique. C'est celui de l'*Évangile selon
Philippe*, tout autant que celui de l'*Évangile selon Thomas* (log. 22, 37).
Et c'est dans cette perspective qu'il faut interpréter les pages 131,13-
132,2 de l'*Exégèse de l'âme*, dont nous avons extrait plus haut une brève

---

[18] Cf. W.-C. ROBINSON, « The Exegesis of the Soul », *Novum Testamentum* XII,
2 (1970) 102-117 ; M. KRAUSE, PAHOR LABIB, *op. cit.*, pp. 68-87.

citation (p. 131, 27-30). Il s'agit du retour de l'âme en son intérieur, pour éviter le commerce avec les Puissances extérieures.

Bien des éléments particuliers rapprochent l'*Exégèse de l'âme* de la théorie des Naassènes (cf. HIPPOLYTE, *Elenchos* V, 6-7), ainsi que l'a souligné W.C. Robinson [19]. Les Naassènes faisaient un emploi élaboré du thème androgynique, ils interdisaient les rapprochements sexuels et soutenaient que la restauration de l'union androgynique ne pouvait s'effectuer que par l'abolition de la sexualité. Leur enseignement s'appuyait tout aussi bien sur une interprétation du mythe d'Attis mutilé par Cybèle que sur les affirmations de Paul proclamant la nécessité de devenir un seul homme nouveau, ni mâle ni femelle. Ils se référaient également à l'histoire d'Isis recherchant Osiris, encore que la présence du symbole phallique ne soit pas apparente dans l'*Exégèse de l'âme*. Ils citaient et réinterprétaient Homère, en y mêlant le thème de l'*Exode* et en identifiant l'Égypte au corps.

Toutefois, ce que dit Hippolyte (*Elenchos* V, 8) trouve aussi un écho dans l'*Exégèse de l'âme*, bien que cette section de l'*Elenchos* ne traite pas directement des Naassènes, mais des Samothraciens, des Thraciens et des Phrygiens. On y retrouve Homère, la régénération, l'androgynie, des passages de l'Écriture comme *Jn* 6,44, cité également dans l'*Exégèse de l'âme* (p. 135, 1 s). Le rapprochement sexuel est une faute; pour entrer dans la maison de Dieu, il faut se dépouiller de ses vêtements, s'identifier à la fiancée redevenue mâle, grâce à l'Esprit-Vierge.

L'*Exégèse de l'âme* nous paraît bel et bien être un traité gnostique. Sa doctrine du retour de l'âme dans l'Esprit, lors de sa remontée au ciel, symbolisé par l'image du mariage spirituel, la rapproche des autres traités gnostiques, plus particulièrement de l'*Évangile selon Philippe*. Si ce mariage est un sacrement pour Philippe, il est certes un sacrement de la fin des temps, comme le pense Gaffron, mais aussi un sacrement qui peut être déjà actualisé dans la vie du gnostique, car l'âme de celui-ci s'est déjà reconnue, elle s'est retournée sur elle-même et en elle-même, pour y redécouvrir l'Esprit qui ne fait maintenant plus qu'Un avec elle.

---

[19] Cf. *art. cit.*, p. 116.

ON EXEGETING «THE EXEGESIS ON THE SOUL»

BY

FREDERIK WISSE

The name « Coptic gnostic library »[1] used for the papyrus codices found some thirty years ago near Nag Hammadi, has raised certain expectations which tend to make the interpretation of these works one-sided. Though the gnostic ownership of the collection cannot be taken for granted[2], most interpreters look at the individual tractates as expressions of some form of Gnosticism. This brings the danger of a gnosticizing interpretation, a kind of « guilt by association ». Statements which otherwise might have passed for orthodox Christian or typically Hellenistic are now searched for a possible gnostic slant. Not a few fall prey to the ingenuity of the modern interpreter. It is revealing of the gnostic movement, or our knowledge of it, that few pagan or Christian religious writings of the first three centuries of our era are immune to being interpreted as showing the influence of Gnosticism or as including a polemic against it.

The presence of a Coptic version of *the Sentences of Sextus* (XII, *1*) among the tractates should serve as a warning against a gnosticizing interpretation of the library[3]. No one would want to claim that these ethical maxims were written by a Gnostic, though it is possible to imagine that a Gnostic would have found much in them with which he could sympathize. The Coptic translation shows no gnostic bias, and it seems to have been made by someone who was mainly interested in being accurate and intelligible[4]. A good number of other works

---

[1] This title was used by JAMES M. ROBINSON for his inventory article « The Coptic Gnostic Library Today », *NTS* 14 (1968) 383-401, and for the international English edition of the Nag Hammadi Codices being published in the *Nag Hammadi Studies* monograph series by E. J. Brill, Leiden.

[2] Cf. T. SÄVE-SÖDERBERGH, « Holy Scriptures or Apologetic Documentations. The 'Sitz im Leben' of the Nag Hammadi Library », in this volume.

[3] Cf. F. WISSE, « Die Sextus-Sprüche und das Problem der gnostischen Ethik », in : *Göttinger Orient Forschungen*, *VI-2*, Wiesbaden 1975.

[4] See my introduction to the forthcoming text edition of the Coptic version of *the Sentences of Sextus* in : *The Coptic Gnostic Library, Codices XI, XII, XIII*, ed. John Turner. (*Nag Hammadi Studies*), E. J. Brill, Leiden.

contained in the Nag Hammadi codices are not obviously gnostic and deserve to be considered « innocent until proven guilty ». It is significant that the tractates which come into question are at the same time clearly Christian.

Without wanting to minimize the importance of the library for our understanding of Gnosticism, the contribution it makes to our knowledge of early Christian literature may well prove to be more significant. What is left of the Christian writings of the first three centuries is mainly what proved to be useful to later orthodoxy. The great majority are apologetic, heresiological and theological works. That this was only a limited and one-sided selection of what was available is suggested by the apocryphal Acts of the Apostles which have survived. While one can disagree with details of Walter Bauer's reconstruction of early Christianity, he appears to be right in picturing pluralism and heterodoxy in at least a part of the church [5]. It is reasonable to expect that the religious writings of the period reflect this situation. The paucity of nonorthodox works can be attributed to the suppression of such literature by later orthodoxy.

It appears now that the Nag Hammadi collection has given us a number of outstanding examples of early Christian heterodoxy. There is, for example, *the Teachings of Silvanus* (VII, *4*), a wisdom text which reflects Stoic ethics against a middle-Platonic background [6]. This pseudophilosophical form of Christianity may have been an offshoot of Alexandrian theology. Another prominent example is *Authentic Teaching* (VI, *3*), a homily on the fate of the soul in this world [7]. Like *the Teachings of Silvanus*, this work is in many ways unique in early Christian literature, yet it is not obviously heretical. There are also a number of works attributed to apostles which are more

---

[5] WALTER BAUER, *Rechtgläubigkeit und Ketzerei im ältesten Christentum.* (*Beiträge zur historischen Theologie*, 10), Tübingen 1964².

[6] Cf. J. ZANDEE, « Die Lehren des Silvanus », in : *Essays on the Nag Hammadi Text in Honour of Alexander Böhlig.* (*Nag Hammadi Studies*, III). Leiden 1972, pp. 144-155, and J. ZANDEE and M. PEEL, « The Teachings of Silvanus from the Library of Nag Hammadi », *NovTest* 14 (1972) 294-311.

[7] The *editio princeps* was published by M. KRAUSE and P. LABIB, *Gnostische und hermetische Schriften aus Codes II und Codex VI.* (*Abhandlungen des Deutschen Archäologischen Instituts Kairo*, Koptische Reihe, Band II), Wiesbaden 1971 (appeared 1972), pp. 133-149. See also the introduction and German translation by W.-P. FUNK, in : *TLZ* 98 (1973) 251-259, and the useful introductory article by G. W. MacRAE, « A Nag Hammadi Tractate on the Soul », in : *Ex Orbe Religionum. Studia Geo Widengren oblata.* (Supplements to *Numen*, XXI), Leiden 1972, pp. 471-479.

clearly heterodox if not in some cases sectarian. They are : *the Acts of Peter and the Twelve Apostles* (VI, *1*), *the Apocryphon of James* (I, *1*), *the Book of Thomas the Contender* (II, *7*), *the Gospel of Thomas* (II, *2*) and *the Gospel of Philip* (II, *3*). Though these works were or would most likely have been rejected by the defenders of orthodoxy, all except the last one could have been written by someone in a part of the church where orthodoxy had not as yet asserted itself. They can, therefore, enrich our limited picture of the variety of beliefs and practices in early Christianity [8].

One of the most interesting Christian writings in the Nag Hammadi collection is *the Exegesis on the Soul* (II, *6*). It has appeared in a text edition with German translation by Martin Krause [9]. Among the Nag Hammadi tractates it shows similarities with *Authentic Teaching* and *the Teachings of Silvanus* [10]. These three writings, each in its own way, direct themselves to the hazardous existence of the soul in this world. It is not the purpose of this article to provide a commentary or an introduction to ExSoul. The study of the tractate has only just begun [11], and the immediate need lies still with understanding the Coptic text. Thus it appears most helpful at this point to comment on problem passages in the text and the translation. In addition to this, some basic issues raised by William C. Robinson Jr. concerning the make up of the work will be discussed.

The text and translation of Krause will serve as the basis of the discussion. The present author was able to check Krause's text against the originals in the Coptic Museum in Cairo. When there is no question

---

[8] Also *the Gospel of Truth* (I, *2*), *On the Resurrection* (I, *3*), *the Apocalypse of Paul* (V, *2*) and *the Apocalypse of James II* (V, *4*) come into question. The other Christian-gnostic writings in the library are representatives of mythological gnosis or appear to be of too late a date to be of interest here.

[9] M. KRAUSE and P. LABIB, *Gnostische und hermetische Schriften*, pp. 68-87. Krause published a virtually identical translation with a few introductory comments in : *Die Gnosis*, Zweiter Band : *Koptische und mandäische Quellen*. (*Die Bibliothek der alten Welt*, Reihe Antike und Christentum), Zürich and Stuttgart 1971, pp. 127-135.

[10] Compared with most other Nag Hammadi tractates, these three stand out in being written in good, idiomatic Coptic.

[11] An introductory article by WILLIAM C. ROBINSON Jr., « The Exegesis on the Soul» , *NovTest* 12 (1970) 102-117, has appeared. HEDDA BETHGE of the *Berliner Arbeitskreis* is preparing a dissertation, and M. KRAUSE has announced plans for a commentary on the tractate. A detail study by P. NAGEL, « Die Septuaginta-Zitate in der koptisch-gnostischen 'Exegese über die Seele' (Nag Hammadi Codex II) », *Archiv für Papyrusforschung*, is scheduled for publication in 1975.

about the reading such differences with Krause's text involving word
division, supralinear strokes, articulation and punctuation marks, and
the placement of dots or brackets with letters in or near lacunae will
not be noted [12].

The « narrative section », which tells of the fall of the soul from
her heavenly home, her entanglement in evil company, her suffering
and desolation, her repentance and prayer for mercy and finally the
willingness of the Father to hear her prayer (127,22-129,5), presents
few problems. Only Krause's reconstruction in 127,29, ⲁⲩ[ⲱ ⲁⲩⲭⲱϩⲙ
ⲙ̄ⲙ]ⲟⲥ, is too long and the alternative, ⲁⲩ[ⲭⲱϩⲙ ⲙ̄ⲙ]ⲟⲥ, is too
short. At this point in the narrative it is explained in what ways the
soul fell into the hands of her abusers. Then in 127,32 it is said that
she was defiled. Thus one does not expect ⲭⲱϩⲙ in 127,29, but some
other verb. The meaning of the sentence does not depend on the reconstruction.

In the first block of Biblical quotations the reconstruction of *Hos*
2 : 5 and 7 in 129,32 and 34 is problematic. The Septuagint reading,
ἀποκτενῶ αὐτὴν ἐν δίψει, at the end of verse 5 has been given a
different meaning in the Coptic, probably because it does not fit
the narrative where the soul is not killed but comes to repentance.
The Coptic states that she will be made childless. Since the next sentence in Greek and Coptic says that her children will not receive mercy
it is clear that the childlessness is not barrenness but refers to the death
of her children of fornication. In the narrative section such children
were mentioned as being « deaf, blind and sick with retarded minds »
(128,24-26). Most likely the author of ExSoul purposely read ἀτεκνῶ
for ἀποκτενῶ. Also in verse 7 b it is clear that he read πορνεύσομαι
for πορεύσομαι. The reconstruction of 129,34 is uncertain, since the
Greek κατῄσχυνεν ἡ τεκοῦσα αὐτά was apparently rather freely
translated. Remnants of two letters visible near the end of the line
could fit ⲏⲣ in Krause's reconstruction : ϯϣ[ⲓⲡⲉ ⲛ̄ⲛⲉⲥϣⲏⲣⲉ].

The exegetical method used by the author of ExSoul comes to
the surface in the interpretation of *Ez* 16:26. The ⲛⲁⲛⲓⲛⲟϭ
ⲛ̄ⲥⲁⲣⲝ [13] in 130,20.21, which characterizes the sons of Egypt,
translates μεγαλόσαρκος. The Coptic translator interpreted it to
mean « very fleshly ». The fornication of the soul with the « men of

---

[12] ExSoul is now available in fascimile : *The Facsimile Edition of the Nag Hammadi
Codices, Codex II*, E. J. Brill, Leiden 1974, plates 139-149 (= Coptic pp. 127-137).
[13] KRAUSE's reading ⲛ̄ϭⲁⲣⲝ in 130,20 is a printing mistake.

great flesh » becomes thus the pollution with « the fleshly and per-
ceptible things and the things of the earth » (130,22 f.).

The lacuna in 130,33 f. is left unreconstructed by Krause. His
problem was that he thought that the words of the apostles began
in 130,33 after « the apostles wrote ». The following reconstruction
solves this problem : ⲉⲩⲥ2ⲁ[ⲓ ⲛ̄ⲧⲉⲕⲕⲗⲏⲥⲓⲁ] ⲙ̄ⲡⲛⲟⲩⲧⲉ ⲱⲓⲛⲁ ⲭⲉ
ⲛⲉ[ⲛ2ⲃⲏⲩ]ⲉ̣ ⲛ̄ⲧⲉⲉⲓ ⲙ[ⲓ]ⲛⲉ etc. The sentence reads then :

> Therefore, the apostles write [to the church] of God that [things] of this kind may
> not happen in it (130,32-35).

The allusion is to *Acts* 15 : 29 [14].

A serious misunderstanding lies at the basis of Krause's translation
of the section 130,35-131,13. He translates the quotation of 1 *Cor* 5 : 9 :
« Verkehrt nicht mit Hurern, auf keinen Fall mit Hurern dieser Welt
... ». Yet the context demands that the verse be read the way Paul
meant it : « Do not mix with fornicators, not at all (meaning) the
fornicators [15] of this world ... ». Furthermore, the ⲧⲁⲉⲓ ⲧⲉ ⲑⲉ in
131,8 does not refer to what follows, but to the preceding quotation
of 1 *Cor* 5 : 9. The passage as a whole should read :

> But the great [struggle] is because of the fornication of the soul; from it comes
> also the fornication of the body. Therefore, Paul, writing to the Corinthians, said :
> « I wrote to you in the letter : 'Do not mix with fornicators', not at all (meaning) the
> fornicators of this world or the greedy or the robbers or the idolators, since then you
> would have to go out of the world ». Thus he speaks pneumatically, for « our struggle
> is not against flesh and blood », as he said, « but against the worldrulers of this
> darkness and the spiritual powers of wickedness ».

This passage is crucial to the whole tractate. It gives apostolic sanction
to the whole exegetical enterprise of ExSoul. It legitimates taking
the references to πορνεία in Scripture to refer to the spiritual pollution
of the soul. Without 1 *Cor* 5 : 9 f. and *Eph* 6 : 12, the pneumatic-
allegorical interpretation of the Old Testament passages on fornication
would lose its basis. Given the exegetical methods of this time, the
procedure of ExSoul is beyond reproach.

The passage which follows is somewhat obscured by Krause's
too literal translation. We translate :

---

[14] It is better to reconstruct a II Present, ⲉϥϣ]ⲟⲟⲡ, in 130,36 to account for the
available space in the lacuna.

[15] The strange spelling ⲙ̄ⲡⲣ̄ⲛⲟⲥ for ⲙ̄ⲡⲟⲣⲛⲟⲥ may indicate that some text
dropped out due to homoioteleuton ; the Vorlage would then have read : ⲙ̄ⲡⲣ̄⟨ⲧⲱ2
ⲙⲛ̄ ⲙ̄ⲡⲟⲣ⟩ⲛⲟⲥ. The meaning of the sentence does not depend on this emenda-
tion.

As long as the soul goes to and fro, copulating with whomever she meets and being defiled, she is subjected to the « pascha » [16], of the things she deserves to undergo. But when she realizes the sufferings in which she is and cries out to the Father and repents, then the Father will have pity on her and he will turn her womb from the external things and turn it again inward. And the soul will receive again her true character [17] (131,13-22).

ExSoul uses here a difficult and perhaps not entirely successful metaphor. It says that the womb of the fallen soul is like the male genitals, i.e. on the outside of the body. After the soul's repentance the womb is again returned to its original position « on the inside ». This « conversion » is identified with baptism (131,20 and 132,2), and illustrated by the example of the washing of a dirty garment. This illustration is, unfortunately, obscured by a lacuna which appears not to have been reconstructed correctly by Krause. The available space and the remnants of letters are better accounted for by the following reconstruction of 131,32 f. : ϣ[ⲧⲏⲛ ⲉⲩ]ϣⲁ[ⲗ]ⲱⲱⲙ ϣⲁⲩⲧⲉⲗⲟⲟⲩ ⲉⲡ[ⲱⲛⲉ (?) ⲁⲩⲱ ⲛ̄ⲥ]ⲉⲕⲧⲟⲟⲩ. This translates as :

Just as a [garment [18], when it is] dirty, is set upon a [stone (?) and] turned until its dirtiness is brought out and it is clean (131,31-34).

The point of comparison appears to be that the garment is turned inside out and treated until it is clean [19]. This corresponds to the turning and cleansing of the womb. The external position of the womb probably symbolizes that the soul has unnaturally exposed its intimate parts, almost to invite defilement. Such « indecent exposure » was described in the narrative section (128,29 f.) and especially in the Old Testament quotations (129,19; 130,17 f. 26 f.) [20].

The section on the turning of the womb is followed by another difficult metaphor, that of giving birth (132,2-5). It could be that the excursus on the womb became the occasion for an ad hoc use of this

---

[16] The exact use and meaning of ⲡⲁⲥⲭⲁ is unclear. The context suggests that it is related to the verb πάσχειν « suffer ».

[17] The word μερικόν refers most likely to the proper or original state of the soul. Since 127, 22 states that the soul has by nature a womb, the point would be that the womb has returned to the position it had in her pre-fallen state.

[18] In comparisons the Coptic syntax normally demands a plural (ⲛ̄ⲑⲉ ⲛ̄ⲛⲓ-) where the Greek — and most modern languages — would use a noun in the singular. The Sahidic prefers in this construction the demonstrative article ⲛⲓ.

[19] The wet clothes were probably beaten or scrubbed on a stone in a river.

[20] For the last word in 131,36 I agree with the reading ⲟⲛ suggested by H.-M. Schenke.

metaphor. We propose the following free rendering of this problematic
sentence :

> Then she (i.e. the soul) will begin to rave at herself like she who gives birth turns
> herself in agony when she delivers the child (132,2-5).

One expects that the τότε in 132,2 resumes the theme of repentance
last mentioned in 131,18. The birth metaphor would then illustrate
the intensity of the penance and plea for mercy. Yet it could also
refer to the theme of rebirth discussed in 134,6 ff. For the soul must
recover her former state by giving birth to herself. The moving of the
soul in 134,8 could then be the same as the writhing in pain in 132,5.

The birth metaphor becomes in turn the transition to the important
section dealing with the marriage and reunion of the soul with her
heavenly husband (132,6-134,6). Troublesome is the translation of
132,15-23 :

> No longer does she go on the market place to copulate with whomever she desires,
> but she continually looks forward to the day he will come, since she is anxious about
> it ; for she did not know ⟨it⟩ (i.e. the day). His looks she no longer remembers
> since the time she fell from her Father's house. {And by the Father's will ...} And
> she dreamt about him like a woman who loves a man.

This translation assumes that in 132,19 f. the Coptic translator by
mistake made « his looks » the object of « know » instead of « remember ».
The γάρ in 132,19 explains why the soul looked anxiously forward
to the day of her bridegroom's arrival. The reason is that she does
not know on what day he will come. This detail is probably dependent
on the parable of the ten virgins (*Mt* 25 : 1-13). The verb « remember »
in 132,20 has at present no object. If in the Greek Vorlage the object
preceded the verb, for the sake of emphasis, the confusion in these
lines is understandable. « And by the will of the Father » in 132,21 f.
is anacoluthic and does not appear to belong in this place.

It is peculiar to read in 132,26 f. that the groom decorated the
bridal chamber (νυμφών) after it had been stated in the preceding
sentence that he came down to the ready (!) bridal chamber (ⲙⲁ
ⲛ̄ϣⲉⲗⲉⲉⲧ). To assume that two different kinds of chambers are
meant only shifts the problem. There is also little basis to see here
a conflation of two sources.

A key passage is the description of the heavenly γάμος (132,27-35).
Krause takes this passage apparently to refer to the fleshly marriage !
We translate :

For that (heavenly) marriage is not like the fleshly marriage. Those who have relations with each other are satisfied with that union and, like a burden, they leave the plague of lust behind them and they do not [separate from] [21] each other. But this [   ] [22] is this marriage, but [once] [23] they unite with each other they become a single life.

In Krause's reading it is hard to understand how the author of ExSoul could have said of the fleshly marriage that it is satisfying, or that those who engage in it have abandoned the plague of lust. On the contrary, carnal intercourse was thought not to give lasting satisfaction and it makes those who practice it the slaves of their passions. Only the heavenly marriage can be said to be free from desire and to bring a perfect, satisfying and lasting union. The spiritual intercourse is further described in 133,35-134,3.

The heavenly marriage is not the climax of the tractate, for the theme throughout the tractate remains repentance. The preparations for the coming of the bridegroom are part of the penance and self-cleansing of the soul. Even after the reunion with her husband, the soul continues to bemoan her former life (133,11-13). Furthermore, the discussion of the heavenly marriage of the soul serves as introduction to several Old Testament quotations which speak of the need for a woman to leave her people and her father's house in order to join her husband [24]. Since « Father's house » was in the narrative section the heavenly home of the soul, the author has to make here a distinction between the soul's heavenly and earthly father (133,25-28). That the idea of an earthly father does not fit the earlier narrative should not be given much weight. The author's purpose was not to tell a consistent story but to bring out the need for repentance as forcefully and as clearly as possible. Everything useful to this end is permissible in the composition. The wording of 133,26 f. reminds strongly of the parable of the prodigal son (*Lk* 15 : 11 ff.). The ethical implication of this section is that repentance includes the renunciation of this world.

---

[21] Read in 132,32 : N̄CETM̄[ΠΟΡΧΟΥ ΕΒ]ΟΛ. KRAUSE's reconstruction ϨΜϨ]ΑΛ is not possible, since the supralinear stroke over ϨΑΛ should have been visible; see 128,10 and 144,6.

[22] KRAUSE's reconstruction of 132,33 is far too short.

[23] I adopt here the reconstruction of 132,34, ϢΑ[ΡϢ]Ϩ, suggested by HEDDA BETHGE in her forthcoming translation of the tractate made in conjunction with the *Berliner Arbeitskreis für koptisch-gnostische Schriften*.

[24] KRAUSE translates 133,20 incorrectly : « Er würdigt sie nämlich ... » instead of « For he asks her ... ».

The meaning and purpose of 133,31-34 remains unclear in Krause's translation. The passage probably means :

Thus the soul adorned herself again in her beauty. [Again she found] pleasure in her beloved, and he also loved her [25].

It clearly serves as a transition to the discussion of the spiritual κοινωνία which follows. The adorning mentioned in 133,14 f. becomes here the preparation for the « love act » and the begetting of spiritual children, who are the opposite of the children who issued from the soul's earlier fornication (128,23-25).

The mentioning of the birth of the spiritual children leads to the theme of rebirth (134,4-29). This is also a conscious return to the main theme of repentance, which is now approached from the viewpoint of renewal. The soul must give birth to herself in order to receive the divine nature which allows her to return to her heavenly home. The author takes pains to make clear that the soul's own efforts at regeneration are not the real basis for her salvation. The tractate specifically rejects the idea that salvation comes « through words of practice (ἄσκησις), or through skills (τέχνη) or written teachings » (134,30-32). What precisely is meant is not clear. Since the next sentence states that salvation is a gift of God one expects that it expresses that all human effort is excluded. The three terms perhaps mean that salvation does not come through ascetic practices, (cultic) acts or (the belief in) written doctrines. Yet the sentence does not seem to say this. Though the general meaning of 134,31-35 is clear, the lacunae resist reconstruction in places [26]. The fact that salvation comes only through grace is used by the author as a further ground for the soul to repent and call upon God for mercy (135,4-15). This prayer should not be made « with external lips but through the inward spirit who came from the depth, while we sigh ... » (135,5-8). The allusion to 1 *Cor* 2 : 10-13 and *Rom* 8 : 26 f. is obvious.

It is not immediately clear why *Mt* 5 : 6 is quoted along with verse 4 (135,16-19). *Mt* 5 : 4 provided the Scriptural basis for the need to

---

[25] Read in 133,32 : X[H ⳕK]O̲[C]MEI and in 133,33 : ON [ⲡⲁⲗⲓⲛ ⲁⲥ†] ⲙⲉⲉⲧⲉ.

[26] Read at the end of 134,31 : ⲟⲩ[ⲁ]ⲉ̣ N̄ instead of Krause's ⲟⲩ[ⲁⲉ] ⳕN̄. Krause's reconstruction of line 33 is too long. The ⲦⲈ could be left out, but one would have expected to see the tail of the ⲣ in ⲣⲱⲙⲉ. With ⲟⲩⲉⲓⲉⲓⲡⲉⲕ.[in line 34 we have either an unattested word or a scribal error. Read in 134,35 : ⲧⲟⲩⲧⲟ̣ ⲅ[ⲁ]ⲱ ⲕⲁⲕ.

mourn oneself in order to receive mercy, but nothing was said in the preceding context about hungering or about being filled. It is likely that hungering is part of the penance which is expected from the soul. This could mean that fasting or some other form of self-denial is demanded. After the quotation of *Lk* 14 : 26 (135,20 f.) [27] follows a sentence which summarizes the main theme of the tractate : « For repentance is the beginning of salvation » (135,21 f.).

The introduction to the quotation from 1 *Clem* 8 : 3 is ambiguous. One could read : « Therefore, he (i.e. the Father) said through the Spirit of the prophet » or « Therefore, he said through the Spirit to the prophet ». The latter translation expresses more likely what was meant. There can be little doubt that the prophet referred to is supposed to be Isaiah. This is, first of all, implied by 1 *Clem* 8 : 4, for right after the above mentioned quotation it reads : Καὶ ἐν ἑτέρῳ τόπῳ λέγει οὕτως, and then *Is* 1 : 16-20 follows. The reader naturally expects that the previous quotation is also from Isaiah. Since it contains allusions to *Is* 1 : 18 and 50 : 3 it could easily be mistaken for the words of this prophet [28]. Secondly, the author of ExSoul clearly assumed that these are Isaiah's words. This is seen from the formulas introducing the two following quotations, ⲡⲁⲗⲓⲛ ⲕⲉⲙⲁ (136,4) and ⲡⲁⲗⲓⲛ ⲡⲉⲭⲁϥ ⲛ̅ⲕⲉⲙⲁ (136,8 f.) [29]. Since both quotations are from Isaiah the author of ExSoul must have believed that the unidentified quotation in 1 *Clem* 8 : 3 was also from Isaiah.

The need to pray day and night for mercy is illustrated by the example of a person who is in danger of drowning. Krause's translation misses the point; it should read : « as one who is afloat in the middle of the sea prays to God with his whole heart » (136,18-20). Hypocritical prayer is useless « for God examines the kidneys (cf. *Jer* 17 : 10) and he investigates the heart to the bottom » (136, 23 f.) [30].

ExSoul shows next by means of two Homeric examples that genuine repentance demands the abandonment of all love for « the place of deceit » :

> Odysseus sat crying on the island. With grief he turned his face from the words of Calypso and her deceits, and he wished to see his (home) town and the smoke

---

[27] Read at the end of 135,19 : ⲭⲉ ⲉ̣[ⲣ].

[28] Read in 135,32 : ⲭ[ⲉ ⲉⲣ]ϣ[ⲁ]ⲛⲉ̣[ⲧ]ⲛ̅ⲛⲟⲃⲉ, and in line 35 : ⲉⲩϭⲟ [ⲟ]ⲩ[ⲛⲉ ⲁⲩⲱ ⲛ̄ⲧⲉ].

[29] The same quotation technique can be observed in 134,34 f. followed by 135,15 f. and 135,19.

[30] The words at the end of 136,24 should be divided : ⲉⲧⲙ̄ ⲡⲥⲁⲙⲡⲓⲧⲛ̄.

which came forth from it. And had he not [received] [31] help from heaven, he [would] not [have been able to return] [32] to his town. So also Helena says : «[my heart] [33] has turned from me; I want to go again to my house». For she sighed and said, « It was Aphrodite who deceived me and she brought me out of my town. My only daughter I left behind as well as my good and wise and handsome husband » (136,28-137,5).

The quotation from *Od* 4,260 ff. is followed by an explanatory comment on the role of Aphrodite. The translation causes problems; we propose :

For when the soul abandoned her perfect husband — because of the guile of Aphrodite which consists in this worldly begetting — then she will be injured ... (137,5-9).

The difficulty lies with the phrase between the dashes. ⲘⲠⲉⲉⲓⲘⲀ is an adverb meaning « here». ⲡⲉⲭⲡⲟ normally refers to the act of giving birth or begetting. The point of the phrase would be that carnal begetting keeps the soul enslaved in this world [34]. The same encratic teaching is suggested by the Calypso story. This puts the important πορνεία metaphor of ExSoul in a new light. Only celibacy would be consistent with the teaching of the tractate. Repentance remains, of course, the dominant theme, but an ascetic way of life appears to be a part of it. This ethical emphasis provides also a link with *the Gospel of Thomas* and *the Book of Thomas the Contender* in Codex II, as well as with a number of other writings in the library [35].

The evaluation of ExSoul has not been able to free itself from the dubious stamp put upon the tractate by Jean Doresse [36]. This is astonishing in light of the fact that Doresse could not have had more than a cursory knowledge of the work, and that his assessment of the content of the Nag Hammadi library has often proved to be wrong [37]. The fact alone that he groups ExSoul whith such abstruse representatives of mythological gnosis as *the Paraphrase of Shem* (VII, *1*) and

---

[31] Read in 136,33 : ⲤⲀⲂⲏ[ⲗ ⲭⲉ ⲁϥⲭⲓ ⲚⲚⲟⲩ]Ⲃⲟ.

[32] Read in 136,34 : Ⲛ[ⲉϥⲛⲁⲱ]ⲕⲧ[ⲟϥ] ⲀⲚ. The final Ⲛ is indicated by a stroke over the alpha.

[33] The reading : ⲦⲕⲉⲢ[ⲉⲗⲏ]Ⲛⲏ in 136,35 was correctly intimated by H.-M. SCHENKE. Read in 136,36 : [ⲘⲘⲟⲤ ⲭⲉ ⲡⲀⲢ]ⲏⲦ.

[34] This is the dominant theme of the encratic tractate *the Testimony of Truth* (IX, *3*).

[35] Cf. F. WISSE, « Die Sextus-Sprüche und das Problem der gnostischen Ethik ».

[36] J. DORESSE, *The Secret Books of the Egyptian Gnostics*, New York and London 1960, pp. 190-192.

[37] See M. KRAUSE, « Der Stand der Veröffentlichung der Nag Hammadi-Texte », in : *Le Origini dello gnosticismo : Colloquio di Messina 13-18 Aprile 1966*; *Testi e discussioni*. (Supplements to *Numen*, XII), Leiden 1967, pp. 70 ff.

Zostrianos (VIII, *1*) is enough reason to disqualify his opinion in this case. Yet it has been generally assumed ever since that the work is gnostic. Doresse's offhand remark on the composition of ExSoul has proved to be equally ominous. He states that « various eclectic glosses and references have been inserted by the compiler of the manuscript » — he means the compiler of Codex II ! [38] Though he would most likely not have adopted such an implausible view had he known the tractate and the codex better, yet the issue of the secondary insertion of the Biblical quotations has remained with us.

Krause, in his Messina report, objected to Doresse's classification of ExSoul, but he did not put forward an evaluation of his own. He also seemed to assume the unity of the tractate [39]. Later, in the brief introductory note to his translation, he posed that ExSoul is a product of one of the Valentinian schools at the end of the second century. As a basis he mentions the gnostic interpretation of baptism, resurrection from the dead, the ascension and rebirth of the soul in the work. He considers the role of the bridal chamber in the tractate as very similar to the « sacrament » of the bridal chamber in the Valentinian *Gospel of Philip* [40].

What exactly is gnostic about the use of these concepts in ExSoul is far from clear. For example, it is not baptism which is reinterpreted in 131,29 and 132,2, but rather the purification of the soul and her womb in the allegory are interpreted to refer to baptism. The baptism of John is the Biblical proof for the connection between baptism and repentance (135,22-24). Also in the case of the references to the resurrection from the dead, ascension and rebirth, elements in the allegory of the soul are identified with concepts known to the Christian reader. The Christian content of these terms is not denied or changed but assumed. It is also difficult to see what the marriage imagery in ExSoul has in common with the Valentinian sacrament of the bridal chamber. The use of marriage symbolism to express the relationship between Christ and the soul was no invention of the Valentinians, and it is common in patristic literature [41]. There is no hint in ExSoul that the bridal chamber has something to do with a sacrament, nor does it reflect any of the peculiarities of the use of the word in, for example, *the Gospel of Philip*. In the allegory of the soul the bridal chamber

---

[38] *The Secret Books*, pp. 170 and 190 f.

[39] « Der Stand der Veröffentlichung », p. 72.

[40] *Die Gnosis*, pp. 125 f.

[41] Cf. G. W. H. LAMPE, *A Patristic Lexicon*, London 1961, νύμφη, νυμφίος and νυμφών.

plays a role in the purification and preparation of the soul to receive
her bridegroom. It helps to bring out an important aspect of repentance.

The question whether or not ExSoul is gnostic is closely linked
to the problem of the composition of the tractate. William C. Robinson
Jr. has argued for a complex literary history in which there was a non-
christian narrative on the soul's sojourn in this world followed by some
exhortations as well as some exegetical comments and further exhortations. These additions need not all have been made by one redactor [42].
The basic claim Robinson makes is that « the quotations are not integral
to the narrative but are catchword insertions ». Their removal « leaves
a narrative which, while not entirely clear, is relatively intact [43] ».
Though Robinson's argumentation appears to me to be unconvincing
and, at places, faulty, to counter his and similar attempts at isolating
the narrative from the rest of the work, it suffices to show that the
narrative depends for its content on the quotations.

It should be kept in mind that similar « myths » about the fall and
return to heaven of the soul were current in the ancient world. Though
Gnostics appear to have made use of such myths, they are in themselves
not gnostic [44]. It is thus possible that the author of ExSoul was familiar
with a non-Christian form of the myth and that it influenced his
composition to some extent. The issue is, however, whether the narrative sections in ExSoul were once an independent composition which
was taken over by the « redactor », or whether they were composed
by the author of the whole tractate.

The main narrative section (127,22-129,5) is complete in itself and
demands as such no continuation. It effectively sets the background
of the repentance of the soul and extensively describes the repentance
itself as well as the Father's acceptance of the pleas for mercy. In the
introduction (127,19-22) the foundation for the allegory had been
laid by showing that the soul is a woman [45]. The allegory has three
sections :

a) The fall of the soul, her defilement by evil men, her own shameless
   behavior and resulting desolation.

---

[42] « The Exegesis on the Soul », pp. 103-108.

[43] *Ibid.*, p. 104.

[44] See the important article by C. COLPE, « Die 'Himmelsreise der Seele ' ausserhalb
und innerhalb der Gnosis », in : *Le Origini dello Gnosticismo*, pp. 429-445.

[45] Also the excursus on the turning of the womb is already prepared for by the
claim that the soul has a womb.

b) The repentance of the soul and her pleas for mercy.
c) The Father's acceptance of the soul's penance.

The first section summarizes the content of the first block of quotations (129,5-130,30), on which it is completely dependent for its details, i.e. the soul's virgin existence in her father's house (129,21 f.), her defilement by many evil adulterers (129,11 ff.; 130,7), the gifts of deception she receives (130,2 ff.), her own shameless behavior (129,15-20; 130,13-20), her halfhearted repentance (130,9 ff.), her desolation (129,30), her children of fornication (129,33). These vivid details are not a standard part of the « myth » of the fall and return of the soul and only find their explanation in the Old Testament passages which follow the narrative. The importance of 1 *Cor* 5 : 9 f. and *Eph* 6 : 12 for the relationship between the narrative and the πορνεία quotations has already been shown in the comments on the text and translation (*supra*, p. 72).

The allegorical sections which follow, e.g. 131,13 ff., are not parts of a continuing narrative but elaborations on the repentance of the soul introduced in the first narrative section. The development is not systematic or chronological but determined by further aspects of repentance which the author sees and develops; at times, it seems at the spur of the moment [46]. The allegory of the fall and salvation of the soul is only auxiliary to this main theme. Thus he explores cleansing and baptism in connection with the turning of the womb, the intensity of penance in connection with birth pains, purification and « adorning » in connection with the coming of the bridegroom, renewal in connection with rebirth, ceaseless prayers for mercy in connection with the free gift of salvation, rejection of « the place of deceit » and « Aphrodite » in connection with the examples of Odysseus and Helen. Finally, at the end of the tractate, the author states once more what he has been trying to say with his « exegesis on the soul » : « If we truly repent, God, who is longsuffering and great in mercy, will hear us ».

---

[46] See the comments on the text and translation.

JEWISH GNOSIS AND MANDAEAN GNOSTICISM

Some Reflections on the Writing Brontè

BY

GILLES QUISPEL

I

The writing *The Thunder, The Perfect Mind* is the most impressive writing that I know. It was found in one of the codices of Nag Hammadi in 1945 or 1946 (VI, page 13-page 21) and published by Martin Krause and Pahor Labib in 1971 [1]. Its title is uncertain : instead of *ţebrontè*, the thunder, one can also read : *ņebrontè*, a name similar to that used by Mandaeans and Manichaeans to indicate a female deity [2]. Moreover, its content seems to suggest that « Nous teleios» should rather be translated as « Complete Mind » than as « Perfect Mind ».

Be that as it may, the text itself is fascinating. In it Sophia introduces herself as the beginning and the end, the prostitute and the saint, the woman and the virgin, and so on and so forth in an almost endless continuation of paradoxes.

There is nothing explicitly and perhaps even implicitly Christian in this text. At first sight one might even think that it could even be pre-Christian.

Nor is there anything typically gnostic in *The Thunder or the Complete Mind*. In it Wisdom declares :

> For I am the Sophia of the Greeks
> and the Gnosis of the barbarians.
>
> (16, 3-5)

> I am unwise
> and I am wise.
>
> (15, 29-30)

---

[1] M. KRAUSE and P. LABIB, *Gnostische und hermetische Schriften aus Codes II und Codex VI* (*Abhandlungen des Deutschen Archäologischen Instituts Kairo*, Koptische Reihe, Band 2), Glückstadt 1971, 122-132.

[2] See C. COLPE, « Heidnische, jüdische und christliche Überlieferung in den Schriften aus Nag Hammadi », I, *Jahrbuch für Antike und Christentum*, 15 (1972) 11-12.

> I am without wisdom
> and they receive wisdom from me.
>
> (16, 28-29)

But there is nothing to suggest that according to the author Wisdom has fallen from the spiritual world, as is the case in the Gnosis of Simon the Magician, or in the *Apocryphon of John*, or in the myth of Valentinus. And this might tend to indicate that *Brontè* is pre-gnostic.

It would be much more difficult to deny that it is Jewish. Its remarkable style, the endless repetition of antithetical parallelisms, « I am ... I am not », has its counterpart in *Ecclesiastes* 3 :

> a time to be born
> and a time to die;
> a time to plant
> and a time to uproot;
>
>   and so on and so forth.

I may be mistaken or misinformed, but I do not know of any document in any other literature where we find the same fatiguing and monotonous device.

Moreover, it is in the Hebrew literature that we find similar self-proclamations of Wisdom :

> *Prov.* 8, 4 :   Men, it is to you I call,
>   I appeal to every man.
> *Prov.* 8, 12 :   I am Wisdom, I bestow shrewdness
>   and show the way to knowledge and prudence.
> *Prov.* 8, 30-31 : Then (sc. at the creation) I was at his side each day,
>   his darling and his delight,
>   playing in his presence continually,
>   playing on the earth when he had finished it,
>   while my delight was in mankind.

The same may be observed in *Siracides* 24 :

> 3 I (ἐγώ) came forth from the mouth of the most high ...
> 4 I (ἐγώ) put my tent on high.
> 16 I (ἐγώ) stretched out my branches as a terebinth.
> 17 I (ἐγώ) blossomed grace like a vine.

Generally speaking, many parallels with *Brontè* are to be found in the sapiential literature of the Hebrews, both in style and in thought.

So *Siracides* 33, 13 seems to observe that good and evil, life and death, piety and sin originate in God, because his works consist always of opposites. This may be relevant for *Brontè* 19, 15:

> I, I am sinless and the root of sin is in me.

And also for 16, 11-13:

> I am the one who is called Life, and you have called me Death.

Such paradoxes can also be found elsewhere in the Bible. For our purposes it may suffice to quote two passages:

Is. 45, 7	*Brontè* 21, 4
I form the light and create darkness,	<I am> the light <and the darkness>.
	Brontè 14, 31;32
I make peace and create evil.	I am the war and the peace.
Deut. 32, 39	*Brontè* 16, 11-13
I put to death and I keep alive,	I am the one who is called Life and you
I wound and I heal.	have called me death.
	<I am the healer that heals, and I am
	the wounder that wounds>.

But even if these passages are the ultimate roots from which the views of *Brontè* have grown, it seems clear that the wisdom literature served as an intermediary.

In the mean time much had happened. God was no longer the lonely male of the desert, he had got a wife. This view is clearly enounced by the author of the *Wisdom of Solomon*, viz. that Sophia is the house-wife of God, who lives with him (8, 3: συμβίωσιν θεοῦ ἔχουσα). Moreover, she is She who at the same time treats the wise man like a sweet mother, spoils her best boy, and receives her lover with the tenderness and unexpected wildness of a young mistress:

> She will come out to meet him like a mother;
> She will receive him like a young bride.
> (*Siracides* 15, 2)

This is not different from what another Jewish poet, Christian Morgen-stern, later wrote:

> Du, trotz aller Abseitsrolle,
> Göttin mit den Möglichkeiten
> Allerletzten Tragischkeiten,
> allerletzten Glücks und Leides,
> Mutter und Geliebte, beides.

Christians know their own tradition so poorly, and have such a distorted view of Israel's religion, that they cannot believe this to be Jewish. And yet it is, or ought to be, inspired scripture and living faith of all Catholics. Moreover, it can be integrated easily into the existing system of orthodoxy, if Sophia is identified with the Holy Spirit. This, however, is already the case in the *Wisdom of Solomon* (1, 4-5; 1, 6; 7, 7; 7, 22; 9, 17).

In a sense this is an inner-Jewish process, that can be observed in Hebrew Scripture and announces the trinitarian convictions of Christianity. And for a while, Old Testament scholars have been reluctant to admit that this process has been stimulated by the beliefs of Israel's surrounding nations, Egypt, Canaan, Mesopotamia. And it is true that the existence of a consistent Sophia myth and an underlying myth of the Saved Saviour, which was supposed to have influenced the biblical notions, cannot be proved.

But recently some undisputable facts have been adduced, which refuted the fancies of the radicals and the scepticism of the conservatives. Attention was drawn to the Isis inscriptions in the temple of Memphis, Egypt, copies of which have been found at several places in the Hellenistic world. In this so-called aretalogy Isis reveals who she is and what her gifts are with an ever recurrent « egô eimi ». Very careful and solid studies have established that this aretalogy has influenced both *Siracides* (3rd century B.C., Jerusalem) and the author of the *Wisdom of Solomon* (1st century B.C., Alexandria), when they describe Wisdom [3]. This is important.

It had rightly been observed that « Ego eimi » is not correct Greek. *Odysseus* says :

εἰμ' 'Οδυσσεὺς Λαερτιάδης

(Od. 9, 19)

when he wants to introduce himself in the palace of Alkinoos. It was said then that this expression was Oriental and Semitic.

Eduard Schweizer drew attention to Mandaean texts, which contained parallels with the Johannine Gospel : « I am the Life ... I am the Kusta (= Truth) ... I am the Light », etc. [4]. He concluded that the

---

[3] J. MARBÖCK, *Weisheit im Wandel. Untersuchungen zur Weisheitstheologie bei Ben Sira (Bonner Biblische Beiträge, 37)*, Bonn 1971; J. M. REESE, *Hellenistic Influence on the Book of Wisdom and its Consequences (Analecta Biblica, 41)*, Rome 1970.

[4] E. SCHWEIZER, *Ego Eimi. Die religionsgeschichtliche Herkunft und theologische Bedeutung der johanneischen Bildreden (Forschungen zur Religion und Literatur des Alten und des Neuen Testaments, 56)*, 2nd ed., Göttingen 1965, 37.

Mandaean material was older than the Gospel of John and had influenced its author.

But now we can offer an alternative that is much less hypothetical and vague. The origin of the « Ego eimi » style is to be found in the Egyptian Isis aretalogy. It was applied to Sophia by Jewish authors who were thoroughly familiar with Hellenistic culture. This happened either in the « I am » style (*Siracides* 24) or in the related « She it is who … » style (*Wisdom of Solomon* 10).

We know nowadays that these speculations about Wisdom were very important for the formulation of Christology. When Jesus says :

> Come unto me, all ye that labour and are heavy laden, and I will give
> you rest (*Matth.* 11, 28),

he speaks as the embodiment of divine Wisdom. When the Johannine Christ says : « I am » (the true vine, the good shepherd, etc.), he would seem to be in the same Wisdom tradition. We see that now clearer than before, because Sophia in the writing *Brontè* anticipates John in several respects :

> I am the voice, whose sound is multiple
> and the *Logos*, whose appearance is numerous (14, 12-13);
> I am the one who is called *Life* (16, 11-12);
> I am the one who is called *Truth* (20, 7-8);
> I am the *Light* (20, 4).

It is quite clear that *Brontè* has been inspired by the Isis aretalogy. Nevertheless it may be a Jewish writing about Wisdom, like *Siracides* and the *Wisdom of Solomon*. It might have been written in the third century B.C., like *Siracides*, when Palestine was a part of Ptolemaic, Hellenistic Egypt and the national reaction of the Maccabees had not yet begun. On the other hand, the writing is so sophisticated that a later date, the first century B.C., and a Hellenistic milieu, Alexandria, all seem preferable. But there are, as far as I can see, no indications which lead us to suppose that the text, in its original form, is not Jewish and is not pre-Christian.

This would imply that John and the Mandaeans are mutually independent continuations of the same Wisdom tradition.

What does that mean ?

In *Brontè* Sophia exclaims :

> I am the Gnosis and the Ignorance.
>   (14, 26-27)

This is understandable as an amplification of a view already expounded in *Proverbs* 8, 14, where Wisdom styles herself as « bina », understanding :

Counsel is mine, and sound wisdom;
I am understanding; I have strength.

Now, if the Mandaean bearer of revelation is called Manda d'Haijē, Gnosis of Life (= God), this is very much in the trend of Jewish Wisdom, and so akin to John; but nothing obliges us to suppose that the Mandaean Manda d'Haijē is behind the Johannine Christ. We rather must suppose that the author of *John* was familiar with the idea contained in *Brontè*, that Sophia is the absolute consciousness of God, who reflects and reveals this hidden mystery.

This « Egyptian » solution seems much more plausible than the Mandaean hypothesis of Eduard Schweizer; it is more precise, firmer based upon chronological facts and explains more phenomena. We suppose that it might be right.

And then we see that *Brontè* is not only composed in the same way as the aretalogy, whith its endless repetition of « Ego eimi », but in some cases is clearly related in content :

Kyme-Memphis inscr. (Bergman 301) [5]	*Brontè* 13, 30-31
6. I am the wife and the sister of king Osiris (ἐγώ εἰμι γυνὴ καὶ ἀδελφὴ ᾿Οσείριδος βασιλέως).	I am the sister of my husband.
41. I am the lady of war (ἐγώ εἰμι πολέμου κυρία).	14, 31-32 I am war and peace. 18, 24-25 I am peace, and war came into being because of me.

And this relation of our text to Egypt and its religion encourages us to find some affinity between Sophia and the interpretation of Isis found in Plutarch. In his work *Isis and Osiris* he discusses among other things the problem of evil, mentions the solution of dualism, quotes Heraclitus's dialectics of the resilient harmony of the universe, « like that of a lyre or bow », and seems to find this monism in the figure of Isis. She, as a matter of fact, is concerned with « matter, which becomes everything :

---

[5] J. BERGMAN, *Ich bin Isis* (*Acta Universitatis Upsaliensis*, Hist. Relig., 3) Uppsala 1968.

light, darkness,
day, night,
fire, water,
life, death,
beginning, end » (*De Iside*, 77).

In ch. 38 Isis is thought to be the earth : « they hold and believe the earth to be the body of Isis, not all of it, but so much of it as the Nile covers, fertilizing it and uniting with it » [6]. This is somewhat different from the interpretation given in ch. 77. In ch. 53 Isis is in fact the female principle of nature and is receptive of every form of generation. This would seem the same interpretation as in ch. 77 [7].

Some of the paradoxes of ch. 77 do occur in *Brontè* :

13, 16 : for I am the first and the last;
16, 13 : I am the one that is called Life and you have called me Death;
21, 4 : I am the light and I am the darkness.

And it is perhaps owing to this Egyptian, Isiac inspiration that the author of *Brontè* goes much further than any other Hebrew prophet or sage.

For if Isaiah says that God creates light and darkness, peace and catastrophe, and if the Deuteronomist observes that God wounds and heals, it was reserved for *Brontè* to say that Wisdom *is* life and death, war and peace, good and evil.

On the whole, then, we may say that the Egyptian influence on *Brontè* is sure. It is here much clearer than in the *Siracides* or in the *Wisdom of Solomon*, and in this respect *Brontè* confirms the studies which established a special relationship of the last-mentioned texts with the Isis aretalogy. On the other hand, comparison of *Brontè* with these and other sapiential writings of the Hebrews makes it sufficiently clear that its author was a Jewish sage. Perhaps he alludes to this affinity between Isis, whose image is to be found in Egypt,

---

[6] See also below p. 94.

[7] PLUTARCH continues : « in accord with which she is called by Plato the « gentle nurse » and the all receptive ». According to ALEXANDER OF LYCOPOLIS, *Adv. Man.* PLATO calls matter « all receiving » (*Timaeus* 51a, 7) and « mother » (*Tim.* 50d, 3) and « nurse » (*Tim.* 49a, 6). J. MANSVELD has shown that ALEXANDER reflects the earlier traditions of Alexandrian Middle Platonism ; cf. P. W. VAN DER HORST and J. MANSVELD, « An Alexandrian Platonist against Dualism, » *Theta Pi*, 3 (1974) 6-47. He may do so in this passage too. Then Plutarch possibly uses an Alexandrian source. This is relevant for *Brontè*, if this writing originates in Alexandria.

and Wisdom, whose image is taboo among the iconoclastic Jews, in the following passage :

> Why did you hate me, ye Greeks ?
> Because I am a barbarian (Jew ?) among the barbarians ?
> I am namely the Sophia of the Greeks and the Gnosis of the barbarians.
> I am the crisis of the Greeks and the barbarians.
> I am she whose image is numerous in Egypt
> and who has no image among the barbarians.
>
> (16, 1-9)

II

It is much more difficult to establish, if and to what extent Jewish speculations about Wisdom have been influenced by that other power-ful deity of the Near East, the goddess of love and war, who was known under different names but for convenience's sake may be called here Ishtar.

Perhaps the writing *Brontè* may be of some help to solve this very controversial problem. In this book Wisdom says :

> I am the first and the last,
> I am the honoured one and the despised one,
> *I am the prostitute (πόρνη) and the saint (σεμνή),*
> I am the woman and the virgin.
>
> (13, 16-20)
> I am the bride and the bridegroom.
>
> (13, 27-28)

The last remark seems to suggest that Sophia is androgynous. The concept, however, that Sophia is a prostitute reminds us of the fact that quite often Ishtar in Sumerian and Akkadian texts is called « the prostitute » [8].

From Sumer to Alexandria is a very long way, from 3000 B.C. until 100 B.C. is an exceedingly long period. And though we may admit

---

[8] My late colleague R. FRANKENA has given me some valuable references on this point, for instance *The Assyrian Dictionary*, 6, Chicago 1956, 101 : « When I sit at the entrance of the tavern *I* (Ishtar) *am a loving prostitute* » (in a Ishtar hymn). The word *ištarītu*, an epithet of Ishtar, means « hierodoule », cf. W. VON SODEN, *Akkadisches Handwörterbuch* (fasc. 5, 1963), 399. In Sumerian texts Inanna (Ishtar) is sometimes called *nugig-* (*qadiš-tum*) or *ištarītu* (EDZARD, *Zeitschrift für Assyriologie*, 55, 104-105 ; FALKENSTEIN, *ibid.*, 56, 119 ff.) ; B. LANDSBERGER, *Materialien zum Sumerischen Lexikon*, IV, Rome 1956, p. 17 (78), translates *nu.gig* with « tabooed woman ».

that Astarte in the West-Semitic world had very much the same function as Ishtar in the East, the impact of this fertility deity upon Wisdom
is still very controversial.

In Sumer and Akkad the king at the New Year festival had conjugal
relations with a sacred prostitute to ensure the fertility of the earth
through sympathetic magic. To this rite the love of Ishtar and Tammuz
furnished the myth. New fragments of their lovesong have been found,
which sometimes show a word for word agreement with the biblical
Song of Songs [9].

I have not the slightest doubt that this book is a description of
the love between the Lord and his bride, coined after the love of Tammuz and Ishtar. In this sense the *Song of Songs* is mythological and
symbolic, because a myth is a story about gods. Those who say that
the *Song of Songs* contains profane love songs and sings the praise of
profanity and secularisation, are wrong in my view.

But was Chokma coined after Isthar?

There does exist an Assyrian hymn (and a Babylonian doublet) in
which Ishtar proclaims herself:

> Ishtar, the goddess of the evening *am I*,
> Ishtar, the goddess of the morning am I [10].

This has undoubtedly a formal similarity to the self-proclamation of
Wisdom in *Proverbs* 8 and in *Brontè*.

Nevertheless Gershom Scholem flatly denies that Wisdom has a
mythological background. She is a creature, not divine, an allegory,
not a myth, hardly an aspect of God, not to speak of her being his wife.

Scholem cannot deny that in Philo God is the husband of Sophia.
But he stresses the fact that Shechinah, a related character, nowhere
shows the slightest trace of being female. And yet he ruefully admits
that already in Talmudic times Jewish speech about Shechinah tended
towards a gnostic hypostatisation: this is proved by the fact that the
Mandaeans have inherited from the Jews the pluralistic use of Shechinah and speak about *Shechināthā* [11].

Gerhard von Rad is more careful. He points to the Egyptian goddess
Maat (Truth, Sense), the daughter of the sungod Atum, later identified

---

[9] S. N. KRAMER, *The Sacred Marriage Rite. Aspects of Faith, Myth and Ritual in Ancient Sumer*, Bloominton-London 1969, pp. 85-106.

[10] A. UNGNAD, *Die Religion der Babylonier und Assyrer*, Jena 1921, 201.

[11] G. SCHOLEM, « Zur Entwicklungsgeschichte der Kabbalistischen Konzeption der Schechinah », *Eranos Jahrbuch*, 12 (1952) 45-107.

with Isis, who is represented as embracing her father and kissed by him, after « he has put her before his nose » [12]. In the same way Wisdom is a child, a pet :

> The Lord brought me forth as the beginning of his works,
> before all else that he made, long ago.
> Alone, I was fashioned in times long past,
> at the beginning, long before earth itself.
> When there was yet no ocean I was born,
> no springs brimming with water.
> Before the mountains were settled in their place,
> long before the hills I was born,
> when as yet he had made neither land nor lake
> nor the first clod of earth.
> When he set the heavens in their place I was there,
> when he girdled the ocean with the horizon,
> when he fixed the canopy of clouds overhead
> and set the springs of ocean firm in their place,
> when he prescribed its limits for the sea
> and knit together earth's foundations,
> then I was at his side each day,
> his darling and delight,
> playing in his presence continually,
> playing on the earth, when he had finished it,
> while my delight was in mankind.
>
> (*Proverbs* 8, 22-31)

But then Sophia is quite a person, visualized in a very imaginative and poetic way, a little princess playing in her father's presence, sitting as it were on his knee. Certainly she is the child of God, not his creature.

When discussing the well-known passage in *Proverbs* 9 about the house Sophia built with the seven pillars of wisdom, von Rad observes that here Chokma is a sort of photographic negative (*Kontrastbild*), made by the teachers of wisdom to suppress rites like temple prostitution or sacred fornication that under the influence of Astarte's cult had penetrated into Israel [13].

Certainly the counterpart of Wisdom, « Mrs. Folly », is painted with the colours of Astarte :

> The Lady Stupidity is a flighty creature;
> the simpleton, she cares for nothing.
> She sits at the door of her house,

---

[12] G. VON RAD, *Weisheit in Israel*, Neukirchen-Vluyn 1970, 199.
[13] G. VON RAD, *o.c.*, 217.

on a seat on the highest part of the town,
to invite the passers-by indoors
as they hurry on their way;
« Come in, you simpletons », she says.
She says also to the fool,
« Stolen water is sweet
and bread got by stealth tastes good ».
Little does she know that death lurks there,
that her guests are in the depths of Sheol.

                                        (*Proverbs* 9, 13-18)

In *Brontè* Wisdom styles herself as the saint and the prostitute.
Must we assume, then, that in certain liberal quarters in Israel Wisdom
had preserved some of the ambivalence of her anti-type Astarte ? The
latter, as a matter of fact, was sophisticated, the goddess of love and
of war, female and male, saintly and fornicating. Could it be that the
author of *Proverbs* is polemicizing against some people in Israel, in
the North or in the South, according to whom the spouse of God was
both positive and negative, wise and wanton ?

Until now parallels to this paradoxical concept could only be adduced
from the *Zohar* and the *Kabbalah of Safed* [14]. Therefore, it seemed
adventurous to suppose that Wisdom was once conceived in Israel
as being a prostitute. But now that we have this view in *Brontè*, the
whole problem should be taken up again. The more so, because we
find a related concept in Mandaeanism. And this too would seem to
be a heritage of Judaism. *Rūhā dQudša*, the Holy Ghost, the
Mother of the Seven (planets), is a figure much related to Chokma,
who builds her house with seven pillars. She is called the prostitute, *kadišta*, in two passages of the *Right Ginza*, 80, 31 and 494, 11.
Equally Libat, the planet Venus or Ishtar, is called prostitute in the
Book of John, 183, 13.

Is it thinkable that two religions, Cabbalism and Mandaeanism,
both dependent upon Judaism, have developped spontaneously a
very peculiar view on the same subject, without any relation with
Ishtar ? And yet *qadištu*, the devotee, is also an epitheton of Ishtar [15].
Or is it more probable that at a certain moment, under the influence
of Astarte's cult, Wisdom was represented in its ambivalence ?

---

[14] G. SCHOLEM, *o.c.*, 102.

[15] W. VON SODEN, *Akkadishes Wörterbuch* (fasc. 10, 1971), 891, s.v. *qadištu(m)*, 4c
(Ištar).

The Hebrew language shows some awareness of this ambiguity; *kadēšā*, prostitute, lit. devotee, is related to *kadoš*, holy.

We will never know with certainty whether the holy and fornicating Wisdom was already known to Israel when the book of *Proverbs* was written. It seems, however, rather sure that the writing *Brontè* is ultimately indebted to the cult of Astarte when it calls Wisdom a prostitute, as we shall see more clearly below. And this prefigures at a very early date some very important developments which were to take place later on both in Cabbalism and in Mandaeanism. Sophia at a certain moment and in certain quarters was a very ambivalent figure.

For this reason we cannot believe that the shocking and coarse erotic language which Philo of Alexandria uses when speaking about Sophia, is the first outbreak of a mythological consciousness, which had been absent in Israel before the first century A.D. We consider this rather to be a revival and survival of older views, suppressed and repressed by the violence of prophets and scribes to such an extent that it seemed to have almost completely vanished.

According to Philo, Sophia is the *wife* of God. The sexual imagery is so drastic that the Alexandrian philosopher can even speak about the sperma of God, which is conceived by Sophia and from which she brings forth a son, the world, in birth pangs :

> With his Knowledge God had union, not as man have it, and begat created being. And Knowledge, having received the divine seed, when her travail was consummated, bore the only beloved son who is apprehended by the senses, the world which we see.
>
> (*De ebrietate* 30)

On the other hand, Sophia is also the *daughter* of God, even a virginal daughter :

> and it is Wisdom's name that the holy oracles proclaim by « Bethuel », a name meaning in our speech « Daughter of God »; yea, a true-born and ever-virgin daughter, who, by reason alike of her own modesty and of the glory of Him that begat her, hath obtained a nature free from every defiling touch.
>
> (*De fuga et inventione* 50)

These are good parallels for the concept of *Brontè* :

> I am the woman and the virgin,
> I am the mother and the daughter.
>
> (13, 19-21)

This makes it more probable that *Brontè* was written in Alexandria, where Philo lived in the first century A.D. The comparison shows,

that such passages are not isolated outbreaks in one author, but
reflect current views in certain Jewish quarters, which have been
eliminated later on by the victorious Talmudists. So *Brontè* helps
us to recover an unknown and forgotten aspect of Judaism. For what
does it mean that Sophia is called by Philo « earth » [16] ? Isis in a sense
symbolizes the earth, her images sometimes are black [17]. Philo lived
in exile, in the Diaspora, and had no roots in Palestinian soil, like the
Jewish people after him for almost two millennia. Is not, as Scholem
has suggested in his masterly article, this quest for the tender, female
aspects of God at the same time an expression of the Jew's aspiration
to return to his origin and finish the exile ?

If we see the importance of such utterances for the Jewish existence,
we clearly discern that these speculations are not exclusively due to
the influence of Egyptian religion, but also are a valid expression of
the existential situation of the Jewish people.

We are not amazed to hear in the last-quoted passage that Sophia
is (also) male and therefore a father :

> He called Bethuel Rebecca's father. How, ... can Wisdom, the daughter of God,
> be rightly spoken of as a father ? Is it because, while Wisdom's name is feminine,
> her nature is manly ? ... Let us, then, pay no heed to the discrepancy in the gender
> of the words, and say that the daughter of God, even Wisdom, is not only masculine
> but father, sowing and begetting in souls aptness to learn, discipline, knowledge,
> sound sense, good and laudable actions.
>
>   (*De fuga et inventione* 51-52)

This passage more than any other makes it clear that Barbelo, the
spouse of God in the *Apocryphon of John*, is none other than Sophia.
And we understand that Barbelo (Sophia) is called Metro-pator,
the mother who is at the same time father, and Holy Spirit (because
Spirit and Sophia have been identified already in the *Wisdom of
Solomon*), and also androgynous (53, 4-10).

We can make these connections now without leaving any doubt.
And we see clearly that it is in the context of these historical developments that the word of *Brontè* : « I am the bride and the bridegroom»
should be understood.

We expect much greater opposition when we suggest that the view

---

[16] *De Cherubim*, 49 : « ... that He is the father of all things, for He begat them, and
the husband of Wisdom, dropping the seed of happiness for the race of mortals into
good and virgin soil ».

[17] G. VANDEBEEK, *De Interpretatio Graeca van de Isisfiguur* (*Studia Hellenistica*, 4),
Louvain 1946, 98.

of these Alexandrian Jews that God has a wife has very archaic antecedents in the history of Israel.

The facts are clear : this is what the book *Wisdom of Solomon* says (8,3). There Sophia is said to live with God, and the word « symbiosis » clearly has matrimonial and sexual connotations. Philo is more than clear in the quoted passages. And *Brontè* means very much the same, when Sophia proclaims : « And my husband it is who engendered me » (13,29). This is only understandable in the perspective of the sapiential tradition, according to which Sophia was brought forth before all ages as the daughter of God (*Proverbs* 8) and is at the same time God's spouse.

But our admittedly bold hypothesis is that the Alexandrians have not invented this spontaneously, but have preserved the more unorthodox view, not unknown in ancient Israel, namely that the Lord had a spouse called Anat Jahu.

In order to silence in advance all too understandable protests, we draw the attention of our readers to the rather unknown fact that Anath-Haijē continued to exist as a female being in the Mandaean pantheon. Haijē, Life, being a designation of God in the Mandaean religion, we may safely assume that she is none other than Anat Jahu.

The passage in the *Ginza* (Lidzbarski, 118, 3), where she is mentioned, is not perfectly clear. It is said there that Anath-Haijē was born together with Hibil (Abel) from the secret Adam and the « cloud of light ». But for our aim is is sufficient to prove that Anat Jahu was not completely suppressed but continued to exist even until the rise of the Mandaean religion, that is either some time before or some time after the beginning of our era.

Anat, Ashera and Astarte were the three great deities of the Phenician, Canaanite religion long before the Israelite tribes entered the promised land. The three are different from each other and related at the same time.

Anat was considered to be the sister and the wife of Baal. She is consummating the Hieros Gamos with Baal. At the division of the kingdom of Israel the Northern part developed a syncretistic Jahwe cult at the instigation of Jeroboam, especially in the royal town Samaria. It was here, it seems, that at an unknown date the Canaanite deity was integrated into Jahwism under the name of Anat Jahu, the spouse, it would seem, of the Lord. If we want to appreciate to what extent the cult of love, sex and fertility coloured the convictions of true believers, we have only to read the prophet *Hosea*, the only

scriptural prophet from Northern Israel, who lived before the exile.
There God prophesies that his people one day will call Him « my
husband » and no longer « my Baal » (2,16). And one can suppose that
in certain quarters Anat Jahu was supposed to say both.

In 722, when the Northern Kingdom came to its end, much of the
syncretism seems to have been transferred to Bethel, in what later
was to be called Samaria, where the cult continued to exist.

It was from there that the Jewish military colony at Jeb-Elefantine
(near Assuan, Egypt) can have come. The correspondence of this
community is to be dated about 410 B.C., when their sanctuary had
been destroyed. It reveals that these people considered themselves
to be Jews, but at the same time continued the syncretism that existed
at Bethel and in the former Northern Kingdom. They venerated
Jahu, a special form of the name of the Lord, but also Anat Jahu or
Anat Bethel, whom one would guess to be the spouse of the Lord [18].
It is, however, equally possible that the veneration of Anat Jahu
did exist in the Southern Kingdom too. This is suggested by such
names of places as Anathot and Beth Anat, both in the South. Then
the Elephantine papyri might reflect the atmosphere of popular religion
in Juda and Benjamin, untouched by the criticism of the prophets.
In any case there must have been a period in the religion of Israel
in which, according to some, the Lord had a divine spouse, called Anat,
with whom he was celebrating the Hieros Gamos. Already Jeremiah
had complained that all the Jews, who dwell in the land of Egypt,
have burned incense to the Queen of Heaven, a practice known even
in the cities of Judah and in the streets of Jerusalem (*Jeremiah* 44,17).

It is my hypothesis that the erotic flavour of the Alexandrian views
on Sophia somehow is an echo of these quite unorthodox beliefs.
After all, the Jews in Elephantine were living in Egypt. Why could
not later Jews like the author of the *Wisdom of Solomon* or Philo,
or the author of *Brontè*, have continued their views rather than those
of official Jerusalem ? It gave them the opportunity to integrate the
warm mother religiosity of their surroundings, the ever more prevalent
cult of Isis, into their traditional faith.

The name Jahu, an abbreviation of the tetragrammaton, lies behind
the Greek name Iao, under which so many Greek and Roman authors,
not only writers of magical papyri, knew the Jewish God [19]. The same

---

[18] TH. C. VRIEZEN, *De godsdienst van Israel*, Zeist 1963, 214.
[19] Cf. GANSCHINIETZ, « Iao », in Pauly-Wissowa, *Realencyclopädie*, 9, 1916, 689-721.

name Iao is now even found in a papyrus manuscript of the Septuagint, thus showing that it was current among the Jews of Egypt. And compound names like Io rabba (= Great Iao) in Mandaean suggest that it was known among the ancestors or forerunners of these Mesopotamian Gnostics. In the same way the West-Semitic love goddess, integrated into the religion of Israel as Anat Jahu and still familiar to the Mandaeans as Anath Haijē, can have persisted among the Egyptian Jews as Sophia, the spouse of God [20].

To confirm this view, I refer to a Jew of the first centuries of our era, namely Justinus the Gnostic, who most probably lived in Egypt and was in fact a Christian Jew.

He quotes the words of *Hosea* 1, 2 in the wording of the Septuagint and understands this as alluding to a mythical figure called Edem, who « whored away from behind the Lord » :

> And, he says, when the prophet is said « to take to himself a wife of harlotry, because the land will go a-whoring from the following of the Lord » (*Hos.* 1, 2), in these words, he says, the prophet clearly speaks the whole mystery, and is not heard because of the wickedness of Naas.
>
> (Hippolytus, *Ref.* V, 27, 4)

> For Edem, the consort of Elohim, is also called Israel.
>
> (*Ibid.* V, 26, 36)

It has become clear only recently, who this Edem really is. She is depicted as having the same outward appearance as the Egyptian goddess Thermouthis, who at that time had been identified with Isis : a virgin above her groin, a viper below [21]. So it was established for the first time that such Jewish speculations on a gnostic goddess were somehow inspired by the concept of Isis.

This connection becomes still more clear if we keep in mind that Edem in Hebrew means « earth », as Justinus the Gnostic still knows quite well :

> When the paradise had come into being out of the mutual good pleasure of Elohim and Edem, then the angels of Elohim took of the finest earth — that is, not of the

---

[20] H. Schmid, « Altes Testament. Exilische und nachexilische Literatur », in *Theologie und Religionswissenschaft*. Edited by U. Mann, Darmstadt 1973, 277 : « Meines Erachtens ersetzte die Weisheit eine Göttin (wohl Aschera), die in heterodoxen Kreisen Jahwe zugeordnet wurde ».

[21] R. van den Broek, « The Shape of Edem according to Justin the Gnostic », *Vigiliae Christianae*, 27 (1973) 35-45.

animal part of Edem, but from the human and civilized regions of the earth above the groin — and made man.

(Hippolytus, Ref. V, 26, 7)

« Increase and multiply, and inherit the earth, i.e. Edem ».

(Ibid. V, 26, 9)

For he (sc. Elohim) aspired upwards, leaving Edem behind; being earth, she did not wish to follow her consort upwards.

(Ibid. V, 26, 14)

It was, however, Isis who was interpreted by the Hellenistic authors as being earth. Among the many witnesses we quote Varro, who in De lingua latina V, 10, says :

principes dei caelum et terra, hi dei idem qui Aegypti Serapis et Isis [22].

Firmicus Maternus, De errore profanarum religionum 2, 6, affirms the same : Isin terram. According to the Neoplatonist philosopher Porphyry, Osiris is the river Nile, and Isis is the Egyptian land which is fertilized by it :

Ἶσις ἡ Αἰγυπτία ἐστὶν γῆ

(Eusebius, Praeparatio Evangelica III, 11, 51).

If any doubt about the meaning of Edem still lingers in the mind of some scholars, this can now be dispelled : Edem means « earth » and resembles Isis.

But at the same time Edem is called Israel and is a symbol of the Jewish people like in Hosea :

This maiden is called « Edem » and « Israel ».

(Hippolytus, Ref. V, 26, 2)

The myth of Justinus, however, describes the sacred marriage between Elohim and Edem, that is between God and Israel :

When the father saw that half-woman Edem, since he was without foreknowledge, he came to a desire for her. Now this father, he says, is called « Elohim ». Edem was no less desirous for Elohim, and the desire brought them together in heart-felt love.

(Ibid. V, 26, 2)

Edem is not intrinsically evil. It is only when her husband leaves her that she makes herself up in order to make him return to her. When

---

[22] Cf. TH. HOFFNER, Plutarch über Isis und Osiris, II, Prague 1941, 176; J. GWYN GRIFFITHS, Plutarch's De Iside et Osiride, University of Wales, 1970, 445-446.

he does not come back, she instructs her daughter, the goddess of love Aphrodite, to create fornication and separation among men :

> Then Edem, knowing that she had been abandoned by Elohim, in her grief set her own angels beside her and adorned herself becomingly, in the hope that Elohim might fall into desire and come to her. But as Elohim, held fast by « the Good », came down no more to Edem, Edem commanded Babel (who is Aphrodite) to effect adulteries and divorces among men, in order that, just as she herself had been separated from Elohim, so also the spirit of Elohim might be pained and tormented by such separations, and suffer the same as the abandoned Edem.
>
> (*Ibid.* V, 26, 19-20)

Here the blasphemous view that Israel is at the same time a goddess and a prostitute is only thinly veiled.

And it would seem that this can be explained in a satisfactory way by supposing that among the Jews of Egypt the view persisted that the Lord had a divine spouse who is at the same time the cause and symbol of all fornication.

Holy prostitution was unknown to the Egyptian religion. It is impossible that some Egyptian myth about Isis-Thermouthis as a prostitute inspired the myth of Edem-Israel. Isis was steadfast to her husband and for ever faithful. This leads us to suppose that Justinus used traditional material already existing before him, describing Israel as the divine and unfaithful spouse of the Lord, which he welded with the concept of Isis as earth and anguipede.

There is a decisive proof that at one time the West-Semitic love goddess, the Egyptian Isis and the Jewish Wisdom were all welded together. Epiphanius tells us that Isis has been prostituting herself for ten years in Tyrus [23]. Contacts between Isis and the Phoenician female deity were old and persisted in the Hellenistic period [24]. And yet this is the only passage known to me where it is said that Isis was a harlot. This is very unusual.

And therefore it is this specific legend which must be responsible for the report that the gnostic Helena had been prostituting herself in the same city of Tyrus. But this means that according to these Gnostics it was Sophia herself who had done this, because Helena was another name of Sophia.

---

[23] EPIPHANIUS, *Ancoratus* 104; W. BOUSSET, *Hauptprobleme der Gnosis*, Göttingen 1907, 81. For the cult of Astarte in Tyrus see H. GESE, *Die Religionen Altsyriens* (*Die Religionen der Menschheit*, 10, 2), Stuttgart 1970, 173.

[24] VANDEBEEK, *o.c.*, 83-84; R. E. WITT, *Isis in the Graeco-Roman World*, London 1971, 69, 109, 131.

Irenaeus tells us the following story about Helena, the companion
of Simon the Magician. She had come forth from God as his First
Idea, the Mother of the All, through whom he conceived in the begin-
ing to make angels and archangels, the celestial powers that rule this
world. In the process, however, this divine being has been made captive
by these Archons and migrated from one incarnation to another.
It was she who was in Helen of Troy and who at last prostituted herself
in a brothel in Tyrus [25].

This is a curious mixture of Greek and Jewish lore. It was the Pytha-
goreans who taught that Helena, abducted by Paris and brought
home by the Greeks, symbolized the soul, which was once on the moon
(Helena-Selènè), now is living in exile in this world, and will return
to her original abode [26].

There is, however, no Greek evidence to show that Helena ever had
a cosmogonic function. And therefore Helena in Simonian Gnosis
really is a covername for Chokma. For Sophia's role in creation is
mentioned in other Jewish sapiential sources too.

As a matter of fact we learn from another source that Helena,
according to Simon the Magician, was none other than Sophia :

κυρίαν οὖσαν, ὡς παμμήτορα οὐσίαν καὶ σοφίαν
(Pseudo-Clementine *Hom.* 2, 25, 2, Rehm 45)

Still more illuminating is a report of Epiphanius, which has not
received the attention it deserves. According to this, Simon identified
Helena-Sophia with the Holy Spirit [27]. This equation, Sophia = Holy
Spirit, of course, is found in many Christian Fathers; but it seems
to have been known also to the Jewish Christians, for in the Pseudo-
Clementine *Homilies* 16, 12, 1, it is said : ἡ δὲ σοφία, ᾗ ὥσπερ ἰδίῳ
πνεύματι αὐτὸς ἀεὶ συνέχαιρεν. But already in the *Wisdom of
Solomon* this equation seems to have taken place. So it is a pre-Christian
and Jewish view that Wisdom and the Holy Spirit are the same.
The presuppositions of Simon or the Simonians are Jewish. But because
they had preserved the older view that the female deity was a harlot,
they came to the paradoxical conclusion that the Holy Spirit was a
prostitute.

---

[25] IRENAEUS, *Adv. Haer.* I, 23, 2.

[26] M. DETIENNE, « La légende pythagoricienne d'Hélène », *Revue de l'Histoire des
Religions*, 152 (1957) 129-152.

[27] EPIPHANIUS, *Panarion* 21, 2, 4 : ἥτις ἐστὶν αὕτη ἡ καὶ Προύνικος καὶ πνεῦμα ἅγιον
καλουμένη.

This proves that in this case the speculations about Sophia were influenced by views on Isis and the Phoenician deity, which had clearly penetrated Samaritan Judaism. But then thinkers like Philo, or the author of the *Wisdom of Solomon*, or the author of *Brontè* could very well be in the same position. If we hesitate to admit that *Brontè* is a Jewish writing of the first century B.C., we should remember that the same concept of the holy prostitute occurs in the Jewish Gnosis of Simon the Samaritan. With this difference that the Simonian Gnosis knew about the fall of Sophia, the tragic split within the deity, whereas nothing of the kind can be found in *Brontè*.

A later phase has been reached in the *Apocryphon of John*, which in its original form can be dated about 100 A.D.

There we find a very lofty description of the Unknown God, who generates his « first Idea », Barbelo. She has the features of Sophia, being virginal and mother, and Holy Spirit and androgynous. But the more negative aspects have been removed from this saintly figure and attributed to the last aeon of the Pleroma, Sophia. She, in fact, though her name is Wisdom, brings forth a being called Saklas (Aram. : the Fool) owing to her « prounikon », her wantonness. She is even called Prounikos, the whore (*Iren.*, I, 29, 4 : *quem et Sophiam et Prunicum vocant*).

Now it has been said very often and becomes ever more clear that the essential myth of the *Apocryphon of John* has nothing to do with Christianity, but could easily be Jewish.

Should that turn out to be the truth, then Mandaeanism is primarily and mainly the continuation of this Jewish Gnosticism. The « Mother » of the Mandaean faith is the divine Mother, complement of the Father. In her celestial character she has several aspects and several names : she is the « Wellspring », Mother of Life, spouse of the great principle of divine enlightenment; she is the archetype of the pure Bride and she appears too as Nasirutha, the true Nasorean faith [28].

I am the Lord of Greatness (= God), father of the spiritual beings and the « Wellsping » is my spouse. Praised is the great 'zlat, for she is the wellspring of light, for she is my spouse, mine, your Father, the Lord of Greatness ... Praised be the treasure of Life, mother of all worlds, she from whom the upper, middle and lower worlds emanated [29].

---

[28] Cf. E. S. DROWER, *The Secret Adam*, Oxford 1960, 12.
[29] ID., *The Thousand and Twelve Questions*, Berlin 1960, 111.

This Mother is obviously the same as Barbelo, and Chokma, and
ultimately, Anat Jahu. The more negative aspects of the terrible
Great Mother have all been attributed to Ruha, the female devil,
the Mother of the Seven (planets), who is constantly harrassing and
tempting the soul, figuring out new strategies against the Life and
its envoys, and trying to obstruct Mandaean rites [30].

There are however quite a few passages in Mandaean literature,
which prove that Ruha originally belonged to the world of light and
spirit and still has preserved some sparks of her original nature.

In the *Canonical Prayerbook of the Mandaeans* we read the following
reaction of Ruha to the revelation of Life :

> Spirit (*ruha*) lifted up her woice,
> She cried aloud and said, « My Father, my Father,
> Why didst thou create me ? My God, my God,
> My Allah, why hast thou set me afar off
> And cut me off and left me in the depths of the earth
> And in the nether glooms of darkness
> So that I have no strength to rise up thither [31] ? ».

Ruha is perfectly aware that she is cut off from the realm of light and
in exile in this world, like the gnostic Sophia and the Shechina of
later Cabbalism.

It is only in the perspective of Jewish Wisdom speculations that
this ambivalence can be understood. Ruha is called at the same time
the Holy Spirit and the prostitute, just as Sophia in *Brontè* is the saint
and the whore, just as in Simonian Gnosis Sophia is called the Holy
Spirit and the harlot. It would even seem that her dialectical nature
goes back much further than *Brontè* or Simon the Magician or the
Apocryphon of John, to the syncretism of Israel before, during and after
the prophets. In any case we have in Mandaeanism a parallel development as in later Cabbalism, where the Shechina is the divine Mother
and yet shows demonic features.

Much has been written about the Iranian or Babylonian sources
of Mandaeanism. Only recently it has become clear that it preserved
the elements of a Jewish Gnosticism. In the future scholars must reckon
with the fact that this Gnosticism in its turn originated in an Israelitic
Gnosis and a Jewish Wisdom tradition which has left only a few traces
in the Hebrew Bible.

---

[30] From now on I use material from a paper by a student, Jorunn Jacobsen.

[31] E. S. DROWER, *The Canonical Prayerbook of the Mandaeans*, Leiden 1959, 74.

And this is exactly why Mandaeanism is important for the study of Gnostic origins. Our present evidence for the existence of a Jewish Gnosis, the reports about the teaching of Simon the Magician, the *Apocryphon of John* and similar documents are all tinged with the terminology of Greek philosophy. So Helena in Simonian sources, Barbelo in the *Apocryphon of John*, is called « the First Idea », a Stoical and highly philosophical terminology.

This veneer of civilisation is completely absent from the wild and confused mythology of the Mandaean texts. This proves that Mandaeanism does not go back directly to the Simonian lore or the Sethian Gnosis of the *Apocryphon of John*, but rather to its even more mythological Jewish prototype.

The Mandaean literature still reveals the signs of the revolt of the images on Jewish soil at the beginning of our era.

III

These long preliminaries were necessary in order to discuss the simple fact that *Brontè* is quoted in the *Treatise without Title* and in the *Ginza*. Or, to put it more carefully : it would seem that a passage in the Coptic translation of the writing *Brontè, the Complete Mind* shows some similarities with a passage in a gnostic writing which was found at Nag Hammadi, in Codex II, without having a title and was therefore called by its editor *Treatise without Title* and is now mostly called *On the Origins of the World*, and with a passage in the *Book of Dinanukht*, a Mandaean writing contained in the so-called *Right Ginza*.

The passage in *Brontè* 13,2-14,1, can be translated literally as follows :

> They sent me from the power. And I came to those who think of me and they found me among those who seek for me.
> Look at me, you who think of me. And you hearers, hear me. You who expect me, take me to you and do not follow me before your eyes.
> And do not suffer that your voice hate me and your hearing. Do not be ignorant concerning me everywhere and at all times.
> Be careful, do not be ignorant concerning me.
> For I am the first and the end. I am the honoured one and the despised one. I am the harlot and the respectable.
> I am the woman and the virgin. I am the mother and the daughter. I am the members of my mother.
> I am the barren one and numerous are her children.
> I am the midwife and the one that does not bear.
> I am the consolation of my birth pangs.

> I am the bride and the bridegroom. And my husband it is who engendered me.
> I am the mother of my father and the sister of my husband and he is my offspring.
> I am the slave of him that prepared me. I am the mistress of my offspring.

It is not only the English that is clumsy here, the Coptic is too. The passage is almost incomprehensible.

The *Treatise without Title* is not very clear either. It was written in Coptic before $\pm$ 350 A.D., the date of almost all the manuscripts of Nag Hammadi. In its present form the work contains some Christian retouching, but critics agree that its sources, though gnostic, are not Christian at all but rather Jewish. The original language must have been Greek. If the passage we are going to quote has been taken from the *Brontè*, it certainly was not borrowed from its Coptic translation : the Coptic is too different. We must assume that it was the Greek text of *Brontè* which underlies the passage in the *Treatise without Title*.

In it a spriritual being, called Sophia-Zoè (= Eve) and also Eve, the first virgin, is said to have sung the following hymn after having brought Man forth :

> I am the part of my mother and I am the mother,
> I am the woman, *I am* the virgin. I am pregnant, I am the physician.
> I am the consoler of the birth pangs. My husband it is who engendered me and I am his mother and he is my father and my master. He is my force. What he wants, he says it. In a reasonable way I am becoming. But I have brought forth a man that is lord.

These words, obscure as they are, may help us to restore the original wording of *Brontè*. Even the smallest details may be helpful.

Here we read : « *I am* (ⲁⲛⲟⲕ ⲧⲉ) the virgin ». This may lead us to suppose that we should read in *Brontè* : « I am the woman and <*I am*> the virgin ». It is to be remembered that « Ego eimi » is not correct Greek at all and could be easily omitted by a Greek or Coptic scribe.

Moreover the parallelism, so popular among the Jews, was offensive to the Greek ear. Luke, the evangelist, has often broken away the parallelism he found in his source Q, for the obvious reason that he tried to write a correct and elegant Greek [32].

And this fact suggests that the author of *Brontè* built up his text with perfect parallelisms, repeating again and again his « Ego eimi », somewhat like the *Ecclesiastes* in his third chapter ([there is] a time to ... and [there is] a time not to).

---

[32] See, for instance, R. BULTMANN, *Die Geschichte der synoptischen Tradition*, 7th ed., Göttingen 1967, 97.

Moreover, the passage in the *Treatise without Title* seems to suggest that some of the original antithesis have got lost in the Coptic version of *Brontè*.

Sophia-Zoè says she is pregnant. This presupposes a certain climax in *Brontè*, where Sophia must have said that she was married, though unmarried, was pregnant and still barren, brought forth and yet did not engender.

Moreover, Sophia-Zoè says she is a physician. And this presupposes the original parallelism :

> I am the healer that heals
> and I am the wounder that wounds.

As a matter of fact it is this thought that is to be found in the Mandaean writing. Knowing no Mandaean, I must translate here the German version of Lidzbarski :

> Then came Ewath, the Holy Spirit, approached me in my Šhīnā and said to me :
> Why are you lying there, Dīnānūkht ?
> Why did sleep please you ?
> I am the Life that was from old,
> I am the Truth that was already before in the beginning.
> I am the splendour, I am the Light,
> *I am death, I am Life,*
> I am darkness, I am light,
> I am error, I am truth,
> I am destruction, I am construction,
> *I am the blow, I am the healing.*
>
> (Right Ginza, 207)

It should be observed that Ewath, the Holy Spirit, is none other than Ruha, the evil spirit of the Mandaeans, who reveals herself here in her original ambivalence. Because it is unthinkable that two authors independently of each other are putting such extraordinary dialectical language into the mouth of the same divine person, Sophia or the Holy Spirit, we must assume that the Mandaean was inspired by the earlier writing *Brontè*, which must somehow have been familiar to him. Or perhaps we must say that this Mandaean writing here preserved the same thoroughly ungnostic complex of ideas which also underlies the Alexandrian writing.

In any case it is clear that the monistic version of Ewath is older and more primitive than certain dualistic formulations also to be found in Mandaean literature which we shall discuss presently. For her speech, like that of *Brontè*, echoes the words of *Deuteronomy* 32, 39:

> I put to death and I keep alive,
> I wound and I heal.

It was Tertullian who quoted these words against Marcion to refute
the latter's dualism (*Adv. Marc.* IV, 1 : *Ego, inquit, percutiam, et ego
sanabo*; *Ego, inquit, occidam, et ego vivificabo*). And this seems to show
that the quoted passages of Ewath and *Brontè* cannot possibly be
gnostic, because the Gnostics abhorred this view, and therefore could
reflect views which preceded the rise of Gnosticism.

We may try then to restore tentatively the original text of *Brontè*
in this passage :

> I was sent from the Power (= God)
> and I came to those who thought of me
> and I was found by those who sought me.
> Behold me, ye who thought of me,
> and ye who wanted to hear me, listen to me,
> and ye who expected me, accept me
> and do not chase me away from before your eyes.
> And let not your voice and your ear hate me.
> Do not ignore me anywhere or at any time,
> be careful, do not ignore me.

For

> I am the first and <I am> the last,
> I am the honoured one and <I am> the despised one,
> I am the harlot and <I am> the saint,
> I am the woman and <I am> the virgin,
> I am the mother and <I am> the daughter,
> I am part of my mother <and my mother is part of me>,
> I am childless and <I am> having many children,
> I am polyandrous <and I am> unmarried,
> <I am pregnant and I am barren>,
> I am the midwife <and I am the woman in travail>,
> <I am the woman in childbed> and <I am> the one that bears not,
> <I am the one that causes the birth pangs and> I am the consoler of birth pangs,
> <I am the physician that heals and I am the wounder that wounds>,
> I am the bride and <I am> the bridegroom,
> <I am the mother of my husband and my husband is my father,
> I am the daughter of my husband and my husband is my son,
> I am the sister of my husband and my husband is my brother>,
> I am the slave of my father and I am the mistress of my son.

In *Brontè* and in the quoted passage of the *Right Ginza* the same dialectical concept is put into the mouth of Sophia-Ruha. The « I am » formula must be the original version.

In the same Mandaean writing we find a variation on the theme :

> There is brightness, there is light,
> There is death, there is life,
> There is darkness, there is light,
> There is wrong, there is right,
> There is destruction, there is construction,
> There is striking, there is healing.

(Right Ginza VI, Lidzbarski, 206, 24-26) [33]

This, of course, is not only different in style but also in concept. This is the principle of dualism, of an irreconcilable war between the fundamental opposites of reality. This is presented in a rather old section of the *Right Ginza* (Lidzbarski, 48,10 ff.).

There we are told that the Saviour Anos (= the biblical Enos, which means Man) comes to Jerusalem in the time of Pontius Pilate; he heals the sick, makes the blind see again, purifies the lepers, makes the lame walk and gives speech to the deaf and mute. With the force of the high king of light (= God) he even quickens the dead. So he wins faithful ones among the Jews and entrusts them with his revelation :

> There is death and there is life,
> and there is darkness and there is light,
> and there is wrong and there is right.

He converts some Jews to the truth and destroys the city of Jerusalem.

As we shall see in the following pages, this passage may help us to discern that the rise of the Mandaean religion (and there is no Mandaeanism without dualism) can to a certain extent be explained as an inner Jewish process, namely as a reaction against the view that is God who creates light and darkness, life and death, good and evil.

This view was especially characteristic of the Essenes who are responsible for the Dead Sea Scrolls. And then we see what little significance the fact has, that the Scrolls and the writings of the Mandeaeans have some words in common. The section we are discussing is sometimes called the *Mandaean Book of the Lord of Greatness*, because that expression is found here to designate God. « Lord of Greatness, Mar d'Rabutha », is also found in the Dead Sea Scrolls. But that does not mean

---

[33] Similar formulations in 207, 13-16, and 210, 27-30.

that Mandaeanism originated among the Essenes. On the contrary, it is essentially a *reaction* against the monism of the Jewish religion, and so of the Essenes and of the Jewish Christians (who held that the devil was the left hand of God).

There is yet another text that should be discussed in this context. Among the Manichaean Psalms discovered at Medinet Madi in 1930 there is a section called the *Psalms of Thomas*. One of these contains a dialogue between a saviour, here called the Physician, and Hylè or Matter, designed as the Mother of this world.

Matter tells that she hears the cry of the Physician and implores him to heal her. The saviour refuses :

> How shall I heal thee, o Matter, the ..., the Mother of this world. For
> *I am* the physician that heals
> but *thou art* the wounder that wounds,
> I am the ....
> but thou art the striker that lays low ...

Thereupon Matter asks him to give her a single day, an hour only for her to wound (?) the sons of men so that they do not hope for what has been told (?) to them, that there is death, there is life, there is also the Land of Truth. The saviour answers :

> I will not give thee a single day,
> I will not allow thee an hour only.

> (Allberry, 221)

In the foregoing we have seen that the opposites mentioned in this passage go back to *Deuteronomy* 32, 39.

It would seem that this Manichaean Psalm is a protest against this view that good and evil, wounding and healing come forth from the same source. It seems now reasonably certain that in the Jewish writing *Brontè* Sophia proclaimed :

> I am the healer that heals
> and I am the wounder that wounds.

The lines in the *Psalm of Thomas* contradict this :

> *I am* the healer that heals,
> but *thou art* the wounder that wounds.

What are the connections between *Brontè* and Mani ?

In an excellent study Torgny Säve-Söderbergh has shown that the
Manichaean Psalms agree both in style and in wording with certain
Mandaean hymns, to such an extent that the former must depend upon
the latter [34]. The arguments of the Swedish scholar are so numerous
and so convincing that there must be some truth in it.

Writing in 1949 Säve-Söderbergh could not yet know that the hypothesis according to which Mani lived in his youth among the Mandaeans
rested upon shaky foundations indeed. The Cologne Mani Papyrus
proved this theory to be wrong. Mani did not live among the Mandaeans, but among the Elkesaites [35]. And then we can better understand
the existential situation from which his dualism sprang.

The Jewish Christians of the Pseudo-Clementine writings, who are
certainly related to, if not identical with the Elkesaites, stressed the
view that evil originated in God (*Hom.* 20, 3, 6). Among them circulated
a word of Jesus stressing that good and evil are destined to come,
that is, are both willed by God :

> The good is destined to come,
> blessed is he by whose hand it comes;
> the evil is destined to come,
> cursed is he through whom it comes.
>
> (Pseudo-Clementine *Hom.* 12, 29)

This same logion is quoted in a Manichaean source [36]. And the simplest
solution of this problem is to assume that Mani picked this word up
in his youth and transmitted it to his followers.

This does not mean that he agreed with it. On the contrary, there
was no view which Mani disliked more than the concept that evil
originates in God. His dualism of spirit and matter, light and darkness,
good and evil, was meant mainly to unburden God of any responsibility for the evil of this world of which he was so keenly aware.

So I can imagine the possibility that in the Psalm of Thomas which
we discussed above Mani or one of his followers is reacting against
the views also expressed in the writing *Brontè*, with which Mani
may have become familiar in his Jewish-Christian youth. If there are
nevertheless enough parallels left between the Manichaean *Psalms of
Thomas* and certain Mandaean hymns to assume a mutual dependence,

---

[34] T. SÄVE-SÖDERBERGH, *Studies in the Coptic Manichaean Psalm-Book*, Uppsala 1949.

[35] L. KOENEN and A. HENRICHS, « Ein griechischer Mani-Codex », *Zeitschrift für
Papyrologie and Epigraphik*, 5 (1970) 97-216.

[36] *A Manichaean Psalm-Book*, II, edited by C. R. C. ALLBERRY, Stuttgart 1938, 39.

the possibility must be envisaged that the latter were originally Jewish-
Christian hymns or were made after the pattern of these last-mentioned
hymns.

Jewish Christians are said to have laid the foundations of Aramaic
Christianity, they had an enormous impact even upon such typically
Syrian movements as the Messalians. It is now absolutely certain,
since the discovery of the Mani Codex, that they were active in Southern Babylonia.

The time seems to have come to investigate whether these Jewish
Christians might have influenced the Mandaeans.

IV

Mandaean studies have made great progress recently, mainly owing
to the exertions of K. Rudolph and R. Macuch. It is not so much that
they discovered anything new. In fact not much of decisive importance
has been discovered ever since Lidzbarski made known his arguments
for a Jewish, pre-Christian origin of the Mandaean sect now living in
Iraq and Iran. But Mandaean studies had become disreputable,
because R. Reitzenstein, an amateur, had launched the wildest and
most improbable hypotheses about the impact of the early Mandaeans
upon primitive Christianity. Macuch and Rudolph made the work on
Mandaeanism respectable again. The first wrote, together with Lady
Drower, a dictionary on the language of the community which now
numbers about 15,000 members [37]. The second published some excellent books on the history of this group, with that thoroughness one
has learned to admire and to fear [38]. Ever since he writes summaries
on the present state of the question, here and there and everywhere,
and defends his positions ably and agressively.

Macuch and Rudolph do not always agree, but their common views can
be summarized in the following way. Discernible connections with John's

---

[37] E. S. DROWER and R. MACUCH, *A Mandaic Dictionary*, Oxford 1963; R. MACUCH,
« Anfänge der Mandäer », in *Die Araber in der Alten Welt*. Edited by F. ALTHEIM and
R. STIEHL, II, Berlin 1965, 76-190; ID., *Handbook of Classical and Modern Mandaic*,
Berlin 1965.

[38] K. RUDOLPH, *Die Mandäer*, I and II (*Forschungen zur Religion und Literatur des
Alten und Neuen Testaments*, 74-75), Göttingen 1960, 1961; ID., *Theogonie, Kosmogonie
und Anthropogonie in den mandäischen Schriften* (*Forschungen*, etc., 88), Göttingen 1965;
a selection of Mandaic sources by RUDOLPH in W. FOERSTER, *Gnosis. A Selection of
Gnostic Texts*, II. English translation edited by R. McL. WILSON, Oxford 1974.

Gospel, the *Odes of Solomon* and other gnostic writings make it *entirely* probable that Mandaean traditions reach back to the pre-Christian period. Their baptism, *maṣbūtā* (from *ṣb'*, immerse), takes place only in « living » (= flowing) water, which bears the name yardna (Jordan). Certain traits of this rite go back to a pre-Christian period and have their origin in the lustral and baptismal practices of unorthodox Judaism, i.e. in the so-called baptismal sects once living in the neighbourhood of the Jordan in Palestine (cf. John the Baptist). Indications of their Western origin are to be found in the name Jordan for baptismal water, in the name *Nāṣōrāyê* (Nazoraeans = observers) used by the Mandaeans to design themselves, and even by the name *Ṣubbi* (baptists), used by their Arabic neighbours to design the Mandaeans.

Their millennial history can be reconstructed with some certainty.

The sect originated in Jerusalem. In several texts a tradition is preserved which tells of the persecution of the oldest Mandaeans by the Jews, as a consequence of which Jerusalem was destroyed.

Thereupon they must have migrated to Transjordan, not far from the mountain Haurān. This because a genius Harān is mentioned in the Mandaean sources.

From there they moved to Mesopotamia, more specifically to Harran (Carrhae, near Edessa) into the region between Harran and Nisibis, which was then Iranian territory. This took place in the first and second century A.D. under the reign of a Parthian king called Ardbān (Artabanus).

This part of the theory is based on a sort of « History of the Mandaean Movement », called *Diwan of the Great Revelation, called Harran Gawaita (the Inner Harran)* published in 1953 by Lady E.S. Drower [39].

It begins, after a preamble and a lacuna, with the enigmatic words :

> and Harran Gawaita receiveth him and that city in which there were Naṣoraeans, because there was no road for the Jewish rulers. Over them was king Ardban. And sixty thousand Naṣoraeans abandoned the sign of the Seven (planets) and entered the Median hills, a place where we were free from domination by all other races.

Later on they lived in the southern regions of Mesopotamia [40].

---

[39] E. S. DROWER, *The Haran Gawaita and the Baptism of Hibil Ziwa (Studi e Testi, 176)*, Città del Vaticano 1953.

[40] Cf. RUDOLPH in *Gnosis*, II, 140.

All this is very edifying and impressive and could be believed, was also believed by me, until the Cologne Mani Codex was discovered.

According to this writing Mani lived from his fourth to his twenty-fifth year in a commune of Jewish Christians. The founder of their « law » is said to have been Elchasaios. So they belonged to the well-known sect of the Elkesaites, founded by the prophet Elksai ($\pm$ 110 A.D.) as a special sect of Jewish Christianity. They were baptists in the sense that after baptism they knew ritual ablutions [41].

Now the *Fihrist* of the Arabic author An Nadim never had said anything else. It reported that already Mani's father, Fattik, had joined the baptists (Muqtasila) who lived in the marshes of Southern Babylonia and whose chief is said to have been a certain al Ḥasīḥ (Elksai or Elchasai) [42].

But some scholars of Mandaeanism knew better. According to them, Mani grew up among Mandaeans, and upon this pillar their whole theory was built. Even after the announcement of the Mani Codex one of them goes on to speak about « the certain fact that Mani was rooted in Mandaeanism », in the same paper where he pussyfoots (in a footnote) past the recent discovery [43]. Such a procedure certainly does not enhance the confidence in the soundness of the methods applied.

It is, however, a fact that Mani grew up among Jewish Christians who are said to have baptized themselves every day. « Why do you baptize yourself again every day, after having been baptized once and for all and having been purified once and for all ? », asks Mani [44]. He also tells an anecdote about Sabbaios the Baptist ($\acute{o}$ $\beta\alpha\pi\tau\iota\sigma\tau\acute{\eta}s$) [45]. In short this Jewish group must be identified with the « baptists » mentioned under different names (Maṣboteans, from *Maṣbūtā*, baptism ; *Muqtasila*, Ṣebueans). The Koran knows them under the name Ṣabeans and grants them the privilege of being a « people of the book » and herefore tolerates them.

These Jewish Christians originated in Jerusalem, though their

---

[41] This completely new view on Manichaean origins is also to be found in F. DECRET, *Mani et la tradition manichéenne*, Paris 1974, 48.

[42] Cf. G. FLÜGEL, *Mani, seine Lehre und seine Schriften*, Leipzig 1862 (reprinted Osnabrück 1969), 133.

[43] K. RUDOLPH, « Zum gegenwärtigen Stand der mandäischen Religionsgeschichte », in *Gnosis und Neues Testament*. Edited by K.-W-TRÖGER, Berlin 1973, 128.

[44] HENRICHS-KOENEN, *o.c.*, 141.

[45] *Ibid.*, 148.

leaders, among whom James, the Brother of the Lord, was prominent, were all Galilaeans. There was a time when the church of Jerusalem consisted exclusively of « Hebrews », Aramaic speaking Jews from the motherland, who were *all* zelotic practisants of the Law :

> Then they said to Paul : «You see, brother, how many thousands of converts we have among the Jews, all of them staunch upholders of the Law.»
>
> (*Acts* 21, 20)

They were called Nazoraeans :

> We have found this man (sc. Paul) to be a perfect pest, a fomenter of discord among the Jews all over the world, a ringleader of the sect of the Nazoraeans.
>
> (*Acts* 24, 5)

Before the Jewish-Roman war they left Jerusalem and migrated to Transjordan, namely to the city of Pella, quite a long way from Jerusalem, but not so far from Gilead and Mount Haurān. At least that is what Eusebius tells in his *History of the Church* (III, 5, 3).

There is also a tradition that they migrated to Harran, that is to Carrhae, a city in Northern Mesopotamia between Beroea (Aleppo) and Edessa (Urfa). It is told in the allegedly Jewish-Christian source identified by Schlomo Pines in a work of Jabbar. It is true that the historical trustworthiness of this source is rather doubtful. But it does say that the original and authentic Jewish Christians left Jerusalem and migrated to Harran :

> Thereupon they (sc. the Jewish Christians) fled the country. And the Romans wrote concerning them to their governors in the districts of Mosul and in the *Jazīrat Al-'Arab* [46].

In nearby Aleppo there lived, in the fourth century and possibly much earlier, Jewish Christians which called themselves Nazoraeans. They are sometimes distinguished from other groups as orthodox in their faith and judaizing in their way of life :

> They confess that Jesus is the Christ, Son of God, but they live in every way according to the Law.
>
> (Epiphanius, *Anacephalaiôsis* 2, 29) [47]

---

[46] S. PINES, *The Jewish Christians of the Early Centuries of Christianity According to a New Source* (*Proceedings of the Israel Academy of Sciences and Humanities*, II, 13), Jerusalem 1966, 15.

[47] Cf. A. F. J. KLIJN and G. J. REININK, *Patristic Evidence for Jewish-Christian Sects* (Supplements to *Novum Testamentum*, XXXVI), Leiden 1973, 161.

They are said to live both in Coele Syria and in Transjordan :

> This heresy of the Nazoraeans exists in Beroea in the neighbourhood of Coele
> Syria and the Decapolis in the region of Pella and in Basanitis in the so-called Kokaba
> (Chochabe in Hebrew). From there it took its beginning after the exodus from
> Jerusalem when all the disciples went to live in Pella because Christ had told them
> to leave Jerusalem and to go away since it would undergo a siege. Because of this
> advice they lived in Perea after having moved to that place, as I said.
>
> (Epiphanius, *Panarion* 29, 7,7-8) [48]

It is quite possible that there existed such a group, admitting at
least in words the Sonship of Christ, tolerant of St Paul but not accept-
ing his dialectics of Law and grace, the authentic successors of James
and his fellows in Jerusalem. But it would seem that the name Nazoraeans remained the property of *all* Jewish adherents of Messiah
Jesus. Why should they have given up their original name ? Though
this is not attested in so many words, we must assume that the Elkesaites too styled themselves as Nazoraeans. They had several doctrines
of their own, like the doctrine of the True Prophet or the possibility
of a second penance after baptism, accompanied by ritual ablutions.
But they did remain Jewish Christians and must have preserved their
original name, Nazoraeans. The name Christians was an Antiochene
invention, given to a gentile Christian congregation (*Acts* 11, 26).
The original name of the adherents of the new religion in Palestine
was Nazoraeans.

If in the fourth century Jewish Christians in Transjordan and Aleppo
called themselves Nazoraeans, it is rather obvious that they must
have come to Syria from Palestine. As a matter of fact, it must have
been they who gave their name to the Christians of Syria, who were
always called and are still called Nazoraeans. This is one of the many
arguments showing that Aramaic Christianity which centered in
Edessa originated in Jewish Christian foundations. Tradition tells
us that Christianity was brought to this last city by Addai, a Jewish
Christian from Jerusalem. Some scholars tell us that this is nothing
but a legend without any historical value. But the *Gospel of Thomas*,
composed about 140 A.D. in Edessa or its surroundings and containing
in part a Jewish-Christian Gospel tradition, indicates that Christianity
in these regions is of Palestinian origin.

The Mani Codex reveals that Jewish Christians were living in Southern Babylonia at the time of Mani (216-267 A.D.).

---

[48] KLIJN-REININK, *o.c.*, 173.

It is unthinkable that two different sects had the same names (Nazoraeans, baptists) and the same history (including an emigration from Transjordan to Harran) at the same time. The conclusion is inevitable : the present day Mandaeans are indebted to the Elkesaites for the rites and legends and views they have in common with these Jewish Christians. This explains the Western elements undoubtedly contained in their tradition. This, of course, is only one half of the story : Elkesaitism may explain the ritualism of the Mandaeans, not their Gnosticism. But if the story is only half true, this half is true.

It was Schou Pedersen who to the best of my knowledge was the first to envisage this possibility in his book *Bidrag til en Analyse af de mandaeiske skrifter* [49]. He pointed to, among other things, the belief of the Mandaeans, and of the Pseudo-Clementine writings, that the Jews had falsified the Law of Moses.

The same hypothesis would be able to explain much more :

1. the name Nazoraeans of the Mandaeans;
2. their baptism and ablutions, dressed in their clothes. Epiphanius, *Panarion* 30, 2, 5, says of the Jewish Christians : « But also if one meets somebody coming up from immersion in water and from washing, one returns to wash oneself in the same way again, several times and *fully clothed* »;
3. their affirmation of sex and marriage, a characteristic feature of the Pseudo-Clementines and the Jewish-Christian group which is behind them;
4. the precept of love for one's neighbour, not yet unrestricted but valid only for the members of the community; with this should be compared the Saying contained in the *Gospel of Thomas* (log. 25) but of Jewish-Christian origin : « Jesus said : Love thy brother as thy soul, guard him as the apple of thine eye ».
5. the concept of a transcendental Self, the image and counterpart of man. This belief existed already in the primitive community of Jerusalem (the angel of Peter in *Acts* 12, 15) and is attested in the *Gospel of Thomas* (log. 84). There is a difference of terminology here : the Mandaeans say *d'muta*, likeness, whereas the later Syrians speak about the *zaelaem*, the image, and the Jews say : *iqonin*

---

[49] V. SCHOU PEDERSEN, *Bidrag til en Analyse af de mandaeiske Skrifter* (Theol. thesis Copenhagen 1940), Aarhus 1940.

(eikôn) [50]. There is, however, not the slightest doubt that this terminology relates to *Genesis* 1, 26, according to which man is created after the image and the likeness of God;

6. the idea that there are two kings, one of this world, and one of the beyond. According to the Pseudo-Clementine *Homilies* 20, 2, 1-2, the devil is the king of this world and Christ is the king of the next world :

Ps.-Clem. *Hom.* 20, 1-2	*Book of John* 13
God established two kingdoms and two worlds. To the evil one he attributed the present world, because the latter is short and passing away quickly, but to the good one he promised the coming world, because that is great and eternal.	Two kings came into being, two natures were created : a king of this world and a king beyond the world.

There are still many more elements which could be enumerated here in order to establish that the Mandaeans are dependent upon Jewish-Christian views. In this context the given examples may suffice.

This then does mean that it becomes extremely dangerous to use Mandaean material in order to reconstruct the prehistory of Christian baptism. For what seems to have been pre-Christian, can easily have been derived from Jewish Christianity.

V

Macuch and Rudolph were absolutely right when they stressed the western elements in Mandaeanism and assumed that these were due to a migration of a group from Palestine to Mesopotamia. They went astray when they supposed that this also explained the gnostic character of the Mandaean religion. It is much more plausible to assume that it were the Elkesaites who grafted these typically West-Semitic components into another branch. And the Elkesaites were not in the least Gnostics : their problem was sin after baptism and their solution was : ritual ablutions [51].

Recently Edwin Yamauchi has reacted against the theories of Macuch and Rudolph [52]. He suggested that the western elements in

---

[50] Cf. G. QUISPEL, *Makarios, das Thomasevangelium und das Lied von der Perle* (Supplements to *Novum Testamentum*, XV), Leiden 1967.

[51] H. LIETZMANN, *Geschichte der Alten Kirche*, 3rd ed., I, Berlin 1953, 193-197.

[52] E. M. YAMAUCHI, *Gnostic Ethics and Mandaean Origins* (*Harvard Theological Studies*, XXIV), Cambridge (Mass.)-London 1970, 80 ff.

Mandaeanism have been overrated because of the preponderance of western evidence available. He can conceive of a group with the following characteristics :

1. they would be non-Jews who were acquainted with the Old Testament ;
2. they would be antagonistic to the Jews ;
3. they would speak an Aramaic dialect and be familiar with the Nabatean script ;
4. they would be dwellers in Transjordan, who worshipped the god of the Hauran range ;
5. some of them may have been attracted to John the Baptist, but they did not follow Jesus at all.

The eastern component may have been an indigenous Aramaean group living in the marshes of lower Iraq and south-western Iran. Among them persisted the indigenous Mesopotamian cult and magic. We have incontestable evidence of the transmission of Mesopotamian magic traditions in the Mandaean magical texts, even of verbal formulae. Mandaeanism is basically a gnostic interpretation of an indigenous Mesopotamian cult [53].

We agree with Yamauchi that the Mandaean religion came into being as a synthesis of a western and an eastern component. We would prefer to suppose that it must have been Elkesaites who transmitted the Palestinian, West-Aramaic elements. Nor would we deny that the eastern component may have integrated Babylonian and Iranian concepts. But, as we see it, Mandaeanism is basically the survival of a Jewish Gnosticism such as that attested by the *Apocryphon of John* and other writings from Nag Hammadi. There must have existed in Southern Babylonia a group of Jewish Gnostics who were responsible for the primitive myth of the *Apocryphon of John*.

According to the Mandaeans the King of Darkness has the head of a lion, the body of a dragon, the hands and feet of a monster. He is stupid, he knows neither the First nor the Last. He became arrogant and exalted and said : « Is there anyone who is greater than I ? » [54].

According to the *Apocryphon of John* the demiurge Jaldabaoth is a dragon with a lion's face and his eyes were like burning lightning

---

[53] YAMAUCHI, *o.c.*, 86.
[54] *Right Ginza* XII, 6 (Lidzbarski, 277 ff.).

which flashes; one of his names is Saklas, which means « fool ». In his
ignorance he said : « I am God and there is no other God but me » [55].

The story of the creation of Adam by the demiurge and his seven planet
spirits is also very similar in the *Apocryphon of John* and the Mandaean
sources. The inability of the demiurge and his powers to make Adam
stand on his feet is stressed by both [56]. There is no doubt that the
underlying gnostic myth is essentially the same.

It was only after the discovery of the Jung Codex, with its strong
Jewish influences, that people dared to speak about a Jewish Gnosticism [57]. One wonders why these connections were not made before,
because they are so obvious. The fact is, however, that we were all
too intimidated by current theories to dare see clearly. Even today
one meets with stubborn opposition when one observes that there
must have been Jewish Gnostics who distinguished between the
Highest God and an inferior demiurge. And yet, at that time the *Timaeus* of Plato, which does teach a lower creator, the *dèmiourgos*, was
the « livre de chevet » of every philosopher and theosophist. And yet,
in most creation myths the world is made by one of the lower gods.
This is obviously human, and Jews were human, also at that time of
occupation by the Romans and national disaster.

The stories about the creation of the world of the Mandaeans are
confused and contradictory, but very often Ptahil functions as the
demiurge of the earthly world [58]. He is sometimes addressed as :

---

[55] S. GIVERSEN, *Apocryphon Johannis* (*Acta Theologica Danica*, V), Copenhagen 1963,
67 (Nag Hammadi Codex II, 11, 20-21).

[56] K. RUDOLPH, « Ein Grundtyp gnostischer Urmensch-Adam-Spekulation », *Zeitschrift für Religions- und Geistesgeschichte*, 9 (1957) 1-20.

[57] ITHAMAR GRUENWALD has ably shown that both Gnosticism and Merkava-mysticism have their roots, or some of their roots, in Jewish apocalypticism; the latter is a
reaction against the absolute scepticism of Job. Gnosticism and Merkava-mysticism
have in common that they are an anti-eschatological reaction to apocalypticism; cf.
his « Knowledge and Vision. Towards a clarification of two « gnostic » concepts in the
light of their alleged origins », *Israel Oriental Studies*, 3 (1973) 93-107.

[58] The name of this subordinate deity has led to several hypotheses and most people
could not help thinking of the god Ptah, who has a creative function in Egyptian mythology. This hunch is not improbable. There has been found a representation of Ptah in
Lachish accompanied by an inscription in Proto-Canaanite letters which seems to suggest
that Ptah was identified with El, the main God of their pantheon, by some Canaanites
long before the invasion of Palestine by the Hebrews (F. M. CROSS, *Canaanite Myth
and Hebrew Epic*, Cambridge [Mass.] 1974, 19). Now it is an astonishing fact that some
very archaic names like Samašilam (Eternal Sun) have been preserved by some magical
papyri and amulets dating from the first centuries of our era (cf. C. BONNER, *Studies*

« O, you fool » (Sakla, cf. Saklas in the *Apocryphon of John*)[59]. Sometimes he is called Gabriel :

> He called Ptahil-Uthra,
> embraced him, and kissed him like a mighty one.
> He bestowed names on him,
> which are hidden and protected in their place.
> He gave him the name Gabriel, the Messenger ...
>
> > (*Right Ginza* III, Lidzbarski, 98)

« Gabriel the Messenger » is said to be the secret but authentic name of the Mandaean Demiurge. The creator is an angel.

> The wonderful living fire shall be established and Gabriel
> the Messenger shall be called forth.
> He shall be called forth and commissioned,
> he will be sent hither.
> He shall be called forth and commissioned,
> he will call forth the world.
> He shall come and perform solidification
> and call forth the earth skilfully.
> He shall call forth the earth skilfully
> and stop up the springs of the turbid water.
>
> > (*Right Ginza* III, Lidzbarski, 89)

An angel is the demiurge of this world.

Something similar we find in the *Treatise without Title* (Böhlig, 43, 24) : there it is said that the perfect call Jaldabaoth « Ariel », because he has the face of a lion. This could only have been invented by a Jew, because Ariel means : « the lion of God ». We conclude then that in the *Treatise without Title* the demiurge is thought to be an angel.

A magical amulet of Antiquity contains on its observe the names Jaldabaoth and Ariel in Greek letters, together with a lion-headed figure, and on its reverse the names of the seven demonic rulers of the universe [60].

---

in *Magical Amulets, chiefly Graeco-Egyptian* [*University of Michigan Studies*, Humanistic Series, XLIX], Ann Arbor 1950). One of them is precisely Ptahil, cf. K. PREISENDANZ, *Papyri Graecae Magicae*, I, Leipzig-Berlin 1928, 28, 119 : φθᾶηωλι, 106, 972 : φθαήλ (note : « der mandäische Schöpfergott ; Jac. » (= A. JACOBI). It is possible then that the name Ptahil preserves the very old identification of the Egyptian Ptah and the Canaanite El. One must suppose, however, that at the time of Mandaean origins this was just a magical very old word, like our Abracadabra (from Abraxas), rather meant to cover his real significance and meaning than revealing and making understandable.

[59] *Right Ginza* V, 1 (Lidzbarski, 174).

[60] BONNER, *o.c.*, 135-138.

Scholem says : « That Yaldabaoth was also named Ariel was not known before the publication of this amulet. But Ariel as a lion-headed angel could be only a Jewish conception, Ariel meaning 'the lion of God'. Ariel seems to have been, therefore, an older name of Yaldabaoth, and the sectarian who designed that amulet was still aware of the original context and meaning of Ariel » [61]. We add that only a Jew could conceive of the idea that an angel is to be identified as the creator of the world.

Ever since the Jews became theologically conscious, the crude anthropomorphisms of their concept of God have been toned down : the « Angel of the Lord » came to replace the Lord Himself.

There has even been a pre-Christian sect of the Magharians, according to whom the anthropomorphisms of the Old Testament are applied to the angel who created the world [62]. The same doctrine is attributed to Jewish Gnostics like Simon the Magician and Cerinthus. Ever since the beginning of my career I have been quoting the relevant passages, without at that moment seeing their connection with the Mandaean problem. When it becomes clear to one that Ptahil is an esoteric name for Gabriel, the Jewish angel, these pieces of information become still more precious. Qirqisāni, living in the first half of the 10th century, writes in his work *The Book of Lights and Watch-Towers* about the pre-Christian Jewish sect of the Magharians :

> Their interpretations of some passages in the Scriptures are altogether improbable and resemble foolish talk. Daūd ibn Marwān al-Muqammiṣ says in one of his books that the Sadducees ascribe corporeality to God and understand all the Scriptural descriptions of Him which imply anthropomorphism in their literal sense. The Magharians are said to be opposed to this, i.e., they do not profess anthropomorphism ; yet they also do not take these descriptions (of God) out of their literal meaning, but assert instead that these descriptions refer to one of the angels namely to one who created the world. This (opinion) is similar to the view of Benjamin al-Nahāwandi which we shall explain later [63].

Still more illuminating are the words of Shahrastāni, rightly called the first scholar of the history of religions. In his work *The Book of Religions and Sects*, which was composed in 1127, he writes :

---

[61] G. SCHOLEM, *Jewish Gnosticism, Merkabah Mysticism and Talmudic Tradition*, New York 1960, 72.

[62] Cf. G. QUISPEL, *Gnostic Studies*, I, Istanbul 1974, 215.

[63] Translation by A. A. DI LELLA, *The Hebrew Text of Sirach*, The Hague 1966, 85 ; text in L. NEMOY, « Al-Qirqisānī's Account of the Jewish Sects and Christianity », *Hebrew Union College Annual*, 7 (1930) 363 f.

But one sect of the Maqāriba claims that God spoke to the prophets, may peace be upon them, through the agency of an angel whom He had elected and whom He had given precedence over all creatures and had appointed viceroy over them. They say : « Every description of God in the Torah and in the rest of the Books is an account (given) on the authority of this angel. For otherwise it would not be possible to describe God in any way at all ». They also say : « Furthermore, he who addressed Moses, may peace be upon him, is that angel. And God the exalted One is too exalted to address in human fashion mortal man ... [64] ».

If these reports are authentic, it would be clear that this Angel according to the Magharians was the Angel of the Lord, who addressed Moses in the Burning Bush. When we realize what the meaning and function of the Angel of the Lord in the religion of Israel was, we can understand that some Jews said that he had manifested himself to Moses. That is after all what *Exodus* says in the story of the Burning Bush.

They went further when they said it was this Angel who had given the Law. But even that is not remarkable in a Jewish milieu : Stephen and Paul, both Jews, said that the Law had been given by angels, not by God directly (*Acts* 7, 53; *Gal.* 3,19). The motivation seems to have been very much the same.

The view that is really new and unheard of is that according to the Magharians it was this Angel of the Lord who had created the world. But this is only consistent, if you want to keep the Bible intact and yet believe that God is beyond anthropomorphism.

There cannot be any reasonable doubt that the Mandaeans have preserved the Jewish notions of the Magharians. For it does not mean very much whether you name the demiurge Gabriel or Ariel. The important thing is that in both cases the creation of the world is attributed to a Jewish angel.

We therefore conclude that at a certain moment Jewish Gnostics in Southern Babylonia, the heirs of the Magharians, thought it good to cover themselves with the name of the Nazoraeans. They also accepted the baptism and the ritual ablutions characteristic of the Elkesaites. In this way they integrated many western elements into their body

---

[64] Translation by DI LELLA, *o.c.*, 87; text in W. CURETON (ed.), *Book of Religions and Philosophical Sects, by Muhammad al-Sharastani*, I (London 1892), 169.

of doctrine, which have led some to suppose that they reflected a pre-Christian baptism and a pre-Christian Gnosticism.

Now it is quite possible that these Babylonian Gnostics have preserved some archaic views of Jewish Gnosis, such as the concept of Wisdom as the spouse of God who was both attractive and demonic.

The dualism of the sect, however, the complete demonisation of Ruha, the distinction between God as Life and Light on the one hand and the foolish demiurge on the other hand, can only be a later development.

Still later the merger with the Jewish Christians took place. It was only then that Mandaeanism, as a religion at the same time ritual and gnostic, came into being.

We do not know when that happened. The only certain thing is that no evidence from the first, second or third century is available. Ignoramus et ignorabimus.

If these ideas are right, the Mandaeans will be studied in the future without sensationalism but with understanding and sympathy.

For they represent a very curious development of the Jewish religion, namely Jewish Gnosticism. As such they form an important interval between the religion of Israel and the mystical movements within Judaism during the second millennium of our era.

LE SENS DES SYMBOLES SEXUELS
DANS QUELQUES TEXTES HERMÉTIQUES ET GNOSTIQUES [1]

PAR

JEAN-PIERRE MAHÉ

Presqu'au moment même de la découverte de Nag Hammadi, plus
exactement entre 1942 et 1953, paraissait l'ouvrage d'A. J. Festugière
concernant *La Révélation d'Hermès Trismégiste*. Depuis cette date,
bien des études partielles ont été publiées, apportant parfois des précisions intéressantes [2]. Néanmoins, on ne sera pas surpris, à la vue de

---

[1] Nous remercions MM. F. WISSE et M. PHILONENKO pour les remarques qu'ils ont
bien voulu nous adresser après notre conférence, et qui nous ont conduit à modifier
quelques détails de notre rédaction.

Pour les abréviations, on se reportera à l'*Année Philologique*. Nous ajoutons les sigles
suivants : NH = Nag Hammadi ; CH = *Corpus hermeticum* ; SH = *Stobaei hermetica* ;
FH = *Fragmenta hermetica*.

Tous les textes hermétiques sont cités en traduction française (éventuellement retouchée) d'après A. D. NOCK - A. J. FESTUGIÈRE, *Corpus hermeticum*, t. 1-4, Paris 1945-1954.
Pour le commentaire, nous nous référons à A.J. FESTUGIÈRE, *Révélation* (= *La révélation
d'Hermès Trismégiste*, t. 1-4, Paris 1942-1953). L'*Évangile selon Philippe* (= *ÉvPh*)
est cité d'après l'éd. trad. de J.-É. MÉNARD, Paris 1967 (tenir compte de la *retractatio*
de l'auteur, ci-dessous p. 58, quant à la numérotation des pages du Codex II). L'*Exégèse
de l'âme* est citée d'après l'éd. trad. de M. KRAUSE - P. LABIB, *Gnostische und hermetische
Schriften aus Codex II und VI*, Glückstadt 1972. Le *Traité tripartite* est cité d'après
l'éd. trad. de R. KASSER et collaborateurs, Berne 1973.

[2] Cf. l'avis de K. RUDOLPH, « Gnosis und Gnostizismus. Ein Forschungsbericht »,
TheolRdschau 38 (1973) 1, dans un paragraphe intitulé « Zum alexandrinischen Gnostizismus » : « Im weiteren Sinne gehört in diesem Abschnitt auch die Hermetik, doch sind
darüber in letzter Zeit kaum grössere Untersuchungen zu verzeichnen ».

Citons toutefois quelques travaux de moindre étendue publiés après A. J. FESTUGIÈRE,
Révélation ; H. D. BETZ, « Schöpfung und Erlösung im hermetischen Fragment *Kore
Kosmou* », *Zt.f.Theol.u.Kirche* 63 (1966) 160-187 ; ID., « The Delphic Maxim γνῶθι σαυτόν
in Hermetic Interpretation », *HThR* 63 (1970) 465-484 ; P. DERCHAIN, « L'authenticité
de l'inspiration égyptienne dans le *CH* », *RHR* 161-162 (1962) 175-198 ; J. DORESSE,
« Hermès et la Gnose. A propos de l'*Asclepius* copte », *NT* 1 (1956) 54-69 ; ID., « L'hermétisme égyptianisant », in H. Ch. PUECH, *Histoire des religions*, t. 2, Paris 1972, pp. 430-
497 ; H. DRIJVERS, « Bardaisan of Edessa and the *Hermetica* », *Ex oriente lux* 21 (1969-
1970) 190-210 ; F. N. KLEIN, *Die Lichtterminologie in den hermetischen Schriften*, Leyde
1962 ; M. KRAUSE, « Aegyptisches Gedankengut in der Apokalypse des Asklepius »,

ces quatre volumes bien remplis, que personne n'ait de nouveau tenté
une étude d'importance comparable sur l'ensemble de la question.
Car l'œuvre d'A. J. Festugière ne vaut pas seulement par l'ampleur
des matériaux qu'elle nous propose, elle met en cause l'opinion que
l'on s'était formée jusqu'alors de l'intérêt des textes hermétiques.
Mais c'est justement là qu'il convient que nous prenions garde au choix
qui s'offre à nous. En effet, si nous souscrivions à l'une des conclusions
les plus fermes et les plus constantes d'A. J. Festugière, nous devrions
admettre que les textes hermétiques relèvent moins de la compétence
de l'historien des religions (comme le croyaient au début de ce siècle
des savants tels W. Bousset, W. Kroll, R. Reitzenstein) que de l'histoire
de la philosophie. D'après lui, les écrits d'Hermès emploient bien une
terminologie comparable à celle de certaines religions à mystères,
mais en un sens purement métaphorique qui ne recouvre aucune prati-
que réelle. Il n'y a jamais eu, nous dit-on, de rituels, ni de sacrements,
ni de sectes hermétistes : A. J. Festugière qualifie de « roman »[3]
l'opinion contraire, pourtant soutenue par A. Geffcken ou par R. Reit-

---

in *XVII Deutscher Orientalistentag*, Suppl. Bd 1, Vorträge 1 (= *ZDMG*), Wiesbaden
1969, pp. 48-57; G. VAN MOORSEL, *The Mysteries of Hermes Trismegistus*, Utrecht 1955;
ID., « Die Symbolsprache in der hermetischen Gnosis », *Symbolon* 1 (1960) 128-137;
M. P. NILSSON, « *Krater* », *HThR* 51 (1951) 53-58; J. PARLEBAS, « L'origine égyptienne
de l'appellation 'Hermès Trismégiste' », *Göttinger Miszellen* 13 (1974) 25-28; S. SAUNERON,
« La légende des sept propos de Methyer au temple d'Esna », *Bull. Soc. Fr. d'Égyptologie*
32 (1961) 43-48; J. DE SAVIGNAC, « Quelques problèmes de l'ouvrage dit 'Le Pasteur
d'Hermas' », *EThR* 35 (1960) 159-170; G. SFAMENI-GASPARRO, « La gnosi ermetica come
iniziazione e mistero », *SMSR* 36 (1965) 43-61; ID., « L'ermetismo nelle testimonianze
dei Padri » (*TU* 108 = *Studia Patristica* 11) 58-64; ID., « L'ermetismo », in P. TACCHI-
VENTURI, *Storia delle religioni*, 6ᵉ éd. remaniée par G. CASTELLANI, t. 3, Turin 1971,
pp. 395-421; P. SINISCALCO, « Ermete Trismegisto profeta pagano della rivelazione
cristiana », *AAT* 101 (1966-1967) 83-113; A. ŠKRINJAR, « Theologia epistolae I *Ioh.*
comparatur cum philonismo et hermetismo », *Verb. Dom.* 46 (1968) 148-168; B. STRICKER,
De brief van Aristeas, Amsterdam 1956 (cf. recension par C. PRÉAUX, *CE* 65 [1958] 153-
156); K. W. TRÖGER, *CH XIII und Mysterienglaube* (*TU* 110) Berlin 1971; ID., « Die hermetische Gnosis », in *Gnosis und NT* (*Studien zur Religionswissenschaft u. Theologie*),
Berlin 1973, pp. 97-119; M. VALVO, « Considerazioni sù Manilio e l'ermetismo », *SicGymn*
9 (1956) 108-117; A. WLOSOK, *Laktanz und die philosophische Gnosis*, Heidelberg 1960
(cf. les critiques d'A. D. NOCK, « The Exegesis of *Timaeus* 28 c », *VChr* 16 [1962] 79-86).
   Le livre d'A. J. FESTUGIÈRE, *Hermétisme et mystique païenne*, Paris 1967, est, pour
l'essentiel, un recueil d'articles déjà publiés antérieurement par l'auteur.
   [3] Cf. A. J. FESTUGIÈRE, *Révélation*, t. 1, p. 82; et, p. 83 : « on serait parfaitement
naïf de se laisser tromper par cette affabulation ».

zenstein. Si les écrits d'Hermès témoignent de quelque chose, ce ne peut être, d'après lui, que d'une tradition scolaire, un simple Schulbetrieb [4] : ils témoignent de la façon dont on enseignait la philosophie au IIᵉ s. de notre ère [5], et nous permettent, par exemple, de reconstituer le plan-type des manuels sur l'âme qui avaient cours à cette époque, de faire le point sur l'évolution des doctrines et des enseignements concernant le Dieu inconnu et le Dieu cosmique.

A. J. Festugière n'a pu tenir compte, dans son étude, des textes hermétiques figurant dans la bibliothèque gnostique copte de Nag Hammadi. Cependant, la nouvelle de leur découverte n'ébranla pas l'essentiel de ses convictions, comme le prouvent certaines de ses réponses aux premiers articles de J. Doresse [6]. Concédons que ce n'était pas tout à fait une surprise de trouver les écrits d'Hermès voisinant avec ceux des sectes gnostiques, puisqu'à ce sujet on disposait déjà du témoignage d'Hippolyte sur les pérates, ou d'Ephrem, confirmé par Augustin, sur les manichéens [7]. Pourtant, c'était la première fois que l'on pouvait directement observer ce voisinage, et c'eût été sans doute l'occasion de rependre, sur des bases nouvelles, la confrontation entre l'hermétisme et la Gnose.

Par certains côtés, la découverte de Nag Hammadi diminue l'importance relative des écrits d'Hermès. Tant que le gnosticisme n'était connu que par des témoignages indirects et tronqués, certains textes hermétiques, par exemple le *Poimandrès*, *CH* XIII ou le *Cratère*, pouvaient passer pour des documents de premier ordre et tout à fait irremplaçables sur la Gnose païenne. Aujourd'hui, ils doivent s'effacer derrière les 55 écrits gnostiques de la collection de Nag Hammadi. Mais sans aucun doute, l'abondance actuelle de notre documentation nous aidera à mieux les comprendre, à fixer plus exactement la place qui leur revient à l'intérieur ou au dehors des différentes espèces de la Gnose. Ce travail risque d'être long et difficile. A notre avis, une des méthodes possibles pour le mener à bien consisterait à isoler des

---

[4] Pour reprendre le titre de W. BOUSSET, *Jüdisch-christlicher Schulbetrieb in Alexandria und Rom*, Göttingen 1915.

[5] Cf. A. J. FESTUGIÈRE, *Révélation*, t. 2, pp. 28-50 : « Le *logos* hermétique d'enseignement ».

[6] Cf. ID., *ibid.*, t. 1, « additions et corrections de la 2ᵉ édition », p. 427 de la 3ᵉ édition, Paris 1950 : A. J. Festugière refuse les conclusions d'un article de J. DORESSE, publié dans *VChr* 3 (1949) 129 s.

[7] Sur les pérates, cf. HIPPOLYTE, *Elenchos* V, 13, 8 ; sur les manichéens, cf. J. DORESSE, 2ᵉ article cité *supra* n. 2, p. 478.

motifs particuliers, des thèmes, dont on pourrait suivre le traitement
dans plusieurs écrits du *CH* ou de la bibliothèque de Nag Hammadi [8].
Nous nous limiterons aujourd'hui à l'étude d'un seul de ces thèmes : le
sens des symboles sexuels. L'attitude à l'égard de la sexualité est en
effet l'un des points où l'anthropologie rejoint le plus aisément les
conceptions cosmologiques et théologiques. Suivant que l'on valorise
ou que l'on refuse, que l'on accepte, pour elles-mêmes ou pour leur
valeur symbolique, l'existence et les relations des deux sexes, on adopte
du même coup des attitudes extrêmement différentes à l'égard de ce
monde et du Dieu qui l'a institué.

Nous pouvons prendre pour point de départ le début du 8ᵉ écrit
du codex VI, c'est-à-dire le fragment du *Discours Parfait*, appelé
communément Apocalypse d'Asclépius [9]. Ce passage est très difficile

---

[8] Comme exemple d'études thématiques, cf. *supra* n. 2 le 2ᵉ article de H. D. BETZ,
ou le livre d'A. WLOSOK, qui étudie le thème du *status rectus* comme symbole de la condition humaine dans l'hermétisme et chez Lactance.

[9] NH VI, 65,15 — 78,38. Nous avons établi en synopse le texte copte, sa traduction
française, les fragments grecs, et un nouveau texte critique de la version latine. Pour
répondre à une question posée par le Professeur J. M. ROBINSON après notre exposé,
nous ajoutons les précisions suivantes.

On trouvera dans notre article, « La prière d'actions de grâces du Codex VI de Nag
Hammadi et le *Discours Parfait* », *ZPE* 13 (1974) 40-60, un exposé des rapports entre les
écrits 7 et 8 du Codex VI et l'*Asclepius* latin. Sur le caractère fragmentaire de NH VI⁸,
cf. *ibid.*, p. 57 (+ n. 19 et 20) et p. 60. Nous insisterions moins aujourd'hui sur l'hétéro-
généité du contenu de cet extrait : l'excerpteur semble avoir découpé le texte de façon
à faire ressortir que le Créateur, parfaitement bon, qui a doté l'homme de l'intellect et de
la Gnose, n'est en aucun cas responsable du mal, ni dans ce monde (NH VI, 66,22-23 :
ΠΝΟΥΤΕ ΔΕ ϥϢΟΟΠ ΝΑΝΑΙΤΙΟC) ni dans l'autre (NH VI, 78, 39-41:
ΝΑΪ ΓΑΡ ΝΤΜΙΝΕ ΕΥϢΟΟΠ ΑΝ ΕΒΟΛ ϨΝ ΟΥΨΥΧΗ ΝΘΕΙΟΝ).
Tout au plus laisse-t-il agir des divinités secondaires : les démons qui animent les statues,
et qui sont tantôt bons, tantôt mauvais (cf. parallèle latin à NH VI, 70, 1-2 : *inbecillitates
hominibus facientes easque curantes, tristitiam laetitiamque pro meritis*); les démons
étrangleurs de l'enfer qui sont, sans équivoque possible, mauvais et fils de la « pernicieuse
malice » (NH VI, 78, 43 : ϨΕΝΕΒΟΛ ΝΕ ϨΝ ΤΚΑΚΙΑ ΕΘΟΟΥ).

Grâce à notre synopse des textes copte et latin, nous avons pu constater que c'est dans
le texte de l'Apocalypse proprement dite (NH VI, 70,3 - 76,1) qu'on enregistre le moins de
divergences. Quoi qu'en aient pu dire M. KRAUSE ou P. DERCHAIN, dans leurs articles cités
supra n. 2, il est absolument exclu que l'un ou l'autre de ces deux textes soit la traduction
directe d'une apocalypse égyptienne insérée sans grands changements dans le *Discours
Parfait*. Il y a trop de rapports, entre l'anthropologie des ch. 1-14 de l'*Asclepius* et les
motifs de la catastrophe apocalyptique, pour qu'on ne soit pas obligé d'admettre que
l'auteur hermétique, s'il reprend certains thèmes classiques des apocalypses égyptiennes,
les a ordonnés d'une façon tout à fait nouvelle et très personnelle. Quant au fait que

à traduire [10]. Précisons tout d'abord comment nous l'entendons. A côté de la traduction du texte copte, faisons figurer le texte de l'adaptation latine :

Traduction du texte copte	Texte latin
15 Et (δέ) si tu veux voir la réalité de	et dicendum foret quanta sit
16 ce mystère (μυστήριον) regarde-la aussi	eius mysterii uis atque necessitas,
17 l'image (εἰκών) merveilleuse de l'	nisi ex sui contemplatione unicuique
18 union (συνουσία) qui est consommée par	ex intimo sensu
19 l'homme et (par) la femme [11] : une fois	nota esse potuisset.
(ὅταν) donc	Si enim
20 arrivée à (son) terme (ἀκμή),	illud extremum temporis quo ex crebro adtritu peruenimus
la semence (σπέρμα)	ut utraque in utramque fundat natura
21 jaillit.	progeniem animaduertas,
	ut altera auide alterius rapiat <uenerem> interiusque recondat :
A ce moment-	denique eo tempore, ex commixtione communi,
22 là, la femme reçoit la puissance de l'homme	et uirtutem feminae marum adipiscuntur
23 et l'homme, lui aussi,	et mares

son récit, même bien inséré dans la trame logique du *Discours Parfait* se prêtait à être détaché comme un morceau d'anthologie, il suffit de voir en marge des mss latins les traits, les dessins de doigts et les signes de toutes sortes par quoi les lecteurs ont manifesté leur intérêt et leur étonnement devant le texte : qui nous interdit de penser que les lecteurs coptes étaient, sur ce point, différents des clercs du Moyen Âge ou des humanistes occidentaux ?

[10] Cf. notre discussion de la traduction de M. KRAUSE - P. LABIB, « Remarques d'un latiniste sur l'*Asclepius* copte de Nag Hammadi », *RSR* 48 (1974) 136-155.

[11] Il pourrait sembler plus conforme à la syntaxe copte que nous mettions le subjonctif N̄ΓΝΑΥ (17) sur le même plan que l'infinitif ΕΝΑΥ (15).Dans ce cas, le verbe principal serait ΕϢΑСϢⲰⲠΕ (18), et l'on devrait traduire : « Si tu veux voir la réalité de ce mystère et la voir, l'image merveilleuse de l'union, elle est consommée par l'homme et par la femme ... ». Outre que cette traduction présenterait peu de sens, elle est impossible en raison des passages parallèles (cf. ci-dessous p. 131 et n. 23), qui nous assurent que l'apodose du système conditionnel comportait dans l'original grec un verbe à l'impératif. Le texte se serait présenté à peu près ainsi : Εἰ δὲ ἔργῳ τοῦτο τὸ μυστήριον θέλεις θεάσασθαι, καὶ τὴν θαυμάσιαν εἰκόνα ἴδε τὴν τῆς συνουσίας κ.τ.λ. Dans le texte qu'a eu sous les yeux le traducteur copte, ἴδε devait avoir été remplacé par ἰδεῖν. On trouvera l'exemple de cette faute en *CH* XIV, 9 (A. D. NOCK, A. J. FESTUGIÈRE, t. 2, p. 226). Cyrille d'Alexandrie lit ἴδε contre ἰδεῖν des manuscrits. Dans ces conditions, faudrait-il corriger N̄ΓΝΑΥ (17) en{N̄Γ}ΝΑΥ ? De toute façon la traduction de ΑΥⲰ pour le sens adverbial de καί continuerait de poser un problème : on attendrait plutôt ΤΚΕϨΙΚⲰΝ N̄ϢⲠΗΡΕ(ou ΘΙΚⲰΝ ϨⲰⲰС N̄ϢⲠΗΡΕ) ΝΑΥ ΕΡΟС. Nous jugeons qu'il vaut mieux laisser le texte dans son état actuel, et rectifier la traduction en tenant compte de l'état probable de l'original.

24 reçoit sur lui la puissance de la femme, car (ὡς [12])	femineo torpore lassescunt.
25 tel est l'effet (ἐνεργεῖν [13]) de la semence.	Effectus
26 C'est pourquoi le mystère (μυστήριον) de l'	itaque huius tam blandi necessariique
27 union (συνουσία) est accompli en en secret :	mysterii in occulto perpetratur
28 de crainte que les deux sexes (φύσις) [14]	ne,
29 ne paraissent indécents (ἀσχημονεῖν) en face de beaucoup qui	uulgo inridentibus
30 n'ont pas (vraiment) l'expérience [15] de cette œuvre.	inperitis, utriusque naturae diuinitas ex commixtione sexus cogatur erubescere,

Car (γάρ) chacun

31 des (deux sexes) seul à seul transmet
   sa semence.

32 En effet (γάρ) pour ceux qui sont igno-
   rants de cette œuvre,

33 si elle se produit en leur présence <elle devient un objet de> raillerie	si 'uisibus inreligiosorum hominum
34 et d'incrédulité ; mais (δέ), bien plutôt,	subiciantur.

35 il s'agit de mystères (μυστήριον) sacrés,

36 de discours (λόγος) et d'actes :

37 car non seulement (οὐ μόνον) on ne
   saurait les entendre

38 mais (ἀλλά) on ne saurait (même pas)
   les voir [16].

---

[12] ϨⲰⲤ+ présent Π a généralement une valeur conditionnelle « comme si » (TILL, *Sahidische Grammatik*, § 368); la valeur causale que nous supposons présentement est rare, mais elle existe (TILL, *ibid.*, § 369, citant la phrase : ϨⲰⲤ ⲚⲦⲀⲨϪⲈⲔ ⲞⲨ-ϨⲰⲂ ⲈⲂⲞⲖ ⲈⲚⲀⲚⲞⲨϥ, « *Da* sie ja eine gute Tat vollbracht hatten »); cf. R. HAARDT, « Koptologische Miszellen », *Wiener Zt. f. Kunde des Morgenlandes* 57 (1961) 78-101, spécialement p. 81.

[13] Peut-être faut-il voir dans l'opposition ϬⲞⲘ/ϤⲈⲚⲈⲢⲄⲈⲒ la traduction du grec δύναμις/ἐνέργεια.

[14] ⲤⲞⲈⲒⲰ n'est attesté chez CRUM (374 b) qu'au masculin. Il faut donc, ou bien corriger ⲚⲈⲦⲤⲞⲈⲒⲰ en ⲚⲈ<Π>ⲤⲞⲈⲒⲰ, ou bien supposer, comme M. Krause, que nous avons affaire à une nouvelle forme. Pour le sens, on pourrait aussi bien comprendre « le couple de nature », c'est-à-dire « le couple institué par la nature », mais nous supposons que ⲤⲞⲈⲒⲰ fonctionne ici comme un nom de nombre (cf. CRUM, *l.c.*, δύο : ΠⲤⲞⲈⲒⲰ ⲚⲀⲎⲤⲦⲎⲤ) et que ϤⲨⲤⲒⲤ a une signification sexuelle (on rapprochera en NH VI, 64, 26-27 : Ⲱ ⲦⲘⲎⲦⲢⲀ ⲈⲦϪⲠⲞ ϨⲚ ⲦϤⲨⲤⲒⲤ ⲘⲠⲒⲰⲦ).

[15] ⲈⲨϪⲞⲚⲦ ⲀⲚ ⲘϤⲰⲂ ⲈⲦⲘⲘⲀⲨ : littéralement « qui n'essayent pas cette œuvre ». Mais la comparaison avec *inperitis* nous autorise à infléchir le sens habituel de ϪⲞⲚⲦ « essayer » en « expérimenter ».

[16] Nous renonçons ici aux objections que nous avions formulées contre la traduction de M. Krause dans l'article mentionné n. 10. Simplement, à la lin. 33, nous ajouterions <ϥⲞ> devant ⲚⲤⲰⲂⲈ.

Généralement, le copte se tient plus près de l'original grec [17]. L'auteur de l'*Asclepius* latin a été gêné par la crudité de la description. A vrai dire, il se défend même de décrire l'acte de la συνουσία. Il nous appelle à le contempler à l'intérieur de nous-mêmes [18]. Il excuse l'indécence de ces mystères par leur nécessité. Cédant à ses préjugés, il ne peut s'empêcher d'opposer la *uirtus maris* au *femineus torpor* [19]. On remarquera au contraire que le copte ne recule pas devant les mots et assigne aux deux partenaires des rôles parfaitement égaux.

Pourtant, copte et latin restent d'accord sur un point essentiel : l'union de l'homme et de la femme est un mystère sacré (au pluriel : ϩⲉⲛⲙⲩⲥⲧⲏⲣⲓⲟⲛ ⲉⲩⲟⲩⲁⲁⲃ). Sans doute, convient-il d'apprécier prudemment le sens du mot « mystère ». Il ne s'agit pas d'un sacrement, comme le faisait remarquer A. D. Nock. Néanmoins, l'interprétation qu'il propose lui-même, « secret act with a nuance of solemnity [20] », nous paraît trop restrictive. Dans un sens purement métaphorique, le mariage est souvent qualifié de mystère parce qu'il est consommé dans le secret (*in occulto perpetratur*) et constitue une sorte d'initiation pour les époux.

Sans rejeter cette opinion courante, notre texte va plus loin. Les railleurs et les incrédules, qui devraient pourtant savoir à quoi s'en tenir sur la procréation, sont présentés comme incapables de voir et d'entendre la réalité effective de ce mystère. L'union charnelle est pour eux une affaire scabreuse (ἀσχημονεῖν) : ils ne savent pas, apparemment, qu'elle est « image de merveille » (ϩⲓⲕⲱⲛ ⲛ̄ϣⲡⲏⲣⲉ), qu'elle renvoie à une réalité supérieure. Le mot *diuinitas*, employé à ce propos par l'adaptateur latin, n'a pas de correspondant dans la traduction copte ; cependant, nous ne le croyons pas infidèle à l'esprit du texte : l'union de l'homme et de la femme, les réalités physiques de la procréation, constituent vraiment un mystère sacré, non seulement parce que les époux ne s'exposent pas en public, mais parce que leur acte

---

[17] Cf. notre article cité *supra* n. 10.

[18] Comme en *CH* XI, 14 : « Et si tu veux le comprendre par ta propre expérience, vois ce qui se passe *en toi* quand tu veux engendrer ».

[19] *Femineus* est, d'après *TLL* VI, 1, 465 « uocabulum potissimum poetarum » ; Sénèque et surtout Arnobe sont les premiers à l'employer en prose. Noter d'autre part la citation de Virgile, (*Georg.* 3, 137), identifiée par HOUSMAN, *Hermes* 66 (1931) 412, qui confirme le ton poétique du passage.

[20] Cf. A. D. NOCK, « A New Edition of the Hermetic Writings », *JEA* 11 (1925) 126-137. Comparer avec K. W. TRÖGER, *Hermetische Gnosis* (cf. *supra* n. 2), p. 119 : « Das Mysterium der Synousia ist nur ein Vergleich ».

même a une signification symbolique qui tend à dévoiler quelque chose de divin. « Est enim id indultum ad diuinae fecunditatis aemulationem», écrivait Marsile Ficin, le premier éditeur moderne de nos *Hermetica* [21].

Or, certains autres textes de la bibliothèque de Nag Hammadi expriment des conceptions qu'on pourrait croire, au premier abord, assez comparables : notamment l'*Évangile selon Philippe*, étudié sur ce point par R. M. Grant [22]. On sait que, dans cet écrit, le mariage est couramment présenté comme un grand mystère (sent. 60) : « Le mystère du mariage est grand, car sans lui le monde ne sera pas». L'acte de ce mystère (sent. 121-122) est accompli dans le secret, et c'est une impudicité que de le dévoiler : « Celui qui engendre, engendre ses enfants dans le secret. Il n'y a personne qui pourra savoir le jour où l'homme et la femme s'unissent, sauf eux-mêmes … Un mariage, s'il est dévoilé, est devenu de l'impudicité … ». Enfin, ce n'est pas seulement en raison de ces dispositions secrètes que le mariage est qualifié de mystère, mais, plus encore, comme dans notre texte hermétique, parce qu'il est image d'une réalité supérieure : «Connaissez la communauté immaculée, parce qu'elle possède une grande puissance. Son image est dans la souillure du corps … », entendons : dans le corps qui est corruptible. On remarquera cependant que, dans tous ces textes, le mot de συνουσία (ϩΟΤ̄Ρ en copte) n'est pas employé : il n'est question que de γάμος ou de κοινώνια. C'est là une différence de ton qui n'est pas négligeable.

Mais, à vrai dire, nous ne saurions pousser plus loin cette comparaison entre l'*Asclepius* et l'*Évangile selon Philippe*, sans voir apparaître d'autres différences beaucoup plus importantes. Quelle que soit la valeur symbolique de la συνουσία en NH VI, il n'y a pas là néanmoins d'allusion directe aux pratiques rituelles des mystères, dont témoignent parfois d'autres textes gnostiques. Sur ce point comme sur beaucoup d'autres, les écrits d'Hermès se partagent entre deux courants : l'un, auquel appartient l'*Asclepius*, est d'un esprit entièrement opposé au gnosticisme; le second s'en rapproche davantage. Étudions ces deux courants successivement.

Il existe trois passages du *Corpus Hermeticum* (*CH* V, 6; XI, 14; XIV, 9) qui nous invitent à contempler Dieu à travers le processus

---

[21] Cf. M. Ficin, *Mercurii Trismegisti Pimander*, Paris (Henri Ier Estienne) 1505, Bibliothèque Nationale de Strasbourg, R 103950, p. 49.

[22] Cf. R. M. Grant, « The Mystery of Marriage in the *Gospel of Philip* », *VChr* 15 (1961) 129-140.

de la génération, en des termes très proches de l'*Asclepius* [23]. « Dieu est par nature inapparent», écrit l'auteur de *CH* V, 2, «mais comme il donne une image sensible à toutes choses, il apparaît à travers toutes ». Regardons le ciel, le soleil, les étoiles : nous comprendrons qu'il y a un Dieu qui a créé et qui dirige tous ces êtres. Mais il est même inutile d'aller chercher si haut (*CH* V, 6) : « Si tu veux contempler (Dieu) au travers aussi des êtres mortels, ... considère, mon enfant, comment l'homme est façonné dans le ventre, examine avec soin la technique de cette production et apprends à connaître qui est celui qui façonne cette belle, cette divine image qu'est l'homme ».

Il s'agit là d'un lieu commun, dira-t-on : après le macrocosme, on invoque le microcosme, pour prouver, ou plutôt pour constater et contempler la présence de Dieu. Mais pourquoi est-ce précisément la naissance de l'homme, et le moment de la procréation qui constituent l'objet terrestre le plus approprié à nous faire voir Dieu, mieux encore que le spectacle des astres immortels ? Cela s'inscrit, certes, dans la tendance générale de nos textes à l'anthropocentrisme. Toutefois, dans ce cas particulier, l'auteur compare directement l'union de l'homme et de la femme à l'action créatrice de Dieu. Assurément, il y a des différences, explicitées en *CH* XI, 14 : « Quand il s'agit de Dieu, l'acte d'engendrer n'est point pareil. Dieu n'éprouve pas de plaisir sensible ; et il n'a aucun coopérateur. En effet, comme il opère à lui tout seul, il est toujours immanent à son œuvre, étant lui-même ce qu'il produit ». Mais ces différences n'empêchent pas que l'union des époux les rapproche de Dieu ; plus encore, elle les absorbe dans une activité qui les identifie à l'essence même de Dieu.

De quelque façon qu'on appelle cette essence : l'Etre par excellence, l'Un et le Tout, le Bien, elle ne saurait se concevoir sans la génération (*CH* V, 9) : « Si tu me forces à dire quelque chose de plus osé, son essence (à Dieu) est d'enfanter et de produire toutes choses ; ... il n'est pas possible que Dieu existe éternellement, s'il ne crée pas éternellement toutes choses, dans le ciel, dans l'air, sur la terre ». Par conséquent, ceux qui procréent s'identifient à Dieu, et cette identification est encore soulignée par le fait que, comme tous les animaux et végétaux [24]

---

[23] Ces trois passages sont caractérisés par l'emploi de la même tournure stylistique ; conditionnelle : εἰ δέ + verbe «vouloir» ; apodose : impératif d'un verbe indiquant une opération des sens ou de l'esprit, ἴδε ou νόησον. Cela constitue d'ailleurs un indice supplémentaire de la supériorité de la version copte qui, à la différence de la version latine, reproduit exactement cette tournure : ⲉϢϪⲉ ⲕⲟⲩⲱϢ Ⲇⲉ ... {Ⲛⲅ}ⲚⲀⲨ.

[24] Cf. *Ascl.* 21 : « Vtriusque sexus ergo deum dicis, o Trismegiste ? — Non deum solum,

de sa création, Dieu est lui-même doué des deux sexes, *utraque sexus fecunditate plenissimus*, ou, si l'on préfère le mot grec, ἀρρενόθηλυς. Il faut prendre les mots dans leur sens le plus littéral et le plus concret. Quiconque voit l'homme s'accoupler à la femme, ne voit pas seulement un symbole, une image, un reflet de l'essence divine, mais l'être même de Dieu ; et, comme le dit si bien l'auteur de l'*Asclepius* latin, lorsque les impies surprennent les partenaires et les tournent en dérision, c'est Dieu même qu'ils obligent à rougir. Il n'y a donc pas de rupture essentielle entre création et procréation : c'est la même énergie divine qui se propage depuis sa source jusqu'aux limites de l'univers.

Lactance ironise sur cette opinion : faut-il penser que Dieu (*FH* 13) « s'est accouplé à lui-même ou qu'il n'a pu procréer sans accouplement » ? Le vocabulaire des traités hermétiques nous permet de répondre affirmativement. On relève en effet d'innombrables jeux de langage, relatifs aux deux sexes de Dieu. Dieu est ἀπάτωρ et ἀμήτωρ (*FH* 4 b) mais, en même temps, il est αὐτοπάτωρ et αὐτομήτωρ (*FH* 13) et, quand on s'adresse à lui, on peut l'appeler père et mère à la fois (*CH* V, 7). Le verbe κυεῖν lui convient aussi bien que le verbe ποιεῖν (*CH* V, 9) ; il est *praegnans* (*Ascl.* 20) et il est *effector* ou *creator* (*Ascl.* 2-3). Il féconde lui-même sa matrice au moyen de son conseil ou de sa volonté, qui n'est autre que la bonté indissociable de son essence (*Ascl.* 20).

Voilà pourquoi la παιδοποΐα est (*CH* II, 17) μεγίστη ἐν τῷ βίῳ σπουδὴ καὶ εὐσεβεστάτη [25]. Malheur donc aux impies qui n'ont pas d'enfants. Ils s'opposent à une loi à laquelle Dieu lui-même se soumet. Ils oublient qu'ils ont été mis au monde (*CH* III, 4) « pour rendre un témoignage actif à la nature, pour accroître le nombre des hommes, ... (pour) croître en accroissement et multiplier en multitude [26] ». Après leur mort, ils subiront la peine infamante (*CH* II, 17) d'être réincarnés dans le corps d'un être « n'ayant ni la nature d'un homme, ni celle d'une femme, objet d'exécration pour le soleil ». L'absence de sexualité est en quelque sorte le pire des maux, ce qu'il y a de plus offensant au regard de la bi-sexualité ou plutôt de l'hyper-sexualité, caractéristique

---

Asclepi, sed omnia animalia et inanimalia ». Ces *inanimalia* (ἄψυχα) sont évidemment les végétaux, comme le note A. J. FESTUGIÈRE, *CH*, t. 2, p. 376. A l'image de la συνουσία, *CH* XIV, 9 substitue celle de l'agriculteur jetant la semence ou plantant un arbre.

[25] Comparer avec la position de Philon, cf. R. A. BAER Jr., *Philo's Use of the Categories Male and Female*, Leyde 1970, p. 94 s.

[26] Cf. C. H. DODD, *The Bible and the Greeks*, Londres 1935, p. 164 et 210-249, pour les influences bibliques dans ce traité.

de l'être divin [27]. Car la sexualité du Dieu hermétique est plus intense non seulement qualitativement, puisqu'elle totalise la fécondité des deux sexes, mais aussi quantitativement, puisque, loin de se traduire par des actes espacés dans le temps, comme celle de l'homme et de la femme, elle se prolonge perpétuellement, elle ne saurait interrompre ses effets, sans que l'univers cessât aussitôt d'exister [28].

C'est bien là le sens de tous ces développements sur l'excellence de la procréation : ils aboutissent à la valorisation de l'univers (NH VI, 72,2-10), « ce monde magnifique fait par Dieu, œuvre qui n'a pas sa pareille, réalisation pleine de vertu, spectacle multiforme, décor déployé sans envie ». L'Apocalypse d'Asclépius n'a pas de mots assez forts contre le péché de ceux qui méprisent ce monde et « préfèrent la mort à la vie », sans doute pour éviter de le voir se perpétuer (NH VI, 72, 18-19).

Ainsi, dans ce premier groupe de textes hermétiques, nous sommes à l'opposé de l'anti-cosmisme gnostique. Si nous nous plaçons en effet dans la perspective d'un dualisme rigoureux, ce monde est radicalement mauvais, ainsi que tout ce qui contribue à son maintien. On sait, par exemple, que Marcion et son disciple Apellès n'hésitaient pas à dénoncer les horreurs de la chair et de la procréation en des termes extrêmement violents [29]. Pourtant, si mauvais que soient l'univers et la vie que nous y menons, ils constituent la seule expérience dont nous puissions partir pour concevoir par antithèse (selon le titre même de la bible du marcionisme) un monde, une vie et un Dieu supérieurs. La négation, puis le dépassement des réalités matérielles, sont les deux moments essentiels de la formation du gnostique ; et comme toutes les autres réalités, le mariage de la chair ne sera pas seulement rejeté par Marcion, mais en quelque sorte retourné, vidé de son contenu, pour laisser place à un contenu rigoureusement antithétique. On

---

[27] Comme dans les vers d'OVIDE, *Métamorphoses* IV, 378, … « nec femina dici/Nec puer ut possit ; neutrumque et utrumque uidetur », les anciens confondent souvent l'a-sexualité (*neutrumque*) et la bi-sexualité (*utrumque*) ; cf. M. DELCOURT, *Hermaphrodite*, Paris 1958, p. 49. Toutefois il arrive que l'a-sexualité soit conçue distinctement : ou bien comme un état antérieur et supérieur à la division des sexes, par exemple chez Philon, d'après R. A. BAER Jr., *o.c.* (cf. *supra* n. 25), p. 16 s (la nature supérieure de l'homme est asexuée et c'est précisément par là qu'elle ressemble à Dieu), ou dans la *Korè Kosmou*, *SH* XXIV, 8 ; ou bien comme un état inférieur, comme d'après nous, les figures menaçantes des archontes, dans l'*Hypostase des archontes*, NH II, 87, figures animales à peine dégrossies, qui n'ont ni le corps d'un mâle ni celui d'une femelle.

[28] Cf. *CH* XI, 14.

[29] Cf. A. HARNACK, *Marcion. Das Evangelium vom fremden Gott* (*TU* 45 B), 2e éd., Leipzig 1924, p. 273* s ; J.-P. MAHÉ, éd. TERTULLIEN, *La chair du Christ*, Paris 1975 (*SC* 216-217), p. 104.

sait, en effet, que Marcion admettait des gens mariés dans son église, en les invitant à ne plus faire de leur mariage une union en vue de la procréation des enfants, mais, tout au contraire, l'alliance de deux parfaits contre la loi du Créateur, qui a prescrit de croître et de multiplier [30]. On pourrait trouver l'expression d'une hostilité comparable dans des textes encore inédits, notamment le *Témoignage de Vérité* (NH IX) [31].

Toutefois, dans certaines sectes gnostiques, professant un dualisme moins rigoureux, le mariage de la chair ne sera pas rejeté avec la même intensité ; il le sera, néanmoins, dans une certaine mesure, puisqu'il se chargera d'une signification symbolique (éventuellement spirituelle, eschatologique), qui est la négation partielle de sa valeur et de sa réalité présentes. Alors que dans l'*Asclepius* l'union de l'homme et de la femme est directement l'image de la divinité, pour l'auteur valentinien, elle n'est plus, en quelque sorte, qu'une image d'image. Le « mariage de la souillure » (*ÉvPh*, sent. 122) ne conserve sa valeur que dans la mesure où il reflète le mystère du « mariage immaculé ». Et ce dernier, en tant qu'il concerne chaque gnostique en particulier, soit sous sa forme sacramentelle, soit dans la perspective eschatologique de l'union des âmes avec leurs anges, n'est à son tour qu'une image du mariage de l'Éon Sauveur avec la Sagesse dans le Plérôme, également représenté, en dehors du valentinisme, par exemple dans le *Deuxième traité du grand Seth* [32].

Le propre d'une image est de donner une impression équivoque ou imparfaite de l'objet qu'elle représente (sent. 67) : « la Vérité n'est pas venue dans ce monde nue, mais elle est venue dans les types et dans les images », en particulier « il y a une régénération et une image de régénération ». Or, c'est à ces images, non à « ce qui est solide », c'est-à-dire les réalités à quoi elles correspondent, que s'appliquent les noms de notre langage ; c'est pourquoi (sent. 11) « ils renferment une grande

---

[30] Cf. la rectification proposée sur ce point des opinions d'A. Harnack par P. G. VER-WEIJS, *Evangelium und neues Gesetz in der ältesten Christenheit bis auf Marcion*, Utrecht 1960, p. 272 s.

[31] Cf. NH IX, 30-31 (non encore publié) qui unit, comme dans le marcionisme, l'horreur de la chair à celle de ce monde et de la loi du Créateur. Suit une exégèse du baptême du Christ, d'après laquelle le Jourdain est la puissance du corps, c'est-à-dire des sens et du plaisir ; l'eau du Jourdain est le désir de la συνουσία, Jean, l'archonte de la matrice. Jésus est descendu sur le fleuve pour le « retourner » (NH II, 131, 20), comme, dans l'*Exégèse de l'âme*, le Père « retourne » la matrice de l'âme humaine (cf. *infra*, p. 135).

[32] Cf. R. M. GRANT, *o.c.*, (*supra* n. 22), p. 131, et *Deuxième traité du grand Seth*, NH VII, 65,37 - 66,10.

illusion ». Dans l'Éon (sent. 103), « la forme de l'union » diffère de celle qui est consommée ici-bas par l'homme et par la femme : nous sommes pourtant obligés de lui donner le même nom [33]. Combien peuvent se laisser abuser par cette homonymie !

Dans l'*Exégèse de l'âme* qui, comme le montre J.-É. Ménard, complète les indications de l'*Évangile selon Philippe* [34], nous voyons l'âme, déchue de la maison du Père, forniquer avec divers brigands qu'elle prend à chaque fois pour de véritables époux [35]. C'est qu'elle n'a pas compris qui est l'époux et quel est le mariage véritable. Or, ce dernier, on prend soin de nous le décrire comme le contraire d'un mariage charnel. Certes, l'âme est femme et elle a sa matrice. Mais cette matrice n'est pas à l'intérieur de ses entrailles, comme celle des autres femmes : elle est tournée vers l'extérieur. Avant d'avoir reçu l'époux, l'âme ressent les douleurs de l'enfantement, mais sans devenir mère : au contraire, elle redevient vierge, par la grâce du Père qui lui retourne la matrice de l'extérieur vers l'intérieur. L'âme s'unit à son époux dans la chasteté, non point pour rejeter le fardeau du désir, mais pour ne plus former avec lui qu'une seule vie [36]. Enfin, au terme de cette union, elle ne met pas seulement des enfants au monde, mais elle s'enfante elle-même en une nouvelle naissance [37]. Quand on suppose que le mariage charnel est symbole du mariage spirituel, on a peine à mesurer d'emblée la conversion qu'il nous faut imposer aux réalités de la chair pour maintenir cette interprétation. Alors que, dans l'*Asclepius* et les autres textes hermétiques que nous avons lus jusqu'à présent, ces réalités, acceptées comme telles, étaient directement l'image de la vie divine, elles ne le deviennent ici qu'au prix d'une sorte de retournement, de projection inversée comme dans un miroir ; pour devenir symboles, elles se vident de toute leur substance, elles renient tout ce qu'elles sont, tout ce qu'elles représentent dans leur signification immédiate.

Mais l'opposition se poursuit encore plus avant : la répartition de l'humanité en deux sexes différents n'est pas mauvaise aux yeux de l'auteur hermétique. Nous l'avons vu plus haut : les deux sexes sont

---

[33] Cf. K. KOSCHORKE, « Die Namen im Philippusevangelium », *ZNTW* 64 (1973), 307-322.

[34] Cf. J.-É. MÉNARD, « L'*Évangile selon Philippe* et l'*Exégèse de l'âme* », publié dans ce même recueil, p. 56.

[35] Cf. NH II, 127-128.

[36] Cf. *ibid.*, 131-132.

[37] Cf. *ibid.*, 134.

parfaitement égaux. Chacun d'eux a les mêmes titres à représenter la nature humaine dans sa totalité, et non point d'une façon incomplète ou mutilée.

Cela provient du fait que l'homme accepte sa condition d'être mortel et limité ; il n'envie pas le sort des dieux-astres, qui ont payé trop cher leur immortalité : astreints à la nécessité de trajectoires fixes et immuables, les astres sont privés de l'intellect et de la Gnose [38], dont Dieu a fait la grâce au genre humain. Voilà le point essentiel : mortel et immortel à la fois, c'est-à-dire doué d'un corps et de la faculté de connaître, qui n'appartient qu'à Dieu, l'homme est capable de remonter jusqu'au premier principe et de lui rendre grâces pour tout ce qu'il a fait [39]. Qu'importe la mort après cela ? Même s'il ne subsiste plus rien de l'assemblage humain, cela est sans importance. La plupart des traités hermétiques, soit du groupe étudié jusqu'ici, soit de l'autre groupe, professent la survie de l'âme, mais cela n'est pas nécessaire pour l'auteur de *CH* III, 4 qui, après avoir décrit la création des premiers hommes, explique le sens de leur existence : « Dès lors commence pour eux le fait de mener la vie humaine, d'acquérir la sagesse selon le sort que leur assigne la course circulaire des dieux, et de se dissoudre en ce qui restera d'eux, après avoir laissé sur terre de grands monuments de leur industrie ». Quand on accepte aussi aisément sa condition d'être mortel, on ne se plaint pas des autres limites qu'impose l'existence, ni, particulièrement, de la sexualité.

En revanche, les systèmes gnostiques ne sauraient renoncer à l'assurance d'un salut conçu comme une divinisation ou un retour en Dieu de l'âme humaine. Dieu se suffit à lui-même, mais l'être humain est profondément déficient. L'un sans l'autre, l'homme et la femme ne peuvent assurer leur survie. La division des deux sexes est donc un des aspects de cette déficience. Alors que l'*Asclepius* et les autres traités hermétiques du même groupe admettent que la bi-sexualité soit le privilège exclusif de Dieu, le gnosticisme exige que l'homme y ait part également, puisqu'il doit s'égaler à Dieu. Dès lors apparaîtront des mythes de bi-sexualité primordiale ou eschatologique. Entre les deux, la répartition normale des sexes est ressentie comme un amoindrissement, comme une véritable mutilation.

---

[38] Cf. NH VI, 67, 12-21.

[39] Il s'agit là d'une attitude essentielle dans l'hermétisme : il faut noter le nombre des traités qui, comme *CH* I, V, XIII, *Ascl.* 41, se terminent effectivement par une action de grâces. Celle-ci joue un rôle essentiel dans *CH* XIII et dans *L'Ogdoade et l'Ennéade*, opérant presque avec l'efficacité d'un sacrement.

Comprenons néanmoins que, tout de même que le mariage de la chair n'est pas directement image de la divinité, la différence des sexes n'est image de la déficience qu'au deuxième degré. En effet, l'*Évangile selon Philippe* paraîtrait d'abord accepter l'opinion courante que les femmes sont inférieures aux hommes (sent. 103) : « L'union est en ce monde homme et femme, au lieu de la puissance et de la faiblesse ». Dans le *Deuxième traité du grand Seth*, il est recommandé aux parfaits de n'être point comme la femme qui enfante la malice avec ses frères [40]. Mais ce n'est pas au sens propre que la femme est plus faible ou plus mauvaise, c'est en un sens métaphorique, selon quoi on peut affirmer que nous sommes tous « orphelins » (sent. 6), parce que nous n'avons qu'une mère, et non pas un père et une mère comme les élus. Ou encore, en ce même sens métaphorique, on pourrait reprendre la remarque malicieuse de Tertullien [41], que Gaius et Marcus, qui ont de la barbe en ce monde, deviendront femmes dans le Plérôme, pour servir d'épouses aux anges du Sauveur. Au point de vue du salut, hommes et femmes sont donc placés exactement sur le même plan. L'impuissance des deux sexes à survivre l'un sans l'autre, l'infériorité constatée ici-bas de la condition féminine ne constituent pas directement le symptôme ou l'effet de la chute et de la déficience, mais c'est à travers eux que nous déchiffrons le sens de ces deux données spirituelles. De même, ce n'est pas à l'androgynie de la chair qu'aspire le gnostique, mais à celle de l'âme, qui seule peut ressembler à celle des Éons.

Cependant, nous avons laissé de côté jusqu'ici toute une part des textes hermétiques qui présentent de grandes analogies avec les positions gnostiques que nous venons d'exposer, principalement d'après l'*Évangile selon Philippe*. Il est bien connu, par exemple, que le *Poimandrès*, à côté du Dieu ἀρρενόθηλυς, pose l'existence d'un Anthropos primordial, également pourvu des deux sexes, comme son Père divin [42]. La rupture de l'androgynie primordiale se produit par suite d'une chute dans la matière : cédant à l'amour, sans doute illégitime, de Nature, l'Homme devient le père de sept autres hommes d'une essence inférieure, puisqu'ils portent l'empreinte des sept Archontes : androgynes

[40] Cf. NH VII, 65, 24-26.
[41] Cf. Tertullien, *Val.* 32, 4.
[42] Ce mythe est, jusqu'à présent, exclusivement limité au *Poimandrès*, dans le cadre des écrits hermétiques. Sur les différentes hypothèses proposées en guise d'explication, cf. C. H. Dodd, *o.c.* (*supra* n. 26), p. 146 n. 1 et 149-150.

comme leur père, ils ne tarderont pas à être divisés selon les deux sexes par un décret divin [43].

Pour l'auteur de l'*Évangile selon Philippe*, bien que l'imagerie du mythe soit empruntée à un contexte très différent, la chute se produit dans des conditions analogues : c'est le désir illégitime d'Ève pour le serpent, comparable à celui de l'Homme pour Nature, qui rend effective la séparation des deux sexes. On sait que Caïn fut le fruit de cet adultère (sent. 42). Non que les valentiniens aient admis, contrairement à d'autres gnostiques, qu'Ève se soit vraiment unie au serpent [44], elle l'a fait seulement en pensée. Mais cela suffit, d'après la sentence 112, pour que l'adultère soit consommé [45]. C'est cet adultère qui est cause de la chute, représentée comme une rupture de l'androgynie primordiale (sent. 79) : « Ève fut séparée d'Adam parce qu'elle ne s'était pas unie à lui dans la chambre nuptiale ».

Nous pouvons poursuivre sur un autre point notre parallèle entre les textes gnostiques et ce deuxième groupe de textes hermétiques. Dans l'*Exégèse de l'âme*, nous voyons également l'âme déchue accumuler les adultères : elle conçoit ainsi, avec ses divers amants, des enfants muets, aveugles, chétifs, à l'esprit brouillé [46]. Au contraire, quand, repentie, elle s'unit à l'époux et reçoit sa semence, c'est-à-dire l'esprit qui vivifie, « elle met au monde des enfants qui sont bons, afin d'accomplir son mariage selon la volonté du Père [47] ». La même comparaison se rencontre aussi bien chez Philon que dans les écrits hermétiques du second groupe. D'après *CH* IX, 3, « L'Intellect enfante tous les concepts : des concepts bons, quand c'est de Dieu qu'il a reçu les semences, des concepts contraires, quand c'est de l'un des êtres démoniques... [48] ». Nous sommes ici très proche du traité de Philon, *De Cheru-*

---

[43] Cf. *CH* I, 12-18 ; C. H. Dodd, *o.c.* (*supra* n. 26), p. 152 en note : « the moral of the whole story for the Hermetist is that it was love of material nature that caused man to become mortal in becoming sexual ». Cela nous paraît plus probable que l'opinion d'A. J. Festugière, *Révélation*, t. 3, p. 85 s., qui veut à toute force montrer que l'homme est victime du « désir de créer à son tour », et se trouve ainsi conduit à supposer (p. 88) que le texte a été remanié parce qu'il ne se plie pas aisément à son explication.

[44] Cf. R. M. Grant, *o.c.* (*supra* n. 22), p. 135 n. 22.

[45] *ÉvPh*, sent. 112 : « Souvent quand une femme couche avec son mari par nécessité, mais que son cœur est auprès de l'adultère avec qui elle s'unit habituellement, celui qu'elle enfantera, elle l'enfante ressemblant à l'adultère ».

[46] Cf. NH II, 128.

[47] Cf. *ibid.*, 133.

[48] On ajoutera *SH* VI, 11, qui précise que la semence des démons habitant les décans s'appelle « tane ».

bim, qui paraît occuper une position intermédiaire entre les textes gnostiques et les textes hermétiques. C'est Dieu qui donne sa semence aux vertus de l'âme pour qu'elles puissent produire des enfants (§ 44), et, comme nous l'avons vu plus haut dans l'*Exégèse de l'âme*, alors que « chez les hommes, l'union en vue de la création des enfants transforme les vierges en femmes ; au contraire, quand Dieu commence à avoir commerce avec l'âme, de ce qui était auparavant une femme, il refait une vierge (§ 50) [49] ».

Nous savons que, dans les textes gnostiques, cette purification de l'âme se poursuit jusqu'à devenir une nouvelle naissance, qui est une remontée aux cieux vers la maison du Père [50]. Cette conception n'est pas non plus absente des textes hermétiques. Deux d'entre eux nous décrivent une palingénésie : il s'agit de *CH* XIII et de NH VI⁶, sur *L'Ogdoade et l'Ennéade*, qui est, comme on le sait, d'une inspiration très semblable [51]. *CH* XIII, 2 énumère avec netteté les agents qui concourent à la renaissance de l'Homme. La matrice est « la Sagesse intelligente dans le Silence, et la semence est le vrai Bien ». Celui qui sème est « le Vouloir de Dieu ». Quant à l'être nouveau qui naîtra de ce mystère, il sera « Dieu, Fils de Dieu et Tout dans le Tout, composé de toutes les Puissances ». Le titre présumé du traité *L'Ogdoade*

---

[49] Cité d'après l'éd. de J. Gorez, Paris 1963, p. 39-41 (trad. retouchée). Sur le thème « devenir vierge » chez Philon, cf. R. A. Baer Jr., *o.c.* (*supra* n. 25), p. 51-55 et A. J. Festugière, *Révélation*, t. 2, p. 549. Dans un pseudépigraphe de l'A.T., *Joseph et Aséneth*, issu d'un milieu assez comparable à celui de Philon, on lit également (15, 7) que la « repentance est la mère des vierges » (cf. éd. M. Philonenko, Leyde 1968, p. 185, et commentaire, p. 58, 103). Il nous semble d'ailleurs qu'il y aurait lieu de faire d'autres comparaisons entre cet écrit et l'*Exégèse de l'âme* : par exemple, Joseph, 7,11 (p. 153) et 8, est à la fois le frère et le fiancé d'Aséneth, comme le conjoint céleste qui descend sauver l'âme.

[50] Cf. NH II, 133-134. K. W. Tröger, *o.c.* (*supra* n. 2), p. 12, 105 etc. insiste beaucoup, à la suite de H. M. Schenke sur le fait que, dans le gnosticisme, l'homme ne devient pas Dieu, comme dans les textes hermétiques que nous allons examiner ci-dessous, mais qu'il *re*-devient Dieu, car il l'était déjà. Nous ne sommes pas sûr que cette distinction soit si importante. Chez Marcion, par exemple, Dieu est tout à fait étranger à la création. L'homme n'est donc pas d'origine divine. Cependant il accède au salut par l'*agnitio* de l'Évangile et du Dieu inconnu. Dira-t-on alors que le marcionisme est étranger au gnosticisme ? C'était la thèse d'A. Harnack, mais elle est, aujourd'hui, contestée.

[51] Cf. notre article, « Le sens et la composition du traité hermétique *L'Ogdoade et l'Ennéade*, conservé dans le Codex VI de Nag Hammadi », *RSR* 48 (1974) 54-65, qui était déjà sous presse quand nous reçûmes K. W. Tröger, « Die sechste und die siebte Schrift aus Nag Hammadi Codex VI », *ThLZ* 98 (juil. 1973) 495-503, où se trouve une traduction de NH VI⁶⁻⁷ et, dans l'introduction (col. 498) quelques remarques, qui ne recoupent pas tout à fait les nôtres, sur la parenté NH VI⁶/ *CH* XIII. Cf. Id., *Die hermetische Gnosis* (*supra* n. 2), p. 109.

et l'Ennéade [52] suffit à suggérer que, comme dans l'*Exégèse de l'âme*, cette nouvelle naissance est une montée aux cieux. Nous en avons confirmation par *CH* I, 26, où la nature ogdoadique figure l'assemblée des êtres célestes, chantant des hymnes au Père pour accueillir le nouvel élu [53]. L'énumération des agents de la régénération n'a pas tout à fait, en NH VI[6], la rigidité scolastique de *CH* XIII, 2. Nous apprenons néanmoins qu'Hermès engendre ses fils spirituels grâce à la δύναμις qui est en lui, et que ceux-ci ont pour mères les ἐνέργειαι qui font croître les âmes [54]. Car il faut un père et une mère pour constituer un parfait : ce concept nous est devenu familier dans les textes gnostiques [55].

A. J. Festugière concède que *CH* XIII « n'est pas seulement un exposé doctrinal », mais « une initiation ». Il ajoute, d'autre part, qu'il s'agit là « d'un exemple unique dans la littérature hermétique [56] ». Malheureusement, au moment où il écrivait ces lignes, l'exemple avait cessé d'être unique, puisque *L'Ogdoade et l'Ennéade* était déjà connu par les premiers articles de J. Doresse. Seulement, on peut se demander si l'initiation dont il est question dans ces deux traités suppose des pratiques rituelles. Opérant, en face de Tat, comme γενεσιουργός, Hermès peut être comparé au τελεσιουργός des mystères [57]. Cependant, plusieurs objections viennent à l'esprit. Un rite suppose tout d'abord l'existence de certains formulaires ou de certaines prières adaptées à certaines circonstances. Or, même s'il y a une inspiration commune entre les prières de *CH* XIII et celles de *L'Ogdoade et l'Ennéade*, les différences d'expression l'emportent sur les ressemblances : il faudrait donc admettre que dans ce rite hermétiste de régénération (s'il a jamais existé rien de tel), il était de règle, pour l'initiateur comme

---

[52] Le haut du papyrus étant fort endommagé, nous n'avons pas conservé la suscription du titre. Toutefois la matière de l'entretien est bien définie (NH VI, 56,26) comme « la contemplation de l'Ogdoade et de l'Ennéade ».

[53] Cf. A. J. FESTUGIÈRE, *Révélation*, t. 3, p. 133 s. Pour l'ἀνάβασις, cf. NH II, 134, 14 et *CH* X, 15.

[54] A condition de reconnaître en M̄MAY (NH VI, 53, 16-17) le pl. du mot « mère » (K. W. TRÖGER), et non pas l'adverbe de lieu explétif qui suit le verbe OYN (M. KRAUSE) : étant donné le parallèle avec *CH* XIII, il ne devrait pas, à notre avis, y avoir le moindre doute.

[55] Outre l'*ÉvPh*, sent. 6 (et 20,28,116 etc.), cf. *ÉvTh*, éd. A. GUILLAUMONT, H.-Ch. PUECH etc., Paris 1959, log. 15 : « Lorsque vous verrez celui qui n'a pas été enfanté de la femme, prosternez-vous sur votre visage et adorez-le : celui-là est votre Père ».

[56] Cf. A. J. FESTUGIÈRE, *Révélation*, t. 2, p. 15. Pour la discussion qui suit, comparer avec K. W. TRÖGER, (*supra* n. 2), p. 54-58.

[57] Cf. *CH* XIII, 4 et la note d'A. J. FESTUGIÈRE *ad locum* (p. 211).

pour le futur initié, d'improviser le texte des oraisons qu'ils pronon-
çaient. D'autre part, l'accomplissement d'un rite suppose généralement l'existence d'un édifice cultuel : or, si les dialogues hermétiques
sont souvent censés se dérouler à l'intérieur des temples, nos deux
logoi sur la régénération n'indiquent aucun local particulier comparable,
par exemple, au νυμφών de l'*Évangile selon Philippe*. Ce dernier texte
nous offre en outre une succession structurée de sacrements (sent. 68) :
baptême, onction, eucharistie et chambre nuptiale [58]. Or nos textes
hermétiques font bien allusion à des degrés antérieurs de l'initiation [59],
mais ils ne précisent pas si ces degrés sont en nombre déterminé et
canoniquement définis. Enfin, les monuments que, dans *L'Ogdoade
et l'Ennéade*, Tat est censé construire en souvenir de son initiation sont
si grandioses qu'ils relèvent plutôt de la fantaisie d'un auteur que
des possibilités réelles d'un simple fidèle [60].

Un point nous paraît toutefois digne d'être souligné. En *CH* XIII, 8,
la régénération de Tat s'opère après un moment de silence sans que
l'on précise quel est le geste de l'initiateur qui l'a provoquée. Dans
L'Ogdoade et l'Ennéade, au contraire, il nous est précisé que ce geste
est un baiser [61]. A notre avis, on aurait tort de comparer ce baiser
à celui qu'échangent Hermès et son disciple, à la fin de la *Prière d'actions
de grâces* (NH VI, 65, 3-7), avant d'aller manger « une nourriture
pure et qui ne contient pas de sang ». Ce dernier geste est un baiser de

---

[58] Cf. H. GAFFRON, *Studien zum koptischen Philippusevangelium unter besonderer
Berücksichtigung der Sakramente*, Bonn 1969.

[59] Cf. notre article, cité n. 51, p. 58 s; NH VI, 52, 7.13 et *CH* XIII, 1.9.

[60] Cf. NH VI, 61,18 - 62,19. Comparer avec les moyens modestes de Lucius dans
APULÉE, *Métamorphoses* XI, 28, 9. Parmi les monuments mentionnés dans *L'Ogdoade et
l'Ennéade*, il est question (NH VI, 61, 20) d'une inscription ϨΝ ϨΕΝϹϨΑΪ ΝϹΑϨ
ΠΡΑΝϢ; H. M. SCHENKE, *OLZ* 69 (1974) 241, comprend à juste titre : « en écriture
de la maison de vie », c'est-à-dire en hiéroglyphes. On sait en effet (cf. F. DAUMAS, *Les
moyens d'expression du grec et de l'égyptien, comparés dans les décrets de Canope et de
Memphis*, Le Caire 1952, pp. 184-188) que ἱεροῖς γράμμασιν se dit en hiéroglyphique
mss̆ n pr-ʿnḫ et en démotique *n sḫ pr-ʿnḫ*, tandis que ἱερογραμματεῖς est attesté en démotique sous la forme *n' sḫ. w pr-ʿnḫ* et dans la version bohaïrique de l'A.T. (*Gen.* 41, 8. 24,
cf. GUNNS dans *JEA* 4, p. 252), sous la forme ϹϤΡΑΝϢ. Il est intéressant de signaler
que, dans le Codex VI, le mot ΠΡΑΝϢ est aussi attesté sous la forme ΠΡΑΕΙϢ
(NH VI, 61, 30. 62; 15). Cela constituerait, à notre avis, un argument pour admettre,
malgré les doutes de R. KASSER, « Morphologie copte », *BIFAO* 66 (1968) 105-111,
l'existence, dans l'*Évangile selon Philippe*, d'une forme du factitif en *sa*, dérivé de la
même racine, ϹΟΕΙϢ « nourrir », attesté dans le même texte sous la forme normale
ϹΟΝϢ.

[61] Cf. NH VI, 57, 26-27.

paix, qui ne semble avoir aucun effet matériel ou sensible sur les deux protagonistes. En revanche, dans *L'Ogdoade et l'Ennéade*, à peine le père et le fils se sont-ils embrassés, que surviennent les Puissances, qui, d'après *CH* XIII, 8-10, concourent directement à la formation du corps spirituel du nouveau parfait : leur réunion constitue les membres du Verbe, qui remplace le corps matériel forgé par la dodécade des vices. Par conséquent, si vus de l'extérieur, les deux gestes sont identiques, fonctionnellement, leur signification diffère.

Bien plutôt, *L'Ogdoade et l'Ennéade* devrait être rapproché sur ce point des écrits valentiniens. Le *Traité tripartite* (NH I, 58, 22-27) nous décrit la naissance des Éons « qui existent, ayant procédé de lui, le Fils-et-le Père, à la manière de baisers, à cause de la multitude de ceux qui s'embrassent les uns les autres dans une bonne pensée insatiable ». Mais la naissance de l'Église céleste a nécessairement sa contrepartie ici-bas parmi les membres de l'Église terrestre. On se souviendra particulièrement de l'*Évangile selon Philippe* (sent. 31), où, d'après K. Rudolph, le baiser est un rite essentiel du mariage spirituel des valentiniens [62] : « les parfaits deviennent féconds dans un baiser et enfantent. C'est pourquoi nous nous embrassons mutuellement et nous nous concevons, par la grâce qui est en nous, les uns les autres ». Ce simple rapprochement suffit-il à prouver qu'il y a eu un rituel hermétiste de régénération ? On ne saurait l'exclure, mais la question reste difficile à trancher [63].

Cependant, nous venons de déceler une parenté profonde entre ce deuxième groupe de textes hermétiques et le gnosticisme, très différente des rapprochements spécieux mais vite effacés que nous proposions au début entre l'*Asclepius* et l'*Évangile selon Philippe*. Cela n'est certes pas une nouveauté que de distinguer deux classes d'écrits hermétiques, les uns, proches du gnosticisme et du pessimisme dualiste, les autres de tendance philosophique, moniste et optimiste. C'est l'ancienne thèse de W. Bousset [64], reprise et illustrée par A. J. Festugière,

---

[62] Cf. K. RUDOLPH, *Die Mandäer*, t. 2, Göttingen 1961, p. 388. Voir également R. KASSER et collaborateurs, éd. trad. *Traité tripartite* (cf. *supra* n. 1), p. 39-40 et 321.

[63] K. W. TRÖGER, *Hermetische Gnosis* (cf. *supra* n. 2), p. 119, essaie, semble-t-il, de trouver une solution moyenne en suggérant qu'à l'époque où sont rédigés les écrits hermétiques, les mystères ont été complètement spiritualisés : « Das spiritualisierte Mysterium steht im Dienste der Gnosis. Die entsprechenden Mysterienbräuche hingegen wurden bei den hermetischen Gnostikern schon lange nicht mehr praktiziert » (cf. ID., *CH XIII und Mysterienglaube*, p. 57-58).

[64] Cf. W. BOUSSET, dans *GGA* 176 (1914) 697-755 : compte-rendu de la thèse de J. KROLL, *Die Lehren des Hermes Trismegistos*, Münster i. W. 1914.

à l'aide de nombreux exemples. Cependant, si l'on veut dépasser cette simple constatation pour retrouver une sorte de cohérence, on peut tenter de discerner lequel des deux courants est antérieur à l'autre. Cela ne revient pas à se poser la question controversée et probablement insoluble de la date de composition des différents traités. En effet, cette date importe peu, puisque tous nos traités sont d'une inspiration composite, et supposent l'utilisation ou le remaniement d'écrits hermétiques plus anciens que nous n'avons pas conservés [65]. Il nous faut, en fait, poser la question non pas pour chaque traité, mais pour chacun des thèmes, des lieux communs de l'hermétisme. Nul doute que, bien souvent, cette question doive rester sans réponse.

Toutefois, dans le cas précis de symbolisme sexuel dont nous venons de faire l'étude, nous avons peut-être de quoi montrer quelle est l'inspiration la plus ancienne. Cela dépend comment on juge des rapports de l'hermétisme et de l'Égypte. Pour A. J. Festugière, l'Égypte est aussi peu présente dans les écrits hermétiques, qu'elle peut l'être, par exemple, dans les paysages nilotiques ornant les murs des riches villas de Pompéi : ce n'est qu'un cadre, un décor, un simple parfum d'exotisme [66]. Certains égyptologues se sont opposés à cette interprétation [67], notamment P. Derchain qui, après avoir relevé plusieurs passages du *Corpus Hermeticum* dont l'inspiration égyptienne lui paraît du meilleur aloi, conclut que « l'hermétisme a passé pour un phénomène grec aussi longtemps que seuls des hellénistes se sont occupés de lui [68] ».

Nous sommes tenté de le suivre en suggérant que l'*Asclepius* et les textes apparentés, où s'exprime une conception très optimiste de la sexualité, sont beaucoup plus proches des origines présumées égyptiennes de l'hermétisme que *CH* XIII et le groupe des textes d'inspiration gnostique. Quand l'auteur de *CH* V, 6 s'extasie sur le mystère merveilleux de « l'homme façonné dans le ventre maternel », on ne peut s'empêcher d'évoquer non seulement des lieux communs connus depuis

---

[65] Il n'est pas rare, en fait, que les écrits hermétiques eux-mêmes fassent allusion à leurs sources : *Genikoi logoi*, cf. *CH* X, 1.7, *CH* XIII, 1, *SH* III, 1, NH VI, 63, 2-3 ; *Exotica* (ou *Diexodica* ?), cf. *Ascl*. 1, *FH* 30, NH VI, 63,3 ; *Dits d'Agathodémon*, cf. *CH* X, 25, XII, 1 etc.

[66] Cf. A. J. FESTUGIÈRE, *Révélation*, t. 1, p. 85 : « ces touches d'exotisme n'ont guère plus d'importance que les ibis ou les palmiers des fresques pompéiennes … ».

[67] La thèse de B. STRICKER (cf. *supra* n. 2) est une théorie systématique des influences égyptiennes. Les articles de M. KRAUSE et de S. SAUNERON (cités *supra* n. 2) relèvent quelques indices importants et très significatifs.

[68] Cf. P. DERCHAIN (art. cité *supra* n. 2), p. 197.

la sophistique grecque [69], mais aussi le célèbre hymne au dieu Khnoum qui « forma les mâles reproducteurs et mit sur terre la gent femelle ... anima de la vie les jeunes êtres à l'intérieur du sein maternel ... modelant la peau sur les membres » [70]. De même pour la prière d'actions de grâces de NH VI, adressée à celui « qui est honoré de l'appellation de Dieu et béni de l'appellation de Père ... matrice qui conçoit toute semence ... matrice qui conçoit par la nature du Père » [71] ; ces termes font penser à des prières égyptiennes plus anciennes, par exemple l'hymne à Ptah, que nous livre un document de théologie memphite en écriture démotique : «C'est lui le père des Dieux et aussi la mère, et son surnom c'est 'la femme'. C'est lui la matrice où se déverse la semence de tout ce qui est sorti. C'est le grand Hapy, Père des Dieux [72] ». Ces rapprochements pourraient être multipliés, mais nous allons à l'essentiel : s'il est admis que l'hermétisme ait eu des origines égyptiennes, des deux courants de pensée qui parcourent nos textes, celui qui affiche la conception la plus optimiste à l'égard de la sexualité est certainement celui que l'on aura le moins de peine à concilier avec ce que nous savons de l'ancienne religion égyptienne. Il y a donc de très fortes chances qu'il soit le plus ancien, et que l'interprétation gnosticisante des symboles sexuels corresponde à un développement adventice.

Naturellement c'est là une conclusion partielle, strictement limitée au thème que nous avons choisi pour cette étude. Car, s'il n'est pas invraisemblable que l'hermétisme, d'une inspiration d'abord toute contraire, ait été influencé par le gnosticisme dans les deux premiers siècles de notre ère, l'évolution inverse n'est pas à exclure a priori : Platon donne bien l'exemple d'une doctrine dualiste qui se tempère de plus en plus, principalement dans le *Timée* et dans les *Lois* [73]. Il est

---

[69] Cf. A. J. FESTUGIÈRE, *Révélation*, t. 2, p. 80 s.

[70] Cité par P. DERCHAIN, « La religion égyptienne », in H. Ch. PUECH, *Histoire des religions*, t. 1, Paris 1970, p. 68-69.

[71] Cf. NH VI, 64, 1-3.25-27 et notre article cité *supra* n. 9.

[72] Cf. W. ERICHSEN et S. SCHOTT, *Fragmente memphitischer Theologie in demotischer Schrift*, Wiesbaden 1954, p. 362. La bi-sexualité des dieux créateurs donnait d'ailleurs lieu, dans les anciens hiéroglyphes, à des jeux d'écriture, comparables aux jeux de langage que nous avons analysés ci-dessus (p. 132) à propos de l'hermétisme. Cf. B. VAN DE WALLE et J. VERGOTE, «Traduction des *Hieroglyphica* d'HORAPOLLON», *CdE* 18 (1943) 39-89 (spécialement p. 54-55) et *ibid.* p. 199-239. Faits analogues dans le roman *Joseph et Aséneth*, également d'origine égyptienne, cf. M. PHILONENKO, *o.c.* (*supra* n. 49), p. 76 s.

[73] Cf. A. J. FESTUGIÈRE, *Révélation*, t. 2, p. XII.

donc fort possible que, si nous eussions choisi un autre thème, en l'absence de tout rapprochement vraisemblable avec l'ancienne littérature égyptienne, nous eussions été conduit à poser l'antériorité des tendances dualistes ou gnosticisantes sur les tendances optimistes et monistes.

Remarquons pourtant que, de l'aveu des observateurs les plus perspicaces, aucun traité hermétique n'est d'un dualisme rigoureux et sans partage [74]. Et quand R. Reitzenstein estimait que les adeptes d'une *Poimandresgemeinde*, d'abord indépendante d'Hermès, avaient annexé plus tardivement les écrits du *Corpus Hermeticum* et les avaient modifiés à leur usage pour leur donner la forme que nous connaissons actuellement [75], peut-être n'était-il pas loin de la réalité : en tout cas, pour le thème que nous avons choisi, le *Poimandrès*, *CH* XIII, quelques paragraphes manifestement interpolés dans *CH* IX, et le traité sur *L'Ogdoade et l'Ennéade*, constituent très probablement un groupe assez limité, qui tranche sur les positions anciennes d'Hermès, représentées par l'*Asclepius* et les textes apparentés.

Grâce à la découverte de Nag Hammadi, l'histoire aussi bien externe qu'interne de l'hermétisme s'éclaire donc pour nous d'un jour entièrement nouveau. L'*Asclepius* nous laisse entrevoir au prix de quelles ambiguïtés les symboles de l'hermétisme pouvaient être captés et réutilisés, à contre-sens, comme des symboles gnostiques. Mais ces contre-sens mêmes sont instructifs. L'utilisation de l'hermétisme par les gnostiques rejoint l'évolution interne des écrits hermétiques vers des positions de plus en plus gnosticisantes que nous pouvons mieux apprécier désormais grâce à *L'Ogdoade et l'Ennéade*.

---

[74] ID., *ibid.*, t. 3, p. 36 n. 3 : « disons-le une fois pour toutes : en dehors des traités *CH* I et XIII, il n'est aucun des écrits gnostiques de l'hermétisme où le courant gnostique (dualiste) se présente à l'état pur ». Cependant A. J. Festugière admet (cf. *supra* n. 43) que même *CH* I est d'inspiration mêlée.

[75] Cf. R. REITZENSTEIN, *Poimandres*, Leipzig 1904, p. 248.

«PARAPHRASE DE SEM» ET «PARAPHRASE DE SETH»

PAR

DANIEL ALAIN BERTRAND

On aura reconnu dans les deux termes de ce titre les intitulés de deux traités gnostiques de la littérature ancienne. D'une part la *Paraphrase de Sem* : c'est le premier écrit du septième codex de la bibliothèque de Nag Hammadi [1]. D'autre part la *Paraphrase de Seth* : il s'agit de l'ouvrage allégué par l'auteur de l'*Elenchos*, ce monument hérésiologique du troisième siècle généralement attribué à Hippolyte de Rome [2].

C'est à la fin de sa notice sur les séthiens que l'écrivain renvoie son lecteur pour complément d'information à la *Paraphrase de Seth*; il prétend que cet écrit lui révélera toutes les doctrines des hérétiques [3]. La *Paraphrase de Sem* de Nag Hammadi semble, de prime abord tout au moins, devoir être mise en relation avec ces mêmes sectaires. Je ne fais pas allusion à la thèse soutenue naguère selon laquelle l'ensemble des manuscrits de Nag Hammadi aurait appartenu à une communauté séthienne [4]. Cette opinion, avec ce que sa formulation a de tranchant, apparaît maintenant assez contestable. Le caractère composite de la bibliothèque, les problèmes posés par l'implantation supposée d'hétérodoxes à Chénoboskion, entre autres raisons, incitent à la prudence [5]. Je m'appuie plutôt sur le fait que le codex contenant

---

[1] La *Paraphrase de Sem* est aujourd'hui disponible en fac-similé : *The Facsimile Edition of the Nag Hammadi Codices, Codex 7*, Leiden 1972, pp. 7-55; en transcription copte et en traduction allemande : M. KRAUSE, « Die Paraphrase des Sêem », in F. ALTHEIM et RUTH STIEHL, *Christentum am Roten Meer*, vol. 2, Berlin et New York 1973, pp. 2-105 (index pp. 200-229).

[2] L'*Elenchos* a été plusieurs fois édité et traduit, en totalité ou en partie; meilleur texte grec : P. WENDLAND, *Hippolytus Werke*, 3. Band, *Refutatio omnium haeresium*, Leipzig 1916 (*GCS* 26); unique traduction française : A. SIOUVILLE, *Hippolyte de Rome, Philosophoumena* ..., 2 vol., Paris 1928.

[3] *Elenchos* 5, 22.

[4] Voir surtout J. DORESSE, *Les livres secrets des gnostiques d'Égypte*, t. 1 ..., Paris 1958, pp. 281-352.

[5] Voir notamment F. WISSE, « The Nag Hammadi Library and the Heresiologists», *Vig. chr.* 25 (1971) 205-223.

la *Paraphrase de Sem* comporte deux œuvres, sur les cinq qui le constituent, qui sont placées sous le patronage de Seth, à savoir le *2e
Traité du Grand Seth* [6] et les *Trois Stèles de Seth* [7]. On dirait que le
scribe ou le relieur a tenté de regrouper, dans une certaine mesure, des
traités ayant quelque affinité, formelle ou foncière : l'apocalyptique
(codex 5), le valentinisme (codex 1), l'hermétisme (codex 6), etc. Quoi
qu'il en soit, et sans préjuger d'aucune conclusion, la simple possibilité
que la *Paraphrase de Sem* et la *Paraphrase de Seth* proviennent d'un
même milieu, ajoutée à la similitude de titre, autorise, me semble-t-il,
à examiner le problème du rapport littéraire existant éventuellement
entre les deux œuvres [8].

Il n'y a pas, malheureusement, de citation explicite d'un des deux
ouvrages dans l'autre. Aucun d'eux n'est non plus connu par ailleurs.
Seule une comparaison des deux écrits pourra dès lors peut-être permettre d'apporter une solution à la question de leur relation. Je me
propose donc, après les avoir brièvement résumés, de relever leurs
contradictions et leurs ressemblances les plus frappantes. Il faudra
ensuite apprécier le bilan et enfin tirer si possible les conséquences
de ce résultat : en effet, si la *Paraphrase de Sem* et la *Paraphrase de
Seth* sont indépendantes, on aura à justifier leurs points de convergence ;
si par contre elles constituent deux formes d'une œuvre unique, il
restera à tenter de comprendre le processus de différenciation.

Avant de procéder à l'analyse et à la confrontation des textes,
je crois nécessaire de faire quelques observations préliminaires pour
définir plus exactement les deux termes de la comparaison. Prenons
tout d'abord le plus simple à caractériser, la *Paraphrase de Sem*.
C'est donc, je le rappelle, le traité 1 du codex 7. Cependant, et ceci
ne serait pas sans importance pour notre propos, l'écrit a été autrefois
bloqué avec le suivant, c'est-à-dire avec le *2e Traité du Grand Seth*,

---

[6] CG 7, 2.

[7] CG 7, 5.

[8] La question a été abordée à l'occasion d'autres recherches par J. DORESSE, *ibid.*,
pp. 170-178, par C. COLPE, « Heidnische, jüdische und christliche Überlieferung in den
Schriften aus Nag Hammadi 2 », *Jahrb. für Ant. und Chr.* 16 (1973) 109-114, qui concluent
tous les deux à la parenté des deux écrits, et par F. WISSE, « The Redeemer Figure in
the Paraphrase of Shem », *Nov. Test.* 12 (1970) 138-139, qui fait l'hypothèse d'un commentaire séthien intermédiaire entre la *Paraphrase de Sem*, plus primitive, et la *Paraphrase de
Seth*, chistianisée secondairement.

déjà nommé, de façon à ne faire qu'un avec lui [9]. Sem et Seth se trouve-
raient du même coup identifiés. Ce qu'on considère aujourd'hui comme
la *Paraphrase de Sem* ne comporte en effet pas d'*explicit*, contrairement
à l'usage normal de Nag Hammadi. Mais ce découpage n'est pas à
retenir. Sans même invoquer des raisons de langue et de contenu,
on notera que le manuscrit lui-même sépare les deux textes par des
tirets et un blanc [10]. En dépit de cette limitation, la *Paraphrase de Sem*
reste l'un des plus longs ouvrages de la bibliothèque (presque cinquante
pages [11]). L'œuvre originale était-elle si étendue ? L'analyse de l'écrit,
sur laquelle je reviendrai, fait apparaître plusieurs morceaux de genre
littéraire différent. On peut aussi remarquer que le terme de « paraphrase » (παράφρασις) du titre s'appliquait sans doute primitivement
à une partie beaucoup plus restreinte du texte [12]. On lit en effet vers
les trois quarts de l'œuvre l'introduction suivante : « Voici la paraphrase ». Suit, sous la forme d'un catalogue de définitions, une sorte
de décryptage de certaines des notions rencontrées auparavant.
La matière de l'écrit totalement étrangère au champ de ce commentaire
pourrait donc être adventice. Notons par ailleurs que si le fait que
le traité soit connu directement, sans intermédiaire patristique, est
un facteur extrêmement positif, les conditions de transmission de
l'œuvre ne sont en revanche pas idéales : il ne faut pas oublier en particulier que nous n'avons qu'une traduction copte d'un original grec,
dans un manuscrit certes peu lacuneux mais apparemment assez
fautif [13]. La date de la copie peut, semble-t-il, être fixée, grâce aux
documents trouvés dans la reliure, autour de 345 [14].

La *Paraphrase de Seth*, quant à elle, n'est connue que dans des
conditions encore bien moins satisfaisantes. On sait que la partie
concernée de l'*Elenchos*, le livre 5, n'est transmise que par un manuscrit
unique, tardif (probablement du 14e siècle), très abîmé par l'humidité
et assez corrompu dans ses leçons [15]. Par ailleurs, bien que l'*Elenchos*
remonte à une date assez haute (vers 235, selon l'hypothèse la plus

---

[9] Cf. J. Doresse, *ibid.*, p. 166 ; H.-Ch. Puech, « Les nouveaux écrits gnostiques … »,
in *Coptic Studies in Honor of W. E. Crum*, Boston 1950, p. 105.

[10] Voir p. 49, 9-10.

[11] 1, 1 à 49, 9.

[12] 32, 27 à 34, 16 ; cf. F. Wisse, *ibid.*, p. 130.

[13] Voir par exemple la dittographie de 46, 20-29 (= 46, 9-20) ; d'autres méprises
montrent que le scribe ne dominait pas le texte.

[14] Cf. R. Kasser, « Fragments du livre biblique de la *Genèse* cachés dans la reliure
d'un codex gnostique », *Muséon* 85 (1972) 68.

[15] Le *Parisinus suppl. gr. 464* ; cf. P. Wendland, *ibid.*, pp. XI-XVII.

commune), il faut l'utiliser avec circonspection, compte tenu du fait qu'il s'agit d'un ouvrage polémique. La notice ne saurait donc constituer en tout état de cause qu'un témoignage secondaire sur la *Paraphrase de Seth*. De plus, en l'absence d'une étude générale récente sur la méthode éristique de l'hérésiologue, il est difficile de déterminer dans quelle mesure le traité allégué est la source des renseignements présentés. Dans le meilleur des cas, ce ne sont que des extraits de la *Paraphrase de Seth* qui sont reproduits. Enfin, comme l'analyse de la notice le montrera, d'autres documents ont été probablement utilisés concurremment par le compilateur. Par contre, c'est bien évidemment d'un texte grec de l'ouvrage gnostique que celui-ci s'est servi [16].

Il est temps maintenant de résumer dans leurs grandes lignes les deux œuvres à comparer. Le traité de Nag Hammadi se présente pour l'essentiel [17] comme une révélation faite par un Rédempteur nommé Derdékéas, inconnu par ailleurs, au personnage de Sem, en qui il faut certainement reconnaître le fils aîné de Noé, étant donné l'utilisation de la *Genèse* faite d'autre part. Le cadre rappelle celui de l'apocalyptique juive : Sem est ravi en extase au sommet de la création le temps d'entendre le message divin [18]. Le contenu de la révélation proprement dite est assez composite. Entre autres choses, il comprend 1⁰ une description des premiers principes : la Lumière, l'Esprit et les Ténèbres [19] ; 2⁰ un mythe sur la chute métaphysique : le mélange des deux principes inférieurs et l'émanation de divers éons [20] ; 3⁰ un récit de la descente du Rédempteur à travers l'univers : Derdékéas revêtu de différents vêtements et prenant diverses formes lors de son passage d'une sphère à l'autre de la « Nature » [21] ; 4⁰ une relation de la création du monde d'en bas : l'origine du ciel, de la terre, des démons, etc. [22] ; 5⁰ un abrégé d'histoire sainte : le déluge, la tour de Babel, les habitants de Sodome, la venue d'un démon de l'eau appelé Soldas, peut-être un hérésiarque baptiste inconnu [23] ; 6⁰ un aide-mémoire pour le gnostique devant

---

[16] L'existence de jeux de mots dans la source (*Elenchos* 5, 19, 13-14) indique soit qu'elle était transmise dans sa langue originale soit seulement qu'elle avait subi un travail rédactionnel depuis sa traduction.

[17] 1, 18 à 41, 21.

[18] 1, 6-17 ; 41, 21-23.

[19] 1, 18 à 2, 10.

[20] 2, 10 à 10, 19.

[21] 12, 15 à 19, 27.

[22] 19, 27 à 24, 34.

[23] 24, 34 à 31, 4.

après sa mort traverser les mondes intermédiaires et rejoindre le principe d'en haut : le « mémorial » (ὑπόμνησις) de Derdékéas, sorte de formulaire fournissant les mots de passe [24] ; 7° une interprétation de certains noms d'entités intervenant dans la révélation : la « paraphrase » proprement dite, déjà signalée [25] ; 8° une violente polémique contre des rites d'ablution : la critique du baptême pour les péchés pratiqué par une communauté religieuse non identifiée [26]. Tous ces éléments font donc partie de la révélation de Derdékéas à Sem ravi en extase. Mais le traité se poursuit, en ajoutant notamment une apocalypse annonciatrice d'événements catastrophiques [27], une récitation du « mémorial » (ici ὑπόμνημα) enseigné par le Rédempteur [28] et une vision des sphères à travers le ciel ouvert [29]. Ces derniers passages sont plus ou moins nettement mis dans la bouche de Sem, supposé sur le point de mourir [30].

En ce qui concerne la *Paraphrase de Seth,* on pourrait lui attribuer, si l'on éliminait de la notice de l'*Elenchos* uniquement ce qui est à coup sûr un commentaire de l'hérésiologue, 1° une description des premiers principes : également la Lumière, l'Esprit et les Ténèbres [31] ; 2° un développement sur la rupture primordiale : le mélange de l'essence des principes [32] ; 3° une doctrine sur l'origine des idées et des créatures : les empreintes laissées par les chocs réciproques des multiples puissances émanées des principes [33] ; 4° une version de la descente du Rédempteur : l'apparition dans le monde inférieur d'un Verbe, non nommé, mais revêtu de traits chrétiens [34] ; 5° un recueil de *testimonia* vétéro-testamentaires : le nombre trois dans le *Pentateuque* [35] ; 6° un rapprochement avec des données religieuses païennes : l'interprétation séthienne d'une peinture murale dans un sanctuaire attique [36] ;

---

[24] 31, 4 à 32, 5.

[25] 32, 27 à 34, 16.

[26] 36, 25 à 38, 29.

[27] 43, 28 à 45, 31.

[28] 46, 1 à 47, 7.

[29] 47, 20-32.

[30] Toutes les références précédentes n'ont qu'une valeur indicative, en attendant que le plan de l'écrit soit précisé par les études ultérieures.

[31] *Elenchos* 5, 19, 1-5.

[32] 5, 19, 5-7.14-17.

[33] 5, 19, 8-14.

[34] 5, 19, 18-21.

[35] 5, 20, 1-3.

[36] 5, 20, 6-7.

enfin, 7⁰ une théorie sur les combinaisons des éléments : la chimie des corps composés [37]. Il n'y a pas de raison particulière de douter que la *Paraphrase de Seth*, expressément invoquée, ait été une source de la notice, connue de première ou de seconde main. C'est même sans doute la principale, puisqu'elle est la seule nommée et qu'elle est, au dire du compilateur, susceptible de satisfaire toutes les curiosités sur la secte [38]. Mais rien n'indique qu'elle ait été la seule. L'hérésiologue prétend d'ailleurs lui-même que les sectaires utilisaient d'innombrables écrits [39]. Le recueil de *testimonia* et le rapprochement avec l'iconographie païenne d'une part et la théorie sur les combinaisons d'autre part pourraient ainsi provenir de deux autres documents, car autant de conclusions partielles précèdent l'examen de ces thèmes [40]. Les portions de la *Paraphrase de Seth* préservées par l'*Elenchos* ne laissent rien deviner de la fonction ni même de l'identité du personnage choisi pour patronner l'ouvrage, mais on peut considérer comme certain que ce Seth est le fils d'Adam, eu égard au rôle qu'il joue dans le gnosticisme.

J'en arrive donc au relevé des principaux points de divergence et de convergence entre les deux écrits. Bien entendu, il ne s'agit dans un cas comme dans l'autre que de sélectionner les plus probants. Tout d'abord quelques contradictions.
— Le titre : Sem d'un côté, Seth de l'autre [41].
— L'étendue du traité : que toute la matière de la *Paraphrase de Sem* ne soit pas dans la *Paraphrase de Seth* est compréhensible, puisque cette dernière n'est de toute manière pas citée in extenso par l'*Elenchos* ; mais, dans l'hypothèse d'une relation entre les deux œuvres, il resterait à expliquer le bien propre de la *Paraphrase de Seth*.
— Le milieu doctrinal : la *Paraphrase de Sem* est exempte, semble-t-il, de tout contact avec le christianisme, que celui-ci soit orthodoxe ou hétérodoxe, tandis que la *Paraphrase de Seth* présente manifestement des caractères chrétiens.
— La figure du Rédempteur : d'une part le mystérieux Derdékéas,

---

[37] 5, 21, 2-6.8-12.
[38] 5, 22.
[39] 5, 21, 1.
[40] 5, 20, 1 ; 5, 21, 1.
[41] Par contre le terme commun de « paraphrase » est un argument assez fort en faveur du rapport des deux ouvrages ; j'y reviendrai.

type du Sauveur gnostique, de l'autre, comme je l'ai indiqué, un Verbe anonyme qui emprunte certains traits au Christ [42].

— La théologie de l'eau : des deux côtés l'élément liquide est mauvais, « ténébreux », et il est associé au principe inférieur ; mais la *Paraphrase de Sem* en déduit une condamnation radicale de tout baptême, qualifié d'impur [43], alors que la *Paraphrase de Seth* admet au moins un rite utilisant une eau consacrée [44].

Et maintenant quelques rapprochements significatifs entre les deux traités.

— Les « racines » (ΝΟΥΝΕ), selon la *Paraphrase de Sem*, c'est-à-dire les principes (ἀρχαί), selon la *Paraphrase de Seth*, les deux expressions étant strictement équivalentes dans le vocabulaire gnostique : de part et d'autre ils sont trois, ce sont les mêmes (la Lumière, l'Esprit et les Ténèbres), ils sont disposés de la même façon les uns par rapport aux autres (l'Esprit au milieu, au-dessous de la Lumière et au-dessus des Ténèbres) et ils sont décrits en termes identiques (par exemple les Ténèbres comme une « eau redoutable » et un « vent » soufflant dans les eaux) [45].

— L'élément déchu : souvent appelé « Intellect » (*Νοῦς*) par les deux textes, participant de la Lumière et de l'Esprit, il est paradoxalement à la fois l'objet recherché par le Rédempteur pour être sauvé et le fils ou le complice de la puissance des Ténèbres. Cette espèce de dialectique assez caractéristique de la gnose explique à mon avis que les diverses essences apparaissent simultanément comme hétérogènes et inter-dépendantes et que le principe inférieur, en particulier, possède une double nature, portée au bien et mauvaise, perspicace et bornée [46].

— L'univers : il est imaginé comme une gigantesque matrice (ⲀⲦⲈ, μήτρα ou φύσις dans la *Paraphrase de Sem*, μήτρα dans la *Paraphrase de Seth*) [47].

---

[42] Il a la « forme de l'esclave » (*Ph.* 2, 7), il est descendu « dans le sein d'une vierge » (interprétation de l'Incarnation), « il s'est lavé » (allusion au baptême de Jésus dans le Jourdain ; cf. D. A. BERTRAND, *Le baptême de Jésus, Histoire de l'exégèse ...*, Tübingen 1973, pp. 63-64), etc. (*Elenchos* 5, 19, 20-21).

[43] 37, 22 ; 38, 5-6 ; cf. 36, 25 à 38, 29 ; 40, 25-29 ; 48, 8-11.

[44] *Elenchos* 5, 19, 21.

[45] *Par. de Sem* 1, 18 à 2, 10 ; *Elenchos* 5, 19, 1-5 ; comparer *Par. de Sem* 9, 17 ; 14, 11 ; 31, 13 ; 37, 9-10 avec *Elenchos* 5, 19, 5.7.17 ; 5, 20, 10 pour le thème de l'eau redoutable et *Par. de Sem* 2, 1 avec *Elenchos* 5, 19, 13-20 pour celui du vent.

[46] *Par. de Sem* 11, 22-31 et passim ; *Elenchos* 5, 19, 5-7.14-17 ; cf. F. WISSE, *ibid.*, p. 132.

[47] *Par. de Sem*, voir les index ; *Elenchos* 5, 19, 11-12.17.19-21.

— Le processus de constitution du monde supérieur : c'est la collision des puissances entre elles qui provoque les « nuées » (ⲕⲗⲟⲟⲗⲉ), c'est-à-dire les éons, selon la *Paraphrase de Sem*, ou les « idées» (ἰδέαι), conçues comme des empreintes ou des sceaux, selon la *Paraphrase de Seth*, qui serviront de cadre ou de modèle à la création sensible [48].
— La dernière phase de la descente du Rédempteur : celui-ci, au moment où il va pénétrer dans la matrice cosmique, prend pour la tromper l'apparence de la « bête » ou plus exactement du « serpent » (θηρίον dans la *Paraphrase de Sem*, θηρίον et ὄφις dans la *Paraphrase de Seth*) [49].

Le temps est venu de faire une sorte de bilan des facteurs positifs et négatifs. Il me semble que, quel que soit le poids des différences entre les deux traités, et il est lourd, la nature de leurs ressemblances force à admettre qu'ils sont de quelque manière apparentés. Ce qui emporte ma conviction, ce n'est pas le nombre des rapprochements, c'est la pertinence avec laquelle chacun d'eux est en situation. Il ne s'agit pas d'analogies banales, mais de groupes cohérents de parallèles précis. Ainsi par exemple, le fait que dans deux textes gnostiques l'élément déchu soit appelé *Noûs* ne peut être qu'un indice, que ce *Noûs* y procède de la Lumière et de l'Esprit rend la rencontre déjà beaucoup plus significative, mais qu'il joue en outre des deux côtés le même rôle particulier, cela constitue alors quasiment la preuve d'une relation littéraire.

On sera en revanche extrêmement prudent pour définir le rapport exact existant entre les deux écrits. D'une part, les très importantes différences relevées supposent qu'ils ont connu une assez longue histoire indépendamment l'un de l'autre. D'autre part, leurs particularités de transmission évoquées au début de cet exposé font qu'ils ne seront jamais absolument comparables. Ce qui est évident, c'est qu'aucun d'eux ne dérive de l'autre. Il faut donc leur supposer un ancêtre commun, dont l'un au moins soit assez lointain.

Il reste donc à avancer une hypothèse susceptible de rendre compte

---

[48] *Par. de Sem* 5, 14-25 ; *Elenchos* 5, 19, 8-14. Toutefois les deux textes ne s'accordent pas totalement dans le détail ; en outre la formation du ciel et de la terre matériels décrite dans la *Paraphrase de Sem* (19, 27 à 20, 20) n'a pas de véritable parallèle dans la *Paraphrase de Seth*, mais peut-être cette dernière est-elle tronquée.

[49] *Par. de Sem* 19, 13 à 20, 1 ; *Elenchos* 5, 19, 18-21. Θηρίον a bien quelquefois l'acception d'ὄφις : cf. *Ac.* 28, 4-5 ; *L'orig. du monde* (CG 2, 5) 114 (162), 1-2 ; 118 (166), 26.

des contradictions entre les deux œuvres. Reprenons brièvement les principaux points de divergence signalés précédemment.

— Le titre : il est difficile de savoir quel nom a été remplacé par l'autre [50]. On peut seulement affirmer que la substitution est antérieure à l'état actuel des textes. Pour ce qui est de la *Paraphrase de Sem*, le nom de Sem est bien attesté et bien réparti dans l'ensemble du traité, en dehors de quelques interpolations évidentes [51]. Pour ce qui est de la *Paraphrase de Seth*, le nom de Seth est confirmé par le fait que la notice concerne les séthiens. Dans le cas d'une correction de l'hérésiologue, en effet, il faudrait supposer qu'il a modifié un titre pour le conformer à son sujet ; or c'est le contraire qui aurait tendance à se produire, à savoir qu'une secte soit décrite voire inventée sur la foi d'un simple titre [52]. Plutôt que d'une faute, le changement de titre a dû résulter d'une identification volontaire de Sem et de Seth, facilitée par la similitude de leur nom et l'analogie de leur rôle de premier homme d'une ère nouvelle [53]. Une telle assimilation est peut-être suggérée par l'*explicit* du traité suivant immédiatement la *Paraphrase de Sem* dans le codex de Nag Hammadi, intitulé précisément, comme je l'ai déjà rappelé, *2e Traité du Grand Seth*. Cette identification serait antérieure à la traduction de l'écrit, puisque cet *explicit* est conservé intégralement en grec [54]. A propos du titre, je pense devoir aussi souligner que le terme de « paraphrase » est par lui-même extrêmement caractéristique et qu'il fournit un argument supplémentaire pour l'unité originelle des deux œuvres : il n'y a pas pour le moment, à ma connaissance tout au moins, dans la littérature religieuse ancienne en cause d'autre « paraphrase », sous quelque patronage que ce soit.

— Autre point de divergence à examiner, l'étendue du traité : il est clair que chaque ouvrage a pu amplifier la matière primitive ; mais ce qui est commun aux deux indique des développements originels. Faute de pouvoir repérer exactement où l'*Elenchos* cesse d'utiliser la *Paraphrase de Seth* et de savoir ce qu'il en omet, il est cependant

---

[50] La littérature pseudépigraphique conservée semble faire plus grand cas de Seth (voir le cycle d'Adam, la bibliothèque de Nag Hammadi), mais le *Livre des Jubilés* montre que Sem passait aussi pour être le dépositaire d'ouvrages secrets (10, 14).

[51] Cf. F. WISSE, *ibid.*, p. 131.

[52] Cf. F. WISSE, « The Nag Hammadi Library … », p. 219.

[53] Seth comme fils élu d'Adam, après le meurtre d'Abel, Sem comme fils aîné de Noé, après la fin du déluge ; cf. *Par. de Sem* 1, 20-21. Sem et Seth se trouvent déjà associés en *Si.* 49, 16.

[54] *2e Traité du Grand Seth* 70, 11-12.

difficile de déterminer si celle-ci est secondaire ou non au point de vue de la composition.

— Le milieu doctrinal : le « séthianisme » supposé des deux traités, qui leur avait été prêté en vertu de critères purement extérieurs, ne doit en aucune façon masquer l'écart qu'une évolution séparée a creusé entre eux. Ni l'un ni l'autre n'a en fait à être rattaché aux séthiens, tant que la doctrine de ces sectaires n'aura pas été plus nettement définie, si toutefois il en existe bien une sui generis [55]. Toute liberté est donc laissée de faire passer, le temps qu'il se diversifie, le modèle primitif de la *Paraphrase de Sem* et de la *Paraphrase de Seth* par deux milieux différents qui seraient respectivement préchrétien ou dépourvu de relations avec le christianisme et gnosticiste. Il faut dès lors se demander s'il y a eu christianisation ou déchristianisation de l'écrit originel. La question du sens de l'évolution entre gnose et gnosticisme, dans laquelle s'inscrit la nôtre, est, comme on sait, encore controversée. Serait-elle même résolue, il serait hasardeux d'appliquer un schéma général de l'histoire des idées au problème particulier d'une dépendance littéraire. Ce n'est donc pas non plus la différence de milieu doctrinal qui peut permettre de dire quelle est de la *Paraphrase de Sem* et de la *Paraphrase de Seth* celle dont la forme est la plus primitive.

Les autres points de divergence ne sont pas, comme on va le voir, d'interprétation aussi équivoque.

— La figure du Rédempteur : il y a dans l'*Elenchos* des traits qui tout à la fois ne sont certainement pas imputables à l'hérésiologue, proviennent sans aucun doute de la *Paraphrase de Seth*, n'apparaissent pas dans la *Paraphrase de Sem*, n'auraient pas été supprimés dans l'hypothèse d'une déchristianisation mais facilitent le sens dans celle d'une christianisation. On lit par exemple, à propos de la forme animale revêtue par le Sauveur, cette remarque : « ... la bête : telle est, dit le séthien, *la forme de l'esclave*»; et à propos de la matrice où il pénètre, cette précision : « le Verbe de Dieu est descendu dans le sein *d'une vierge*» [56]. Le sens dans lequel s'est opéré le remaniement est clair : c'est la *Paraphrase de Seth* qui a adapté son modèle, en supprimant en outre le nom de Derdékéas si elle l'y trouvait.

— La théologie de l'eau : ici également la *Paraphrase de Seth* est de toute évidence secondaire. Elle a vu en effet dans le combat que le

---

[55] Voir F. Wisse, *ibid.*, pp. 219-223.
[56] *Elenchos* 5, 19, 20.

Rédempteur, descendu jusqu'au fond des Ténèbres primordiales, livre contre les eaux mythiques une allusion à un baptême qu'il aurait reçu ici-bas [57]. C'est un total contresens sur la forme et l'esprit de l'écrit originel, contresens dû naturellement à une exégèse christianisante.

En conclusion, trois points sont à relever, en dehors des remarques qu'on pourrait faire sur la valeur des sources hérésiologiques. Tout d'abord, au sujet du rapport existant entre la *Paraphrase de Sem* et la *Paraphrase de Seth*, c'est-à-dire de la question qui a motivé cet exposé, il faut considérer, me semble-t-il, que les deux traités ne sont pas irréductibles l'un à l'autre. Si on veut bien leur supposer une histoire littéraire suffisamment longue dans des milieux appropriés, il est extrêmement vraisemblable qu'ils remontent en définitive à la même source. Dans la mesure où le modèle primitif était situé hors de la sphère chrétienne, et cela paraît assuré, la *Paraphrase de Sem* reflète un état plus archaïque, ce qui ne veut pas dire que, sur le plan formel, elle soit moins développée que la *Paraphrase de Seth*. Pour ne regarder maintenant que l'état actuel des deux œuvres, la première est à classer parmi les écrits gnostiques non chrétiens de facture juive et la seconde parmi les écrits gnostiques christianisés [58].

En deuxième lieu, on doit noter que ce schéma d'évolution n'est pas sans parallèle à Nag Hammadi. La relation entre la *Paraphrase de Sem* et la *Paraphrase de Seth* est en effet, *mutatis mutandis*, du type de celle existant entre l'*Epître d'Eugnoste* et la *Sophia Iesu Christi* [59]. Une différence importante cependant : dans notre cas, il n'y a pas dépendance directe d'un écrit par rapport à l'autre, mais dérivation à partir d'un ancêtre commun. Ce processus de christianisation d'un texte gnostique préchrétien ou non chrétien est sans doute illustré par bien d'autres exemples. Mais cela est relativement peu apparent, parce que le plus souvent le premier terme du couple manque.

Il faut remarquer enfin que le milieu d'origine de l'ouvrage qui serait donc la source de la *Paraphrase de Sem* et de la *Paraphrase de*

---

[57] Comparer *Par. de Sem* 32, 5-17 (voir F. Wisse, « The Redeemer Figure ... », p. 137) avec *Elenchos* 5, 19, 21 (voir D. A. Bertrand, *ibid.*, pp. 63-64).

[58] Cf. A. Boehlig, « Zur Frage nach den Typen des Gnostizismus und seines Schrifttums », in *Ex orbe religionum, Studia G. Widengren*, t. 1, Leiden 1972, pp. 389-400.

[59] Cf. M. Krause, « Das literarische Verhältnis des Eugnostosbriefes zur Sophia Jesu Christi ... », in *Mullus, Festschrift Th. Klauser*, Münster in Westfalen 1964, pp. 215-223.

Seth relève à la fois de la gnose et du judaïsme hétérodoxe [60]. Son
identification précise reste à faire. Mais on entrevoit déjà, à la lumière
de nos deux écrits et d'autres qui leur sont comparables, comme
l'*Apocalypse d'Adam* copte, qu'une spéculation poussée de type gnostique a été associée très tôt, voire dans une période préchrétienne,
à une réinterprétation radicale de la tradition vetéro-testamentaire [61].

---

[60] Sur les rapports entre judaïsme et gnose, voir notamment A. Boehlig, « Der jüdische und judenchristliche Hintergrund in gnostischen Texten von Nag Hammadi »,
in *Le origini dello gnosticismo* ..., Leiden 1967, pp. 109-140. Il est bien entendu qu'en
dernière analyse, cet ouvrage gnostique hypothétique peut remonter au delà du milieu
évoqué, à des traditions iraniennes particulièrement : cf. C. Colpe, *ibid.*, pp. 109-116.

[61] La rédaction de cet article était pour ainsi dire terminée quand j'ai pris connaissance d'une communication du Professeur Krause présentée en 1973 lors du colloque de
Stockholm sur le gnosticisme et traitant de la même question ; ce travail doit paraître
prochainement avec les actes du colloque dans la collection *Studies in the History of
Religions* (Supplements to *Numen*).

« LES ENSEIGNEMENTS DE SILVAIN »
ET LE PLATONISME

PAR

Jan Zandee

On peut se demander à quel égard les écrits de Nag Hammadi reflètent la philosophie ou la philosophie populaire de l'époque qui les a vu naître, c'est-à-dire le deuxième ou troisième siècle de notre ère environ. Quel que soit leur caractère, gnostique, hermétique ou chrétien, ils ont une tendance à réagir aux idées contemporaines, à parler la langue des gens de l'époque, et à traiter des sujets actuels. Pendant les premiers siècles de notre ère différentes philosophies étaient en vogue, comme le stoïcisme, le platonisme (respectivement le moyen- et le néo-platonisme), le néo-pythagorisme, l'aristotélisme, ou une philosophie éclectique. « Les Enseignements de Silvain » prétendent être un écrit chrétien. Il s'y trouve des idées très orthodoxes, par exemple, quand il est dit qu'on ne peut connaître Dieu sans l'intermédiaire de Jésus-Christ (Sil. 100, 23-29). Notre auteur se réfère à l'apôtre Paul (Sil. 108,30). La forme de l'écrit est celle d'un livre de sagesse comme les *Proverbes* de l'Ancien Testament. D'autre part, il est aussi influencé par les idées philosophiques contemporaines. En général, on peut dire que « Silvain » est stoïcien dans sa morale et platonicien dans sa conception de Dieu. Notre écrit, certainement, ne partage pas l'immanentisme de la Stoa, mais, au contraire, le transcendantalisme platonicien.

Nous nous proposons de décrire d'abord, dans leurs grandes lignes, quelques correspondances avec le platonisme (A), et, après cela, de mentionner en détail quelques passages de « Silvain » plus ou moins comparables au platonisme (B).

A. Correspondances avec le platonisme

1. *La structure de la réalité*

La trichotomie de l'homme en corps ($\sigma\tilde{\omega}\mu\alpha$), âme ($\psi\upsilon\chi\acute{\eta}$) et intelligence ($\nu o \tilde{\upsilon}\varsigma$) (Sil. 92, 19-25), et les conséquences morales qui en résultent rappellent, vaguement, la trichotomie platonicienne des facultés du désir (ἐπιθυμητικόν), de l'irritation (θυμοειδές) et de la réflexion (λογιστικόν). Quand « Silvain » parle de l'intelligence (νοῦς) divine (θεῖος) en l'homme (Sil. 92,25), ceci est comparable à l'enseignement néo-platonicien, que l'intelligence humaine participe de l'Intelligence supra-individuelle (Νοῦς). « Silvain » (92, 32.33) et Plotin (Enn. IV, 3,9.17), [1] tous les deux, prétendent que la matière et le corps peuvent avoir une influence mauvaise sur les facultés rationnelles de l'homme, ce qui aboutit à un « mélange » défavorable (μῖξις, Plotin, Enn. III, 2,2 ; comparer Sil. 92,34).

2. Transcendance de Dieu

La transcendance de Dieu est formulée d'une manière platonicienne, quand « Silvain » dit que Dieu ne peut pas être compris dans un certain endroit (τόπος) (Sil. 99,22-26. 31-33).

3. La relation Dieu-Christ

Cette relation ressemble parfois, d'une façon éloignée, à la relation platonicienne entre l'Un et l'Intelligence (Νοῦς). Chez « Silvain » le Christ est le « Premier-né » (Sil. 112,35) de Dieu, et chez Plotin le Νοῦς s'appelle « fils » (παῖς) de l'Un (Enn. III, 8,11). Selon « Silvain » le Christ est « la lumière de la Lumière éternelle » (Sil. 113,6.7) et chez Plotin l'Intelligence (νοῦς) est une émanation de l'Un, source de toute lumière noétique comme le soleil dans le monde visible (Plotin, Enn. V, 1,4 ; 3,12). Le Νοῦς cosmique éclaire les intelligences indivi-duelles (φωτίζειν) (Enn. V, 3, 17), et chez « Silvain », le Christ, la lumière de la Lumière divine, éclaire le coeur des hommes (Sil. 98,22-28).

4. Quelques autres idées comparables au platonisme

L'ignorance est parfois désignée comme « oubli » par « Silvain » (Sil. 88,21-25), ce qui rappelle la λήθη, l'oubli des idées, dans le plato-nisme (Plotin, Enn. IV, 3,26).

« La mort » est comme une métaphore pour l'ignorance (Sil. 90,23.24 ; Plotin, Enn. I, 8,13).

« Silvain » exhorte son disciple à retourner à sa nature divine (Sil. 90,29.30) et chez Plotin, on trouve la conception de retourner à son vrai Soi (Enn. V, 1,1 ; 2,1 ; VI, 7,16).

---

[1] Pour les citations nous avons fait usage de l'œuvre de É. BRÉHIER, Plotin, Ennéades, texte établi et traduit, Paris, 1924-1938.

5. *Rapprochements entre « Silvain » et le moyen-platonisme (Albinus)*

La philosophie d'Albinus est un système éclectique. Dans le *Didas-kalikos*, il suit principalement le *Timée* de Platon, mais il y mêle beaucoup d'idées d'Aristote et de la Stoa. A cet égard, Antiochus d'Ascalon était son prédécesseur. Tout comme Platon, Albinus dit que la contemplation du philosophe est orientée vers le monde intelligible (*Didaskalikos* I, 2 ; 152,9). L'être le plus élevé dans ce monde est le Premier Dieu (πρῶτος θεός), qui est tout à fait transcendant (*Didaskalikos* X, 3 ; 164,27.28).

Les opinions sur Albinus dans l'Antiquité étaient divisées. Proclus le prend pour un platonicien, mais, selon Philostratus d'Athènes, il était un stoïcien. A l'égard de l'éclectisme, il y a une correspondance entre Albinus et « Silvain », puisque le dernier était stoïcien dans sa morale et plus proche du platonisme dans sa conception du dieu transcendant.

Voici quelques correspondances entre Albinus et « Silvain » qui seront reprises en détail ci-dessous.

a. L'intelligence est supérieure à la raison (Sil. 85,25.26).

b. La mort, comme métaphore de l'ignorance (Sil. 90,9-13).

c. La métaphore du « pilote » pour la faculté rationnelle (Sil, 90,12.13).

d. Par l'intelligence (νοῦς), l'homme participe à la divinité (Sil. 92, 25-27).

e. Chaque chose dans le monde visible est l'empreinte d'un prototype dans l'intelligence de Dieu (Sil. 99,5-7).

f. Le dieu suprême transcende l'espace (Sil. 99,21-100, 3).

g. Dieu est incorporel (Sil. 100, 5-12).

h. « Intelligence » et « Raison » comme noms de Dieu (Sil. 102,13-16).

i. L'homme s'assimile à Dieu par une conduite rationnelle (Sil. 108, 26 ; 111,8-13).

B. Passages des « Enseignements de Silvain »
comparables au platonisme

85,1. « Ton intelligence (νοῦς) comme principe directeur (ἡγεμονικόν) ». Quoique le terme ἡγεμονικόν soit caractéristique de la Stoa, il n'est pas absent du platonisme. Selon Platon le Démiurge crée dans l'homme le principe directeur divin (θεῖον ἡγεμονοῦν, *Timée* 41 c). Le moyen-platonicien Albinus localisait le principe directeur dans la tête. « Après avoir ainsi construit l'homme et lié au corps l'âme destinée à en être la maîtresse, les dieux ont naturellement placé la partie dirigeante (τὸ ἡγεμονικόν) de cette âme dans la tête, où se trouve le point de départ de la moelle et des nerfs et où les passions mettent des causes de trouble. Les sensations occupent également la tête, où elles sont «comme les gardiens de la partie dirigeante» (ὥσπερ δορυφορουσῶν τὸ ἡγεμονικόν) (Albinus, *Didaskalikos* XVII, 4; 173, 4-14)[2]. Dans un passage (Sil. 84,16-31), notre auteur décrit comment l'intelligence (νοῦς) est capable de maîtriser les passions (πάθος). De même, chez Albinus, le principe directeur contrôle les facultés inférieures de l'âme. « La sagesse (φρόνησις) est la science du bien et du mal, ainsi de ce qui est ni l'un ni l'autre, la tempérance (σωφροσύνη) consiste à régler les désirs (ἐπιθυμίας) et les aspirations (ὀρέξεις) et à les soumettre à l'obéisance du principe directeur (τὸ ἡγεμονικόν), c'est-à-dire la raison (τὸ λογιστικόν)» (Albinus, *Didaskalikos* XXIX, 2; 182,23-27).

85, 25.26. « L'intelligence (νοῦς) est le guide (ἡγούμενος), mais la raison (λόγος) est l'instituteur».

Quoique notre auteur utilise d'habitude les termes νοῦς et λόγος sans distinction, il semble qu'il y ait ici une subordination du λόγος au νοῦς. Ce phénomène présente des parallèles dans le moyen- et le néo-platonisme.

Chez Albinus l'intelligence est le principe actif (νοῦς ποιητικός) qui se sert de la raison comme instrument[3]. «L'intellection est l'opération de l'intelligence qui contemple les premiers intelligibles» (Νόησις δ' ἐστὶ νοῦ ἐνέργεια θεωροῦντος τὰ πρῶτα νοητά, Albinus, *Didaskalikos* IV, 6; 155,17.18). «L'intellection est le principe de la raison scientifique» (τὴν νόησιν ἀρχὴν εἶναι τοῦ ἐπιστημονικοῦ λόγου, Albinus, *Didaskalikos* IV, 6; 155,24.25). C'est ainsi que, chez Albinus, l'intelligence a une priorité par rapport à la raison. Selon Plotin l'âme est le λόγος du νοῦς, l'instrument par lequel l'intelligence parvient à s'exprimer elle-même (*Enn.* V, 1,3). La raison est «comme un rayon lumineux issu à la fois de l'intelligence (νοῦς) et de l'âme» (*Enn.* III, 2,16). «De l'intelligence émane la raison» (*Enn.* III, 2,2).

88,25.26. « Éloigne-toi de l'oubli qui te remplit de ténèbres».

C'est une admonition du maître de la sagesse à son disciple. L'expression « oubli » pourrait être empruntée à la philosophie platonicienne.

---

[2] Edition du texte grec du *Didaskalikos* avec traduction française : P. LOUIS, *Albinos, Epitomé*, Rennes, 1945. Le texte grec est aussi cité selon l'édition de C. F. HERMANN, *Platonis Dialogi VI, Bibliotheca Scriptorum Graecorum et Romanorum Teubneriana*, Lipsiae MCMXXI, *ΑΛΚΙΝΟΟΥ διδασκαλικὸς τῶν Πλάτωνος δογμάτων*, pp. 152-189.

[3] R. E. WITT, *Albinus and the History of Middle Platonism*, Cambridge, 1937 (*Cambridge Classical Studies. Transactions of the Cambridge Philological Society*, vol. VII), p. 55.

L'âme qui, dans sa préexistence, a vu les Idées, les a oubliées après avoir été enchaînée à la matière. Plotin dit : « D'autre part le corps est un obstacle à la mémoire, nous voyons bien actuellement l'oubli (λήθη) de produire, quand on absorbe certaines boissons ; et souvent, dès que le corps en est purgé, la mémoire reparaît » (*Enn.* IV, 3,26). Comme chez « Silvain », dans le *Tractatus Tripartitus* du Codex Jung l'oubli est un équivalent de l'ignorance (CG I, 4 ; 105, 14.15).

89,20-23. « Revêts-toi de la sagesse (σοφία) comme d'une robe (στολή), pose sur toi la science (ἐπιστήμη) comme une couronne ».

Pour Albinus la sagesse et la science sont des capacités du philosophe et elles le rendent indépendant des influences du corps. « La philosophie est une aspiration vers la sagesse (ὄρεξις σοφίας) ou encore l'affranchissement de l'âme qui se détourne du corps [4] quand nous nous dirigeons vers le monde intelligible et vers la vérité : La sagesse (σοφία) est la science (ἐπιστήμη) des choses divines et humaines » (Albinus, *Didaskalikos* I, 1 ; 152,2-5).

90,9-13. « L'homme misérable qui va à travers toutes ces choses mourra parce qu'il ne possède pas l'intelligence, le pilote ».

« Silvain » utilise, pour l'ignorance, la métaphore de la mort [5]. Dans le moyen-platonisme, on était convaincu que l'âme ignorante est mortelle et que seules les âmes qui se laissent diriger par l'intelligence héritent de la vie éternelle. « Il est vraisemblable, en effet, que les âmes dépourvues de raison (ἀλόγους ψυχάς) ne sont conduites que par l'imagination et ne se servent ni du raisonnement ni du jugement ni des représentations ou de leurs rapprochements ni des distinctions générales : elles sont incapables de se faire une idée de ce qu'est la nature intelligible ; elles ne sont pas de la même essence que les âmes raisonnables : elles sont mortelles (θνητάς) et périssables » (Albinus, *Didaskalikos* XXV, 5 ; 178,21-26). Selon Plotin, l'âme qui est plongée dans la matière est morte (ἐν ὕλῃ καταδῦναι ; θάνατος) (*Enn.* I, 8,13). Dans des passages néo-platoniciens comme celui-ci, le mot « mort » a une signification métaphorique et se réfère à la vie dans le corps.

Dans le *Tractatus Tripartitus* du Codex Jung la mort est également une métaphore de l'ignorance : « ... ce grand mal qu'est la mort, c'est-à-dire l'ignorance du Tout » (CG I, 4 ; 107, 30.31).

90,13. La métaphore du pilote pour la sagesse comme guide de l'âme se trouve aussi chez Albinus. « Au contraire, la sagesse (φρόνησις) qui,

---

[4] Comparer le refus du corps chez « Silvain », 92, 29-33 ; 94, 22-24 ; 98, 28.29.
[5] Comparer aussi Sil. 89, 13 ; 91, 10-12 ; 105, 4.5.

elle, est une science (ἐπιστήμη), fixe à chacune des autres vertus ce qui lui appartient ; de même le pilote (κυβερνήτης) révèle aux matelots ce que leurs yeux n'aperçoivent pas, et ils obéissent » (Albinus, *Didaskalikos* XXX, 3 ; 184, 5-8).

90,13-18. « Mais il est comme un navire que le vent jette par-ci par-là, et comme un cheval abandonné qui n'a pas de cocher (ἡνίοχος). Car celui-ci avait besoin du cocher (ἡνίοχος) qui est la raison » (λόγος).

Platon a été le premier à utiliser la métaphore du cocher (ἡνίοχος), qui fut empruntée plus tard par d'autres auteurs. L'homme est comme un cocher qui mène deux chevaux, l'un obéissant, l'autre désobéissant. Il réussira à les contrôler, s'il suit la juste compréhension. « Rappelons-nous qu'au commencement de cette fable nous avons dans chaque âme distingué trois sortes de choses : il y en a deux qui sont du type cheval, tandis que la troisième a fonction de cocher (ἡνιοχικὸν δὲ εἶδος τρίτον) ... Et maintenant, de ces chevaux l'un, disons-nous, est bon, non pas l'autre ; mais en quoi consiste l'excellence du bon ou, chez le vicieux, son vice, c'est ce que nous n'avons pas expliqué et qu'à présent nous avons à dire. Eh bien ! le premier des deux, et qui est celui dont la condition est plus belle, a le port droit ... puisqu' il est compagnon de l'opinion vraie, pour être conduit il n'a pas besoin qu'on le frappe ... Le second, par contre, est de travers, massif ... compagnon de la démesure et de la gloriole, ses oreilles, pleines de poils, sont sourdes et c'est à peine si le fouet garni de pointes le fait obéir ... Cela étant, quand à la vue de l'amoureuse apparition le cocher, qui par la sensation a répandu de la chaleur dans la totalité de son âme (ὅταν δ' οὖν ὁ ἡνίοχος ἰδὼν τὸ ἐρωτικὸν ὄμμα, πᾶσαν αἰσθήσει διαθερμήνας τὴν ψυχήν), a presque son compte du chatouillement et des piqûres causées par le regret, alors celui des chevaux qui obéit docilement au cocher ... Mais l'autre ... d'un bond violent s'élance ... ils finissent pourtant ... par se laisser sans résistance mener de l'avant ... Mais, à sa vue, les souvenirs du cocher (ἡνίοχος) se portent vers la réalité de la Beauté » (Platon, *Phèdre* 253 d-254 b) [6].

91,7-9. « Dieu, le Père saint, la vraie Vie, la Source (Πηγή) de la vie ».

L'idée que Dieu est la source de la vie se trouve aussi dans le néoplatonisme, où elle est liée à la conception de l'émanation. L'intelli-

---

[6] Traduction d'après *Collection des Universités de France, publiée sous le patronage de l'Association Guillaume Budé* ; PLATON, *Œuvres Complètes,* tome IV, 3e partie, *Phèdre,* texte établi et traduit par LÉON ROBIN, Paris, 1966.

gence et l'âme sont situées autour de l'Un comme des cercles concentriques et elles se meuvent autour de lui. « Dans cette danse, on contemple la source de vie, la source (πηγή) de l'intelligence, le principe de l'être, la cause du bien » (Plotin, *Enn.* VI, 9,9). L'Un est comparé à une source. « Imaginez une source, qui n'a point d'origine ; elle donne son eau à tous les fleuves ; mais elle ne s'épuise pas pour cela ; elle reste paisible, au même niveau » (Plotin, *Enn.* III, 8,10).

92,25-27. « L'intelligence (νοῦς) divine (θεῖος) dérive sa substance (οὐσία) du Divin (θεῖον) ».

La faculté supérieure de l'homme, l'intelligence, est de la même substance que le Divin. Pour cette raison elle s'appelle elle-même divine. Selon Albinus, la faculté suprême de l'homme, l'intelligence, est située dans la tête. Par l'intelligence l'homme est apparenté aux dieux, car elle est d'une substance divine. « L'espèce humaine qui devait se rapprocher le plus de la nature des dieux (ὡς συγγενεστάτου θεοῖς), fut l'objet de l'attention particulière du Père du tout et des dieux ses enfants » (Albinus, *Didaskalikos* XVI, 2 ; 172,2-4). Quand l'homme fut créé par les dieux, les facultés rationnelles furent placées dans la tête. « Après avoir ainsi construit l'homme et lié au corps l'âme destinée à en être la maîtresse, les dieux ont naturellement placé la partie dirigeante de cette âme dans la tête » (Albinus, *Didaskalikos* XVII, 4 ; 173,5-6). « La raison (τὸ λογιστικόν) est logée dans le même endroit » (Albinus, *Didaskalikos* XVII, 4 ; 173, 9). Ce qui est situé dans la tête est nommé ailleurs « divin ». « Mais, afin que la partie divine et immortelle (τὸ θεῖον αὐτῆς καὶ ἀθάνατον) de l'âme ne soit pas souillée par les futilités mortelles, ils la placèrent au sommet du corps dans une espèce de citadelle » (Albinus, *Dikaskalikos* XXIII, 1 ; 176,10-12). Il s'ensuit que, selon Albinus. le λογιστικόν est le Divin en l'homme.

Dans le néo-platonisme le νοῦς est divin. Selon Plotin il est un « grand dieu », mais non pas le Dieu suprême, car le Premier Principe siège sur le νοῦς comme sur un beau trône. Le νοῦς est un δεύτερος θεός, qui apparaît avant le Dieu suprême et avant que nous voyions celui-ci (*Enn.* V, 5,3). Quoique ce passage se réfère à l'intelligence cosmique, on peut en conclure que l'intelligence individuelle, elle aussi, participe à la substance divine.

92,32.33. « La matière (ὕλη), au contraire, est la substance du corps (σῶμα) qui est née de la terre ».

L'évaluation, par notre auteur, de la matière et du corps est négative. Elle s'oppose à son évaluation positive de l'intelligence. L'idée de la matière dans le moyen-platonisme est ambiguë. Les

platoniciens acceptaient trois causes : Dieu, la Matière, et l'Idée [7].
Dans le *Timée* la matière est considérée avant les autres causes pre-
mières (ἀρχαί). Le terme ὕλη ne se trouve pas chez Platon [8]. Albinus
se réfère à la doctrine de la matière dans le *Timée* (49 a-52 d) de Platon.
Platon « lui donne les noms de porte-empreintes (ἐκμαγειόν, *Timée*
50 c), de réceptacle universel (πανδεχές, *Timée* 51 a), de nourrice
(τιθήνη, *Timée* 49 a), d'espace (χώρα, *Timée* 52 a, d), de substrat
que ne perçoit point la sensation (ὑποκείμενον ἁπτόν τε μετ' ἀναισ-
θησίας) et qui n'est saisissable que par un raisonnement bâtard
(νόθῳ λογισμῷ ληπτόν, *Timée* 52 b) » (Albinus, *Didaskalikos* VIII,
2 ; 162,25-28). La conception de Platon était que la matière était
espace et non une masse étendue [9]. Albinus, au contraire, déclare,
d'une manière inconséquente, que la matière, avant le commencement
de l'univers « se mouvait en désordre et sans mesure » (ὕλην ... ἀτάκ-
τως καὶ πλημμελῶς κινουμένην) (Albinus, *Didaskalikos* XII, 2 ;
167,12.13). Albinus ne prend jamais la matière pour la cause du mal [10].
Maints platoniciens du second siècle, au contraire, apercevaient une
relation entre la matière et le mal [11]. Celse, par exemple, qui était
un vrai platonicien, déclare que le mal ne provient pas de Dieu, mais
est situé dans la matière [12]. Quoi que fût l'opinion de Platon lui-même
sur la relation de la matière et du mal, l'auteur des « Enseignements
de Silvain » sympathise sans doute avec ces platoniciens qui mépri-
saient la matière, et à qui Albinus n'appartenait pas.

Selon Plotin la matière est la troisième des sphères concentriques
autour du Premier Principe, et la plus éloignée de lui. Elle est identique
à l'absence totale de toute substance intelligible, un non-être complet,
une obscurité (σκότος). La matière a une influence mauvaise sur l'âme,
quand celle-ci se sent attirée vers ce qui est au dehors (*Enn.* IV, 3,9.17).

92,34-93,3. « Si tu te livres au mélange, tu obtiendras les trois parts
(c'est-à-dire, l'intelligence, l'âme et le corps), quand tu tombes de la
vertu dans l'infériorité ».

Cette constatation est un peu énigmatique, mais vraisemblablement
elle se réfère au mélange de l'intelligence avec la matière, et à ses
conséquences défavorables. Dans le néo-platonisme, nous rencontrons

---

[7] R. E. WITT, *Albinus*, p. 75.

[8] ID., *Albinus*, p. 75.

[9] ID., *Albinus*, p. 69.

[10] ID., *Albinus*, p. 120.

[11] ID., *Albinus*, p. 121.

[12] ID., *Albinus*, p. 121. Comparer ORIGÈNE, *Contre Celse* IV, 65.

l'idée de μῖξις qui se réfère au mélange des facultés rationnelles et irrationnelles. Puisque l'homme est un être composé d'intelligence, d'âme et de corps, il est menacé par la domination de la matière sur l'intelligence. Plotin dit : « S'il naît autre chose, ce doit être une chose inférieure à lui et non pas une pure raison (λόγος); ce ne doit pas être non plus la matière puisque la matière n'est pas un monde; c'est donc une chose mélangée (μικτὸν ἄρα) des deux. Elle se décompose donc en matière et en raison; son origine est l'âme qui préside à ce mélange (μεμιγμένον) » (*Enn.* III, 2,2). « Nous aurons donc raison de dire que la laideur de l'âme vient de ce mélange, de cette fusion (μῖξις, κρᾶσις), et de cette inclination vers le corps et vers la matière» (*Enn.* I, 6,5). Probablement, « Silvain » a en vue cette « inclination vers le corps et la matière », qu'il considère comme une menace pour la vertu.

93,5.6. « Acquiers-toi de la force parce que l'intelligence (νοῦς) est forte ».

Plotin, lui aussi, s'occupe de la force de l'intelligence. Pour lui, la faculté intelligible en l'homme (νοῦς; νόησις) n'est pas passive et purement potentielle, mais active (ἐνέργεια) (*Enn.* V, 4,2). Ensuite il dit de l'intelligence : « Oui, elle contient le nombre qui est dans les objets de sa contemplation; elle est une et multiple: sa multiplicité, c'est celle de ses puissances (δυνάμεις), puissances merveilleuses et sans faiblesse, puissances très grandes parce qu'elles sont pures, puissances exubérantes et véritables qui n'ont point de bornes, puissances infinies, infinité et grandeur» (*Enn.* VI, 2,21). Il faut que l'intelligence ait une énergie immanente afin d'avoir prise sur l'homme, autrement elle ne serait pas capable de combattre les passions.

93,10. « L'intellection » (νόησις).

Νόησις est un terme qui se trouve aussi dans le moyen-platonisme. C'est le pouvoir très apprécié de l'intelligence. Albinus en donne la définition suivante : « L'intellection est l'opération de l'intelligence qui contemple les premiers intelligibles » (Νόησις δ᾽ἐστι νοῦ ἐνέργεια θεωροῦντος τὰ πρῶτα νοητά; Albinus, *Didaskalikos* IV, 6; 155,17.18). C'est ainsi que la νόησις pourrait être définie comme l'activité de l'intelligence [13]. Albinus distingue νόησις au sens propre et la νόησις incarnée dans l'homme. La première était préexistante avant que l'âme fût liée au corps. La seconde s'appelle « l'idée innée » (φυσικὴ ἔννοια; Albinus, *Didaskalikos* IV, 6; 155, 18-23). Ces distinctions subtiles ne se trouvent pas chez « Silvain ». Sa méthode est beaucoup

---

[13] ID., *Albinus*, p. 55.

moins « philosophique » que celle du moyen-platonisme et des autres écoles de son époque.

93,24-94,4. « Mais je dis que Dieu est le pneumatique. L'homme a reçu sa forme de la substance de Dieu. L'âme ($\psi\upsilon\chi\acute{\eta}$) divine ($\theta\epsilon\hat{\iota}o\nu$) participe partiellement de Celui-ci (c'est-à-dire de Dieu), ensuite elle participe partiellement de la chair. L'âme mauvaise se tourne de-ci de-là … C'est bon pour toi, ô homme, de te tourner vers la nature humaine plutôt que vers la nature animale — je veux dire vers la nature charnelle. Tu recevras la similitude de la partie vers laquelle tu te tourneras ».

« Silvain » dit que l'âme est dans une situation intermédiaire entre la substance divine et la chair. Comme chez lui, l'âme est considérée être quelque chose de divin ($\theta\epsilon\hat{\iota}o\nu$) dans le néo-platonisme (Plotin, *Enn.* IV, 8,5). L'âme occupe un rang intermédiaire ($\mu\acute{\epsilon}\sigma\eta$ $\tau\acute{\alpha}\xi\iota\varsigma$) entre l'intelligence ($\nu o\hat{\upsilon}\varsigma$) et la matière. « Il est mieux pour l'âme d'être dans l'intelligible, mais il est nécessaire, avec la nature qu'elle a, qu'elle participe à l'être sensible … C'est qu'elle occupe dans les êtres un rang intermédiaire ; elle a une portion d'elle-même qui est divine ; mais placée à l'extrémité des êtres intelligibles et aux confins de la nature sensible, elle lui donne quelque chose d'elle-même. Elle reçoit en échange quelque chose de cette nature (sensible), si elle ne l'organise pas en restant elle-même en sûreté, et si, par trop d'ardeur, elle se plonge en elle sans rester tout entière en elle-même » (Plotin, *Enn.* IV, 8,7). L'âme est soumise à l'inclination ($\nu\epsilon\hat{\upsilon}\sigma\iota\varsigma$), elle peut incliner vers l'intelligence ou vers la matière. Les âmes qui sont liées à la matière « s'éloignent donc dans les profondeurs de l'abîme » (Plotin, *Enn.* IV, 3,6). C'est ce que « Silvain » craint pour « l'âme mauvaise ». « Restée pendant longtemps dans cet éloignement et cette séparation du tout, sans diriger son regard vers l'intelligible, elle devient un fragment, elle s'isole, elle s'affaiblit … appuyée sur un seul objet séparé de l'ensemble, elle s'éloigne de tout le reste … Les âmes ont nécessairement une double vie ($\dot{\alpha}\mu\phi\acute{\iota}\beta\iota o\iota$) ; elles vivent en partie de la vie de là-bas, et en partie de la vie d'ici, davantage de l'une, lorsqu'elles peuvent être en relation plus intime avec l'intelligence, et davantage de l'autre, dans le cas où elles y sont contraintes par leur nature ou par les circonstances accidentelles » (Plotin, *Enn.* IV, 8,4).

98,20-99,4. « Marche avec le Christ et il te sauvera. Car il est la vraie lumière et le soleil de la vie. Car, comme le soleil qui se manifeste et éclaire les yeux charnels, le Christ illumine chaque intelligence et le cœur. Car si un homme méchant qui est dans le corps a une mort mauvaise, combien plus un homme qui a son intelligence aveuglée. Car chaque aveugle va ainsi qu'il est vu comme un homme qui n'a pas d'intelligence saine. Il ne se réjouit pas d'obtenir la lumière du Christ qui est la raison (λόγος) ».

Dans le néo-platonisme nous trouvons aussi le symbolisme de l'illumination (φωτισμός) qui provient du Divin. Pour Plotin la contemplation mystique de l'Un est une telle illumination. « Il faut bien croire que l'on voit, lorsque l'âme perçoit soudainement la lumière : cette lumière vient de lui (le Premier Principe) et elle est lui-même. Il faut penser qu'il nous est présent, lorsqu'il nous éclaire (φωτίζειν), ainsi qu'un autre dieu qui vient dans une demeure à l'appel qu'on lui fait ; s'il n'était venu, il ne nous aurait pas éclairé » (Plotin, *Enn.* V, 3,17). L'Intelligence qui suit l'Un immédiatement s'appelle Son Fils premier-né (comparer le Christ, Sil. 112,35) et il agit comme médiateur de la révélation. Cette relation de l'Intelligence et de l'Un est comparable à celle de Dieu et du Christ chez « Silvain ». L'Un est la lumière absolue, l'Intelligence (*Noûs*) est le soleil et l'Âme est la lune. Chacune de ces deux dernières entités joue un rôle intermédiaire dans le processus de l'illumination (comparer Plotin, *Enn.* V, 6,4).

99,5-7. « Car tout ce qui est manifeste est une empreinte (τύπος) de ce qui est caché ».

Dans le contexte, le Christ, comme entité invisible, est comparé au soleil qui appartient aux choses visibles. De même l'intelligence, qui est une entité noétique, est comparée à une lampe qui illumine l'endroit où elle se trouve.

Dans le platonisme les choses visibles sont les ombres des Idées. Selon Platon, lui-même, les choses sensibles sont des copies (μιμήματα) du monde invisible. Dans le moyen-platonisme le monde intelligible était conçu comme un paradigme du monde sensible. Il y a trois « causes » (ἀρχαί) : la Matière, l'Idée et Dieu [14]. De celles-ci l'Idée est la cause formelle [15]. Elle peut être définie de cinq manières : en relation avec Dieu, avec l'homme, avec la matière, avec le monde sensible, et avec elle-même. En relation avec le monde sensible elle est παράδειγμα. « L'Idée est ..., par rapport au monde sensible, le modèle (ἔστι δὲ ἡ ἰδέα ... ὡς δὲ πρὸς τὸν αἰσθητὸν κόσμον παράδειγμα) ... Car, en général, tout ce qui est fait avec réflexion, est fait en vue d'une fin dont le modèle doit préexister (δεῖ τὸ παράδειγμα προϋπο-

---

[14] Id., *Albinus*, p. 76.
[15] Id., *Albinus*, p. 70.

κεῖσθαι), comme si la chose qui est faite procédait d'une autre » (Albinus, *Didaskalikos* IX, 1; 163,10-18). « On définit l'Idée comme étant
le modèle éternel de ce qui existe naturellement » (ὁρίζονται δὲ τὴν
ἰδέαν παράδειγμα τῶν κατὰ φύσιν αἰώνιον; Albinus, *Didaskalikos* IX,
2; 163,21.22). A l'Idée comme modèle correspond le monde visible
comme empreinte (τύπος). La Matière n'a pas de forme et pour cette
raison elle est propre à recevoir les empreintes des Idées. « En effet,
(la matière) ne serait pas propre à recevoir des empreintes (ἐκτύπωσις)
et des formes diverses, si elle n'était pas elle-même sans qualités ni
absolument exempte des formes (ἀμέτοχον ἐκείνων τῶν εἰδῶν) qu'elle
doit recevoir » (Albinus, *Didaskalikos* VIII, 2; 162,34-36). Dans ce
passage le mot ἐκτύπωσις est un équivalent de τύπος en Sil. 99,6.
La matière non-qualifiée est modelée selon les paradigmes des idées
éternelles.

Plotin était de l'opinion que les choses existantes étaient des images
(εἰκών) faites d'après des archétypes (*Enn.* V, 1,6).

99,7-15. « Car, comme un feu qui brûle dans un endroit (τόπος), le
soleil est dans le ciel et tous ses rayons s'étendent aux endroits terrestres. De même, le Christ a une seule existence (ὑπόστασις), et il illumine
(à la fois) chaque endroit ». Il semble que ce passage reprenne le problème d'unicité et de multiplicité, bien connu du platonisme et du
néo-platonisme.

99,21-100,3. « Ensuite, je parlerai de ce qui est plus élevé que celle-ci
(l'intelligence individuelle) : l'intelligence, par rapport à (κατά) son
existence (ὑπόστασις), est à un endroit, ce qui signifie qu'elle est
dans un corps; mais par rapport à la pensée (ἐπίνοια), l'intelligence
n'est pas à un endroit (τόπος) … Mais nous sommes capables de mentionner ce qui est plus élevé que celle-ci (l'intelligence supra-individuelle) : car, ne pense pas dans ton cœur que Dieu est à un endroit.
Si tu localises le Seigneur du Tout à un endroit, il te permet de dire
que l'endroit est plus élevé que celui qui l'habite. Car ce qui embrasse
est plus élevé que ce qui est embrassé ».

Notre auteur parle pluseurs fois de choses qui sont « plus élevées »
que ce qui était mentionné auparavant. Cela ressemble à la *via eminentiae*, méthode utilisée par Albinus pour parvenir à la suprême divinité
en commençant par les choses visibles. Son argumentation est que,
s'il y a quelque chose de meilleur, il faut qu'il y ait quelque chose qui
soit le mieux. Sa méthode est celle de l'induction [16]. On commence

---

[16] Comparer R. E. WITT, *Albinus*, p. 124.

par considérer la beauté du corps, après cela la beauté de l'âme, et ainsi de suite, jusqu'à ce l'on parvienne à la beauté suprême. « A ces idées on ajoute alors celle de Dieu, qui se distingue par son excellence» (τούτῳ δὲ καὶ θεὸν συνεπινοεῖ διὰ τὴν ἐν τῷ τιμίῳ ὑπεροχήν; Albinus, *Didaskalikos* X, 6; 165,29.30). « Parce que l'intelligence est meilleure que l'âme, et parce qu'au-dessus de l'intelligence en puissance il existe une intelligence en acte, qui pense tout, en même temps et toujours, et parce que la cause de ces choses est encore plus belle, ce qui est plus élevé (ἀνωτέρω) qu'elles doit être le Premier Dieu (ὁ πρῶτος θεός), la cause de l'activité permanente de l'intelligence (τῷ νῷ) du ciel tout entier » (Albinus, *Didaskalikos* X, 2; 164,16-20). L'intelligence est meilleure que l'âme, et le Premier Dieu transcende l'intelligence et tout ce qui lui est inférieur.

La méthode de penser d'Albinus est un procédé de transcendance. Il distingue entre une intelligence (νοῦς) supérieure qui ne se meut pas, et une intelligence inférieure qui se meut [17]. L'intelligence inférieure est céleste (οὐράνιος), c'est-à-dire qu'elle a une demeure dans le ciel. La première intelligence est νοῦς ἐν δυνάμει (intelligence en puissance), et la seconde intelligence est νοῦς κατ' ἐνέργειαν (intelligence en acte) (Albinus, *Didaskalikos* X, 2; 164,17). La première intelligence ou Premier Dieu est ὑπερουράνιος. La seconde intelligence est ἐπουράνιος οὐράνιος. Albinus parle aussi du Dieu qui est dans le ciel et du Dieu qui est au-dessus du ciel (θεὸς ἐπουράνιος et θεὸς ὑπερουράνιος; Albinus, *Didaskalikos* XXVIII, 3; 181,36). Le Dieu supracéleste n'est pas à un endroit (*in casu* le ciel). Ces pensées sont semblables à celles de « Silvain », qui enseigne que Dieu, selon son vrai être, transcende tout endroit, et qu'il est présent à un certain endroit, seulement selon sa puissance ou selon son énergie, c'est-à-dire dans son activité. Dans cette démonstration de la transcendance de Dieu, « Silvain » ressemble au platonisme.

Dans le néo-platonisme aussi, l'Un reste comme il est et il ne se morcelle pas dans les choses visibles. Mais, pour autant que les choses visibles sont émanées de lui, il est le Tout. Aussi l'intelligence a un aspect transcendant, en tant qu'elle est plus que l'intelligence individuelle. Plotin dit : « Leur principe (c'est-à-dire le Premier Principe, l'Un) reste identique à lui-même; il ne se partage pas entre eux, mais il reste entier. C'est pourquoi ses produits (le deuxième principe, l'intelligence, les choses intelligibles) aussi sont permanents, comme

---

[17] R. E. WITT, *Albinus*, p. 128.

la lumière qui subsiste, tant que le soleil subsiste » (Plotin, *Enn.* VI,
9,9). « L'Un est toutes choses et il n'est aucune d'entre elles ; principe
de toutes choses, il n'est pas toutes choses ; mais il est toutes choses ;
car toutes font en quelque sorte retour à lui ; ou plutôt, à son niveau,
elles ne sont pas encore, mais elles seront » (*Enn.* V, 2,1). Cette constatation de Plotin ressemble à celle de « Silvain » : le Premier Principe
ou Dieu transcende tout endroit.

Quant au thème de l'Être le plus élevé, qui contient tout et n'est
contenu par aucune chose, il faut citer ici une étude de W. R.
Schoedel [18], qui se réfère entre autres à Platon [19] qui dit que l'Un
ne peut pas être en quelque chose d'autre, puisque, en ce cas, il serait
« embrassé » par la chose dans laquelle il est. Il faut en conclure que
la sentence de « Silvain » qui dit que ce qui embrasse (ou « contient »)
est plus élevé (ou « transcende ») que ce qui est embrassé (ou « contenu »),
reflète un raisonnement platonicien. La transcendance de Dieu sépare
fondamentalement l'Académie et la Stoa.

100,5-12. « En effet il n'y a pas d'endroit qui s'appelle incorporel.
Car il n'est pas juste que nous disions que Dieu est un corps ($\sigma\hat{\omega}\mu\alpha$).
Car la conséquence en serait que nous attribuons de l'amélioration
et de la détérioration au corps, mais aussi que celui qui souffre de ces
choses ne peut pas rester impérissable » [20].

Le fait que Dieu n'est pas à un endroit (Sil. 99,21-100,3) implique
qu'il est incorporel. Il est impossible que Dieu qui est impérissable
participe au déclin du corps. Ce raisonnement correspond au transcendantalisme platonicien. Le moyen-platonicien Albinus, lui aussi,
affirme que dieu est incorporel. Cela est en rapport avec son idée que
Dieu transcende l'espace parce qu'il est $\dot{v}\pi\epsilon\rho ov\rho\acute{a}v\iota o\varsigma$ et non pas
$\dot{\epsilon}\pi ov\rho\acute{a}v\iota o\varsigma$. « Si Dieu était un corps ($\sigma\hat{\omega}\mu\alpha$), il serait fait de matière ;
il serait donc eau ou terre ou air ou quelque composé de ces éléments.

---

[18] W. R. SCHOEDEL, « *Topological* » *Theology and Some Monistic Tendencies in Gnosticism,* in *Essays on the Nag Hammadi Texts in Honour of Alexander Böhlig* (*Nag Hammadi
Studies,* 3), Leiden, 1972, p. 88-108.

[19] *Parménide* 138 a, b : « Il ne peut être, en effet, ni en autre que soi, ni en soi—Comment
cela ? Etant en autre que soi, il sera enveloppé ($\pi\epsilon\rho\iota\acute{\epsilon}\chi o\iota\tau o$) circulairement par ce en quoi
il est ... Autre donc sera l'enveloppant, autre l'enveloppé ($o\check{v}\kappa ov\nu$ $\check{\epsilon}\tau\epsilon\rho o\nu$ $\mu\grave{\epsilon}\nu$ $\check{a}\nu$ $\tau\iota$ $\epsilon\check{\iota}\eta$
$a\dot{v}\tau\grave{o}$ $\tau\grave{o}$ $\pi\epsilon\rho\iota\acute{\epsilon}\chi o\nu$, $\check{\epsilon}\tau\epsilon\rho o\nu$ $\delta\grave{\epsilon}$ $\tau\grave{o}$ $\pi\epsilon\rho\iota\epsilon\chi\acute{o}\mu\epsilon\nu o\nu$) ». Traduction d'après *Collection des Uni-
versités de France, publiée sous le patronage de l'Association Guillaume Budé* ; PLATON,
Œuvres Complètes, tome VIII, 1re Partie, *Parménide,* Texte établi et traduit par A.
DIÈS, Paris, 1965.

[20] Le copte ⲀⲦⲦⲀⲔⲞ a comme équivalent grec le mot $\check{a}\phi\theta\alpha\rho\tau o\varsigma$, cf. CRUM, *Coptic
Dictionary,* p. 405 f.

Or, en outre, il serait postérieur à la matière, s'il était fait de matière; puisque ces conclusions sont absurdes, il faut bien considérer Dieu comme incorporel (ἀσώματος). De plus, à supposer qu'il soit un corps (σῶμα), il serait corruptible (φθαρτός), engendré et changeant : or, chacune de ces suppositions est inconciliable avec sa nature» (Albinus, *Didaskalikos* X, 8 ; 166,7-13). « De tout cela il résulte également que Dieu est incorporel (ἀσώματος). En voici la démonstration : si Dieu était un corps (σῶμα), il serait fait de matière et aurait une forme ; l'ensemble du corps, en effet, est un assemblage de matière et de forme [21] qui l'accompagne, assemblage qui se conforme aux Idées et y participe d'une façon vraiment difficile à exprimer. Il est absurde de supposer que Dieu soit composé de matière et de forme, car il ne serait ni simple, ni primordial. Aussi Dieu doit-il être incorporel» (Albinus, *Didaskalikos* X, 7 ; 165,37-166,7). Le raisonnement d'Albinus est dirigé contre le matérialisme et le panthéisme de la Stoa qui enseignait que Dieu pénètre tout comme un feu [22]. « Silvain » ressemble à la Stoa en ce qui concerne la morale : l'intelligence comme principe directeur (ἡγεμονικόν) et la raison s'opposent aux passions et aux désirs. En ce qui concerne sa conception du Dieu transcendant, au contraire, il est platonicien.

100,13-31. « Il n'est pas difficile de connaître le Créateur de toute créature, c'est vrai, mais il est impossible de comprendre la ressemblance de celui-ci … Il est nécessaire de connaître Dieu comme il est. Tu ne peux connaître Dieu par personne excepté par le Christ qui possède l'image du Père. Car cette image révèle la vraie similitude en rapport avec ce qui est révélé ».

La transcendance de Dieu implique l'impossibilité de le connaître [23]. Aussi dans le moyen-platonisme Dieu transcende toute compréhension humaine. Albinus dit : « Il faut ensuite parler du troisième principe (ἀρχή, c'est-à-dire « Dieu ») que Platon considère comme presque inexprimable» (ἄρρητον; Albinus, *Didaskalikos* X, 1 ; 164,6.7). Le premier dieu est « inexprimable et parfait en lui-même » (Albinus, *Didaskalikos* X, 3 ; 164,28). Albinus parle de Dieu en termes de théologie négative. Nous ne pouvons pas dire que Dieu a des « qualités » (ποιόν) et aussi nous ne pouvons pas dire qu'il n'a pas de « qualités » (ἄποιον) (Albinus, *Didaskalikos* X, 4 ; 165,9.10). Or, selon Albinus, il y a plusieurs

---

[21] Influence aristotélicienne.
[22] R. E. WITT, *Albinus*, p. 76.
[23] Comparer aussi Sil. 116, 12.13.19.20.

méthodes pour atteindre peu à peu quelque connaissance de Dieu par l'intelligence. Une de ces méthodes est la *via eminentiae*. Commençant par les choses sensibles, on peut s'approcher de l'insensible et ensuite de l'être parfait, Dieu (Albinus, *Didaskalikos* X, 1; 164,6-15). « Dieu est ineffable et saisissable seulement par l'entendement » (ἄρρητος δ'ἐστι καὶ νῷ μονῷ ληπτός; Albinus, *Didaskalikos* X, 4; 165,4-5). Albinus diffère ici de « Silvain », qui prétend que l'homme n'est pas capable d'avoir une pensée de Dieu (νοεῖν; Sil. 116,20). Selon « Silvain » Dieu n'est connaissable que par son image (εἰκών; Sil. 100,27), le Christ. Cette théorie de l'image, bien connue du N.T. (2 *Cor.* 4,4; *Col.* 1,15), pourra avoir été empruntée au platonisme. Platon enseignait que les choses du monde visible étaient des images (εἰκών) des Idées. Ces images rappellent à l'homme le monde d'en-haut. Aussi dans le néo-platonisme les choses de ce monde-ci sont des images du monde transcendant. « Reste donc que la totalité des êtres existe d'abord ailleurs (dans le monde intelligible); puis sans aucun intermédiaire, par le seul voisinage (de cette totalité qui est) dans l'être intelligible avec autre chose, il apparaît une copie, une image (ἴνδαλμα καὶ εἰκών) de cet être; que ce soit spontanément, ou que l'âme s'y emploie (cela n'importe pas pour le moment), je dis l'âme en général, ou bien une certaine âme. Alors, tout ce qui est ici vient de là-bas, mais tout était bien plus beau là-bas; car ici tout est mélange, là-bas tout est sans mélange » (Plotin, *Enn.* V, 8,7). Il est possible que, pour « Silvain », le Christ, comme image (εἰκών) de Dieu, remplace les images platoniciennes comme intermédiaire dans le processus de la connaissance de Dieu.

100,31-110,8. « Considère ces choses par rapport à Dieu. Il est en chaque endroit et, aussi, il n'est en aucun endroit. [Par rapport à sa puissance], c'est vrai, il est en chaque endroit, mais par rapport à sa divinité il n'est en aucun endroit. Car, de cette manière, il est possible de connaître Dieu un peu. Par rapport à sa puissance il remplit chaque endroit, mais dans la sublimité de sa divinité rien ne le contient ».

« Silvain » continue sa démonstration sur la transcendance de Dieu. C'est seulement par sa puissance par laquelle il opère dans le monde que Dieu y est présent. Par les vestiges de sa puissance Dieu est connaissable un peu [24]. Nous trouvons des pensées comparables dans le platonisme. Le moyen-platonisme du deuxième siècle était influencé par

---

[24] Comparer *Rom.* 1, 20. Différemment de Paul, « Silvain » distingue la puissance de Dieu, qui est connaissable, et sa divinité qui transcende la compréhension.

l'aristotélisme. Il acceptait la doctrine de la Première Intelligence
ou du Premier Dieu comme Moteur Immobile. Ce Dieu est absolument
transcendant, mais il opère dans les choses qui viennent de lui. Albinus
parle du « Premier Dieu (ὁ πρῶτος θεός), le moteur qui fait agir
(ἐνεργεῖν) sans cesse l'intelligence du ciel tout entier [25]. Il agit sur elle,
bien qu'il soit lui-même immobile » (ἐνεργεῖ δὲ ἀκίνητος; Albinus,
Didaskalikos X, 2; 164,19-21). « Silvain » s'exprime d'une manière
dialectique. Dieu est transcendant et il est immanent à la fois. Il est
transcendant par rapport à sa divinité, mais il est immanent en tant
que puissance opératrice. De même, selon Albinus, le Premier Dieu
en soi est transcendant, mais son énergie est la source de toute activité
dans le monde. Ce point de vue est une réfutation de l'immanentisme
de la Stoa. Pour le néo-platonicien Plotin l'Un est transcendant.
D'autre part, il existe quelque continuité entre le Premier Principe
et le monde sensible. Car l'un est aussi puissance (δύναμις), et il est lié
au monde par son activité (ἐνέργεια). Il est la puissance de tout
(δύναμις τῶν παντῶν), la puissance dont tout est né (*Enn.* III, 8,10).
Le monde visible et le Premier Principe se contactent l'un l'autre comme
la circonférence et le centre d'un cercle, et ils sont liés par une « puissance ». « L'on reconnaît qu'un cercle tire sa puissance (τὴν δύναμιν) de
son centre, parce qu'il touche ce centre; il en reçoit en quelque sorte
la forme, en tant que ses rayons, convergeant au centre, sont, par celle
de leur extrémité qui est du côté du centre, comme le centre même
auquel ils aboutissent et dont ils sortent » (*Enn.* VI, 8,18). D'une manière
dialectique, on peut dire que le centre est lié à la circonférence et
en est séparé. Le centre est une «puissance illimitée » (δύναμις ἄπειρος;
Enn. III, 7,5) et contient tout ce qui en émane. C'est seulement par
cette « puissance » qu'il y a une unité du centre et de la circonférence.

101,9.10. « Tout est en Dieu, mais Dieu n'est en rien ».

La question si Dieu est en tout ou inversement est aussi abordée
par Albinus. Il dit : « Au gré de sa volonté il (Dieu) a rempli le Tout
de lui-même, car c'est lui qui lui a donné l'intelligence (νοῦ αὐτῆς
αἴτιος ὑπάρχων); celle-ci, une fois organisée par le Père, organise
à son tour l'ensemble de la nature dans notre univers» (Albinus, *Dikaskalikos* X, 3; 164,37-165,4). [26] Dieu, comme la Première Intelligence,
est ὑπερουράνιος, c'est-à-dire qu'il est tout-à-fait transcendant. La
seconde intelligence est ἐπουράνιος et opère dans le monde sensible.

---

[25] La première intelligence supracéleste fait agir la seconde intelligence céleste.
[26] Comparer R. E. WITT, *Albinus*, p. 130.

C'est ainsi qu'elle tient le monde lié à Dieu. Le monde sensible participe à Dieu en tant que l'intelligence cosmique a Dieu comme objet de la pensée. Cette situation, elle aussi, pourrait être caractérisée par les mots : Tout est en Dieu, mais Dieu n'est en rien.

101,12. « Dieu est tout ce qui est dans la vérité ».

Aussi dans le moyen-platonisme il y a une connection entre Dieu et la vérité. « Le Premier Dieu est ... la divinité, l'essence, la vérité (ἀλήθεια), la proportion, le bien » (Albinus, *Didaskalikos* X, 3 ; 164, 29.30). « Il est la vérité (ἀλήθεια) parce qu'il est le principe de toute vérité (πάσης ἀληθείας ἀρχή), comme le soleil est le principe de toute lumière » (Albinus, *Didaskalikos* X, 3 ; 164,34.35).

102,13-16. « En effet, c'est bon de demander et de savoir qui est Dieu. 'Raison' (Λόγος) et 'Intelligence' (Νοῦς) sont des noms masculins ».

Dans ce passage « Raison » et « Intelligence » sont des appellations de Dieu. C'est de même dans le moyen-platonisme. Les Idées sont les pensées de Dieu. On pourrait réduire cette conception à Platon lui-même, qui dit : « Dans la mesure donc où l'intellect aperçoit les Formes comprises dans ce qui est le Vivant, sait quelles elles sont et en quel nombre » (νοῦς ἐνούσας ἰδέας τῷ ὅ ἐστιν ζῷον) (*Timée* 39 e) [27]. Si Dieu pense les Idées, il est, lui-même, intelligence. Albinus parle de « Dieu ou Première Intelligence » (θεόν τε καὶ νοῦν τὸν πρῶτον) (Albinus, *Didaskalikos* XXVII, 1 ; 179,37). Il est la Première Intelligence qui reste immobile (Albinus, *Didaskalikos* X, 2 ; 164,24). Dieu est l'intelligence supra-céleste qui influence l'intelligence céleste. « De la même façon, cette intelligence (νοῦς) mettra en mouvement l'intelligence du ciel tout entier » (Albinus, *Didaskalikos* X, 2 ; 164, 23.24). La raison, elle aussi, est une faculté de Dieu. « La raison (λόγος) se présente sous deux formes : l'une est parfaitement solide et sûre, l'autre n'est à l'abri de l'erreur que dans la connaissance des choses, la première appartient à Dieu et non à l'homme, la seconde peut appartenir à l'homme » (Albinus, *Didaskalikos* IV, 2 ; 154,18-22). Cela signifie que Dieu est le seul qui possède une raison sûre.

De tout cela il ressort que pour Albinus aussi, Dieu s'appelle « Raison » et « Intelligence ».

108,20-27. « Celui qui craint Dieu ne commet aucune témérité (τολμηρία). Celui qui évite de commettre quelque témérité est quelqu'un

---

[27] Traduction d'après *Collection des Universités de France, publiée sous le patronage de l'Association Guillaume Budé*; PLATON, *Oeuvres Complètes*, tome X, *Timée-Critias*. Texte établi et traduit par A. RIVAUD, Paris, 1963.

qui garde son principe directeur (ἡγεμονικόν). Bien qu'il soit un homme existant sur terre, il s'assimile à Dieu».

111,8-13. « Celui qui (c'est-à-dire le Christ) a élevé l'homme s'est assimilé à Dieu, non pas afin qu'il abaissât Dieu jusqu'à l'homme, mais afin que l'homme s'assimilât à Dieu».

Le platonisme du deuxième siècle de notre ère n'était pas une religion, c'est vrai, mais il favorisait des visées religieuses sur le monde. Platon lui-même avait déjà parlé de « l'assimilation à Dieu dans la mesure du possible» (ὁμοίωσις τῷ θεῷ κατὰ τὸ δυνατόν; Platon, *Théétète* 176 b). Albinus suit Platon dans sa morale. Il cite le passage du *Théétète* et il expose les différentes interprétations. « Tantôt il déclare que s'assimiler à Dieu c'est être sensé, juste et saint, comme dans le *Théétète*» (Albinus, *Didaskalikos* XXVIII, 1; 181,17). Parfois ce point de vue a le caractère d'une échappée vers Dieu et une aliénation du monde [28]. La concentration des pensées sur le divin peut résulter dans l'assimilation à Dieu. « L'âme qui contemple la divinité et les notions qui la constituent est dite éprouver du bien-être, et cet état de l'âme est ce qu'on a appelé la pensée; ce n'est pas autre chose, pourrait-on dire, que de s'assimiler à la divinité» (τῆς πρὸς τὸ θεῖον ὁμοιώσεως; Albinus, *Didaskalikos* II, 2; 153, 4-7). La raison et l'enseignement peuvent être utiles dans l'assimilation à Dieu. « Silvain», lui aussi, dit que celui qui tient à son principe directeur, c'est-à-dire l'intelligence, s'assimilera à Dieu, et il est de l'opinion que celui qui se fait guider par la raison et par l'enseignement vaincra les passions et les autres inclinations irrationnelles (Sil. 85,24.26; 87,3-8; 108,24). Albinus dit : « Nous pouvons parvenir à nous assimiler à Dieu (γενέσθαι ὅμοιοι θεῷ), d'abord si nous possédons la nature convenable, et, si ensuite, nous adaptons à ce dessein nos moeurs, notre éducation, notre genre de vie selon les lois, si surtout nous employons pour cela la raison, l'étude (καὶ τὸ κυριώτατον λόγῳ καὶ διδασκαλίαι), les doctrines que l'on se transmet, de manière à nous tenir le plus souvent possible éloignés des affaires humaines et à nous attacher toujours aux choses intelligibles» (πρὸς τοῖς νοητοῖς) (Albinus, *Didaskalikos* XXVIII, 4 : 182,2-7). De tout cela il ressort que « s'assimiler à Dieu » était un thème bien usuel du moyen-platonisme, et on ne s'étonne pas qu'il rentrât dans « Les Enseignements de Silvain». Il ne s'agit pas d'une égalité substantielle à Dieu, mais plutôt d'une similitude morale, c'est-à-dire d'être juste et saint comme Dieu. La thèse de « Silvain » que l'assimila-

---

[28] R. E. WITT, *Albinus*, pp. 123, 143.

tion de l'homme à Dieu est un résultat de l'incarnation du Christ est comparable à une célèbre parole d'Athanase qui dit : « Mais plutôt qu'il admire que les choses divines se soient manifestées à nous par une chose aussi simple et que par la mort l'immortalité se soit étendue à tous, et que l'incarnation du Verbe nous ait fait connaître la providence universelle, et le Verbe de Dieu qui en est le chorège et le démiurge. Il s'est fait homme pour que nous devenions Dieu (αὐτὸς γὰρ ἐνηνθρώπησεν, ἵνα ἡμεῖς θεωποιησῶμεν); il s'est rendu visible en son corps, pour que nous nous fassions une idée du Père invisible; il a supporté les outrages des hommes, afin que nous ayons part à l'immortalité» (Athanase, *Sur l'Incarnation du Verbe* 54; XXV, PG 192 b) [29].

112,1-8 «Si nous ne fûmes pas même capables de comprendre les conseils de nos compagnons, qui sera capable de connaître la divinité ou les divinités du ciel? Si nous trouvons à peine les choses terrestres, qui scrutera les choses célestes? ».

Dans le platonisme le monde transcendant n'est pas accessible à la compréhension humaine usuelle. Platon, dans sa septième Lettre, dit que le monde d'en-haut est ineffable et indescriptible (Platon, *Lettres* 341 c, d; ῥητόν ... οὐδαμῶς) [30]. Plotin dit concernant l'Un : « La plus grande de ces difficultés, c'est que nous ne le comprenons ni par la science ni par une intuition intellectuelle, comme les autres intelligibles, mais par une présence supérieure à la science ... Il faut donc surmonter la science et ne jamais sortir de notre état d'unité ... Mais nos paroles et nos écrits nous orientent vers lui; ils nous font sortir du langage pour nous éveiller à la contemplation» (Plotin, *Enn.* VI, 9,4).

112,35-37. «(Le Christ, le Verbe de Dieu), ton (c'est-à-dire de Dieu) cœur, le Premier Né, la Sagesse, le Prototype (τύπος), la Première Lumière».

Dans le néo-platonisme le *Νοῦς* est considéré comme un autre dieu, qui suit immédiatement l'Un. Il est une lumière de la Lumière, par lequel nous voyons la Lumière suprême. Il est « un second dieu qui apparaît avant le Dieu suprême et avant que nous voyions celui-ci» (Plotin, *Enn.* V, 5, 3). Il est sagesse et connaissance en tant que « la

---

[29] Traduction d'après *Sources Chrétiennes*, ATHANASE D'ALEXANDRIE, II, Tome 18, par P. TH. CAMELOT, Paris, 1946.

[30] « Il n'y a pas moyen, en effet, de les mettre en formules, comme on fait pour les autres sciences ». « Si j'avais cru qu'on pût les décrire et les exprimer pour le peuple d'une manière suffisante, qu'aurais-je pu accomplir de plus beau ? ».

connaissance est dans une nature de second rang» (*Enn.* V, 3,12).
Il est aussi la lumière de la Lumière : « Il est raisonnable d'admettre
que l'acte qui émane en quelque sorte de l'Un est comme la lumière
qui émane du soleil ; toute la nature intelligible est une lumière ; debout,
au sommet de l'intelligible et au-dessus de lui, règne l'Un » (*Enn.*
V, 3,12).

112,37-113,3. « Il (le Christ) est la puissance de Dieu, et il est une
émanation de la gloire pure de l'Omnipotent ».

Le terme «émanation» en copte ⲍⲉϯⲉ (équivalents grecs ῥεῖν, ἔξοδος,
ἀπόρροια)[31], rappelle le néo-platonisme. La conception du Christ
chez « Silvain » est comparable à celle du second dieu, le *Noῦs*, chez
Plotin. Celui-ci utilise le terme « émaner » (ἐξερύειν) pour la manière
dont le monde intelligible provient du Premier Principe et il compare
celui-ci au soleil qui ne se diminue pas par son irradiation (*Enn.* V, 1,6).

113,6-11. « Car il (le Christ) est aussi la lumière de la Lumière éternelle. Il est la vue (ὅρασις) qui contemple le Père invisible, en servant
toujours, et en formant par la volonté du Père ».

Dans le néo-platonisme l'Intelligence (*Noῦs*), fils aîné de l'Un,
contemple le Premier Principe. Cette contemplation incite l'Intelligence à une activité dans le monde intelligible. Plotin dit : « Il y a le
Bien (= le Premier Principe), et il y a l'Intelligence qui est bonne parce
que sa vie (ζῆν) consiste à contempler (θεωρεῖν). Les êtres qu'elle contemple ont la forme du Bien, et elle les possède, dès qu'elle contemple
le Bien … Quand elle le regarde, il n'est pas plus permis à l'intelligence
de ne rien penser que de penser ce qui est en lui ; sinon, elle n'engen-
drerait pas. De lui, elle tient la puissance d'engendrer» (δύναμιν οὖν εἰς
τὸ γεννᾶν εἶχε παρ' ἐκείνου; *Enn.* VI, 7,15). « L'intelligence doit
donc avoir deux pouvoirs, celui de penser, pour voir ce qui est en elle,
et celui de voir ce qui est au delà (ἐπέκεινα) d'elle-même ; c'est une
intuition qui reçoit son objet ; d'abord l'âme le voit seulement ; puis,
en le voyant, elle devient intelligence et s'unit à lui. Le premier de ses
pouvoirs est l'acte de contempler (θέα) qui appartient à une intelligence
sage ; le second, c'est l'intelligence qui aime » (Plotin, *Enn.* VI, 7,35).
L'âme est incapable de voir le Premier Principe directement. C'est
là le privilège de l'Intelligence (*Noῦs*), qui transmet sa connaissance
à l'âme.

116,1.2. « Il (Dieu) sait toutes choses avant qu'elles n'existent ».
On trouve la conception de la prescience de Dieu aussi dans le moyen-

---

[31] CRUM, *Coptic Dictionary*, p. 719.

platonisme. Albinus croyait que Dieu formait un plan d'après lequel le monde fût créé. Il concevait les idées comme modèles d'après lesquels les choses visibles fussent façonnées. « Il est également nécessaire que le plus bel ouvrage qui existe, le monde, ait été fabriqué par Dieu les yeux fixés sur une idée du monde. Cette idée a été le modèle de notre monde qui n'en est que la reproduction (ἀπεικονισμένον). C'est à la ressemblance de cette idée que l'ouvrier a réalisé le monde et c'est par l'effet de la prévoyance (πρόνοια) et de la règle la plus admirable, qu'il en est venu à fabriquer le monde ; c'est parce qu'il était bon » (Albinus, *Didaskalikos* XII, 1 ; 167,5-11 ; comparer Platon, *Timée* 29 e). A côté de la ressemblance, il y a aussi une différence entre « Silvain » et Albinus, en tant que le premier n'est pas optimiste sur la situation actuelle du monde (Sil. 98, 10-13).

INDICES

I. BIBLIOTHÈQUE DE NAG HAMMADI

CODEX I: 16, 17, 18, 19, 26-29, 31, 40, 118, 147

I,1 *L'Apocryphon de Jacques*: 17, 18, 70

I,2 (XII,2) *L'Évangile de Vérité*: 17, 18, 30, 39
   32,31-33: 60
   33,11-14: 37

I,3 *Le Traité sur la Résurrection*: 17, 42
   49,6s: 61

I,4 ⟨*Le traité Tripartite*⟩: 17-18, 123
   58,22-27: 142
   73,6: 38
   75,23: 38
   84,9: 39
   85: 23
   105,14-15: 162
   107,30-31: 162

I,5 *La Prière de l'Apôtre Paul*: 17, 18

CODEX II: 16, 17, 18, 20, 26-30, 79

II,1 (III,1; IV,1) *L'Apocryphon de Jean*: IX, 16, 18, 43, 83, 94, 101-103, 117
   14,20-21: 118
   15,22: 37
   20,3-4: 37
   24,4s: 9
   24,9-36: 9

II,2 *L'Évangile selon Thomas*: 18, 34, 70, 78, 114
   log 1s   32,10s: 35
   log 15   35,27-31: 140
   log 22   37,20-25: 66
            37,26s: 52
   log 25   38,10-12: 115
   log 84   47,24-29: 115
   log 89   48,14s: 52
   log 95-101 49-50: 22

II,3 *L'Évangile selon Philippe*: 18, 34, 56-67, 70, 79, 123, 130, 135, 137, 138, 141, 142

sent 3   52,6: 37
sent 5   52,19: 58
sent 6   52,21: 137
         52,24: 140
sent 7   52,28: 51
sent 8   52,35: 58
sent 9   53,3s: 58
         53,10: 58
sent 11 53,23s: 43
         53,23-54,31: 62
         53,24-25: 134-135
         53,26: 134
sent 12 54,5s: 61
         54,13-18: 61
sent 15 55,6s: 58
         55,12: 58
sent 19 56,3s: 62
sent 20 56,13: 62
sent 21 56,16s: 54
sent 23 56,26s: 57
sent 26 58,11: 63
         58,14: 61
sent 31 59,2-6: 142
         59,3: 64
sent 33 59,12s: 62
sent 42 61,7-10: 138
sent 47 62,10s: 62
sent 53 63,24: 58
sent 54 63,25-30: 59
         63,29: 58
sent 55 63,36: 64
sent 60 64,31-33: 130
         64,32: 33
         64,35-65,1: 130
sent 61 65,8: 60
         65,11-12: 63
         65,12: 61
         65,24: 61-63
         65,28: 60
         65,29: 60
         65,29-32: 60
         65,32: 60
sent 63 66,16s: 54, 63

2,1: 152
2,10 - 10,19: 149
5,3s: 43
5,14-25: 153
9,17: 152
11,22-31: 152
12,15 - 19,27: 149
13 - 14: 123
14,11: 152
19,13 - 20,1: 153
19,27 - 20,20: 153
19,27 - 24,34: 149
24,34 - 31,4: 149
28 - 29: 23
29 - 30: 24
31,4 - 32,5: 150
31,13: 152
32,5-17: 156
32,27 - 34,16: 148, 150
36,25 - 38,29: 150, 152
37,9-10: 152
37,22: 152
38,5-6: 152
40,25-29: 152
41,21-23: 149
43,28 - 45,31: 150
46,1 - 47,7: 150
46,9-20: 148
46,20-29: 148
47,20-32: 150
48,8-11: 152
49,9-10: 148

VII,2 *Deuxième Traité du grand Seth*:
48, 147, 154
65, 24-26: 137
65,37 - 66,10: 134
70,11-12: 154

VII,3 *L'Apocalypse de Pierre*: 16
75: 44

VII,4 *Les Enseignements de Silvain*:
VIII, IX, 69, 70, 158, 165, 170, 176, 179
84,16-31: 161
85,1: 160
85,24-26: 176
85,25-26: 160, 161
87,3-8: 176
88,21-25: 159

88,25-26: 161
89,13: 162
89,20-23: 162
90,9-13: 160-162
90,12-13: 160
90,13: 162
90,13-18: 163
90,23-24: 159
90,29-30: 159
91,7-9: 163
91,10-12: 162
92,19-25: 158
92,25: 159
92,25-27: 160, 164
92,29-33: 162
92,32-33: 159, 164
92,34: 159
92,34 - 93,3: 165
93,5-6: 166
93,10: 166
93,24 - 94,4: 167
94,22-24: 162
98 - 99: 24
98,10-13: 179
98,20 - 99,4: 167
98,22-28: 159
98,28-29: 162
99 - 100: 23
99,5-7: 160, 168
99,6: 169
99,7-15: 169
99,21 - 100,3: 160, 169, 171
99,22-26: 159
99,31-33: 159
100,5-12: 160
100,13-31: 172
100,23-29: 158
100,27: 173
100,31 - 110,8: 173
101,9-10: 174
101,12: 175
102,13-16: 160, 175
105,4-5: 162
108,20-27: 175
108,24: 176
108,26: 160
108,30: 158
111,8-13: 160, 176

II. BP 8502 (= BG): 31, 47

III. CODEX BRUCIANUS

IV. CODEX ASKEWIANUS

V. HERMETICA
(cf. Nag Hammadi VI, 6-8)

CH (= *Corpus hermeticum*):   X, 123-126, 130, 143, 145
CH I (*Poimandrès*):   125, 136, 137, 145
I,12-18:   138
I,26:   140
CH II
II,17:   132
CH III
III,4:   132, 136
CH IV (*Le Cratère*):   124, 125
CH V: 136
V,2:   131
V,6:   130, 131, 143
V,7:   132
V,9:   131, 132
CH IX: 145
IX,3:   138
CH X (*La Clef*)
X,1:   143
X,7:   143
X,15:   140
X,25:   143
CH XI
XI,14:   129, 130, 131, 133
CH XII
XII,1:   143
CH XIII (*Sur la Palingénésie*):   124, 125, 136, 139, 140, 142, 143, 145
XIII,1:   141, 143
XIII,2:   139, 140
XIII,4:   140
XIII,8:   141

XIII,8-10:   142
XIII,9:   141
CH XIV
XIV,9:   127, 130, 132

ASCLEPIVS: 126, 129, 130, 131, 135, 136, 142, 143, 145
c 1:   43
c 1-14:   126
c 2-3:   132
c 20:   132
c 21:   127, 128, 131, 132
c 23:   10
c 24:   126
c 25:   133
c 29:   5
c 41:   5, 6, 136

SH (*Stobaei hermetica*):   123
SH III
III,1:   143
SH VI
VI,11:   138
SH XXIII-XXIV (*Korè Kosmou*):   123, 133
XXIV,8:   133

FH (*Fragmenta hermetica*):   123
FH 4b: 132
FH 13:   132
FH 30:   143

Dits d'*Agathodémon*, *Exotica* (ou *Diexodica?*), *Genikoi logoi*:   143

VI. ÉCRITS MANICHÉENS

Psautier manichéen: 109
(éd. C. R. C. Allberry)
II,221:   108

Papyrus de Cologne: 109, 110, 112, 114
(éd. L. Koenen - A. Henrichs)
141:   112
148:   112

VII. ÉCRITS MANDÉENS

Ginza
(éd. Lidzbarski, 1925)

de droite
II,1   p. 48,10:   107

III   p. 80,31: 92
         p. 89,6-14: 119
         p. 98,7-11: 119
         p. 118,3: 95
V,1   p. 174: 119
VI   p. 206,24-26: 107
         p. 207,13-16: 107
         p. 207,32s: 105
         p. 210,27-30: 107
XII,6   p. 278,18 - p. 279,10: 117
de gauche
II,22   p. 494,11: 92

Livre de Jean
    (éd. M. Lidzbarski, 1915, reprint 1966)
    § 13   p. 55,11: 116
    § 52   p. 183,13: 92

Qolastā (ou Livre canonique de prières)
    (éd. E. S. Drower, 1959)
    p. 74: 102

Mille et douze Questions
    (éd. E. S. Drower, 1960)
    p. 111: 101

Haran Gawaitā
    (éd. E. S. Drower, 1953): 111

VIII. ANCIEN TESTAMENT

Genèse: 9, 10, 121, 149
    2,24: 53
    3,16: 53

Exode: 67
    3: 121

Deutéronome
    32,39: 84, 88, 106, 107

Job: 118 n. 57

Psaumes
    7,19: 66
    44,11-12: 53
    102,1-5: 55

Proverbes: 92, 93, 158
    8: 90, 95
    8,4: 83
    8,12: 83
    8,14: 87
    8,22-31: 91
    8,30-31: 83
    9,1s: 91
    9,13-18: 92, 93

Ecclésiaste
    3,1s: 104
    3,2: 83

Cantique des Cantiques: 90

Sagesse: 85, 86, 88, 94, 96, 100, 101
    1,4-5: 84
    1,6: 84
    7,7: 84

    7,22: 84
    8,3: 84, 95
    9,17: 84
    10: 86

Siracide: 9, 85, 86, 88
    15,2: 84
    24: 83, 86
    24,3: 83, 86
    24,4: 83
    24,16: 83
    24,17: 83
    33,13: 83, 84
    49,16: 154

Isaïe
    1,16-20: 77
    1,18: 77
    30,15: 66
    30,19-20: 66
    45,7: 84, 88
    50,3: 77

Jérémie
    3,1-4: 66
    11,20: 66
    17,10: 66, 77
    44,17: 96

Ézéchiel
    16,23-26: 66
    16,26: 71

Osée: 98
    1,2 (*LXX*): 97

XII. LITTÉRATURE JUIVE ET RABBINIQUE

XIII. LITTÉRATURE ANTIQUE ET PATRISTIQUE

XIV. TABLE DES NOMS PROPRES MYTHOLOGIQUES OU HISTORIQUES

XV. INDEX DES MOTS COPTES

ϫⲓⲥⲉ   ϭⲟⲙ: 128
(ϫⲟⲥⲉ): 60   ϭⲟⲟⲅⲛⲉ: 77
ϫⲱ̄ⲙ: 71

XVI. INDEX DES MOTS GRECS

XVII. LANGUES DIVERSES

XVIII. TABLE DES AUTEURS MODERNES